Systems Analysis for Librarians and Information Professionals

Library and Information Science Text Series

Systems Analysis for Librarians and Information Professionals

Second Edition

Larry N. Osborne
and
Margaret Nakamura

2000
Libraries Unlimited, Inc.
Englewood, Colorado

Libraries Unlimited, Inc.
P.O. Box 6633
Englewood, CO 80155-6633
1-800-237-6124
www.lu.com

Library of Congress Cataloging-in-Publication Data

Osborne, Larry N.
    Systems analysis for librarians and information professionals /
Larry N. Osborne and Margaret Nakamura. -- 2nd ed.
        p. cm. -- (Library and information science text series)
    Includes bibliographical references and index.
    ISBN 1-56308-693-X
    1. Libraries--Automation. 2. System analysis. 3. Library
administration. I. Nakamura, Margaret. II Title. III. Series.
Z678.9.083 1999
025'.00285--dc21   99-39581
                                                            CIP

Contents

Preface to the First Edition

Why This Book Was Written

Like many academic works, this one came to be written because there was a need for it, and no one else had written it. The authors, a practitioner and a teacher, were looking for a text to use: the former to find out how better to design her library systems, the latter to use as a textbook in a library and information systems course. Neither could find a suitable tool. When a craftsman can't buy a tool, he makes one.

Of course there were general systems analysis texts available, but each suffered one or more drawbacks. They were too expensive, too technical, or too concerned with for-profit business practice. Some assumed an undergraduate background in electrical engineering; others, that the reader would be satisfied with a philosophical treatise, and had no need for practical applications.

Audience

No text was suitable for information professionals who would have a need for systems thought, but who would have to balance systems analysis and design activities with the multitude of other demands on their time as they managed their school libraries, cataloged material, operated their information consulting firms, or kept their automated systems up and running. This book was designed for them.

From the authors' standpoint, systems analysis is about problems and their solution. The audience is thus anyone who has, or will have problems: a rather large group. More specifically, the book is intended for information professionals and for students intending to become information professionals. But that limitation is largely because the illustrations used throughout are taken from information environments. The principles illustrated are universal, or nearly so.

Our Approach

The outlook throughout is thus largely practical. Emphasis is on why to do systems analysis, and how to do it. While the authors find the theory and philosophy of systems thought fascinating, it is introduced here only to explain modern practice and to show why one technique is used instead of some other. There is a dangerous tendency among academics to elevate pragmatic concepts to the position of religion. The important uses of the concepts are relegated to second place while discussion takes place on the terpsichorean aspects of the angels involved. Certainly, to the extent that systems analysis involves a way of looking at the world and a way of thinking, it might be compared to religion, but if so, this book is about applied religion.

Organization

Generally this text is organized in a linear fashion: step-by-step through the systems analysis and design process. The general outline is taken directly from the structured analysis and design paradigm developed by Tom DeMarco and Peter Yourdon in the 1970s. To this the authors have added chapters dealing with aspects of systems analysis and design that are of special interest to information professionals.

Instructors using the book as a text may wish to present chapters in a different order. In the course taught in the School of Library and Information Studies at the University of Hawaii the section covering project management (chapter 12) is moved to the third lecture so that students will have the benefit of its guidance as they work through a major project. In general though, chapters four through nine should probably be read or studied in that order, since they present the core of the structured analysis approach.

Conventions Used

The authors have attempted to present the language and symbology actually used by systems analysts. Thus, we have tried to conform to ANSI standards when they are available and appropriate, but if common usage deviates from the "official" standard we have used the form actually used by professionals. Since there are two commonly accepted forms for data flow diagrams, we have presented both, but have shown the one we actually use (the Yourdon symbology) in most of our examples.

In the same vein, a word is in order on the use of the term "data." While pedants point out that data is the Latin plural of the singular datum, and while such usage is normal in academic journals, common practice in the field is to consider data to be singular. We have followed common usage. As foreign words are added to the English language they are adapted. Thus, the Latin agenda is plural (singular agendum), but few would say "the agenda for tonight are...." The authors believe absorption of data into English is well on the way, if not complete.

Thanks

Production of a monograph is a massive undertaking. While there are, perhaps, some who can create such work in isolation, such is certainly not the case for the authors.

We would especially like to thank our families, who put up with much disruption over the course of the past three years, as meeting followed meeting, and revision succeeded revision. They always expressed certainty that eventually we would finish; we were not so sure, and we appreciate their support.

Thanks also go out to all our former instructors who passed on both a belief in the values of the system approach, and an understanding of its limitations. This work would not have been possible without the background we obtained from them. We also thank Gerry Lundeen and Carol Tenopir for encouraging us to write and for helping us in understanding the ways of the publishing industry. From within that industry special thanks go to Kevin W. Perizzolo of Libraries Unlimited for untangling our grammar, removing our redundancies, pointing out our inconsistencies, and putting up with our missed deadlines.

Finally, ultimate thanks go to our former clients. We learned the discipline through the errors we made while being paid to analyze their systems. This is their book as much as ours.

Preface to the Second Edition

The world of information has changed dramatically since the first edition of this work was written. At that time the Internet was still strictly noncommercial, few libraries contained significant numbers of (or even had access to) electronic media, and most information professionals' work was little different from that performed at mid-century. In the intervening years information technology has reached even the most isolated communities. Those who remember the beginnings of today's environment are now in the minority, and it is possible for someone to claim he created the Internet, and for people not to know that he is wrong.

One thing that has not changed is the need for information professionals to determine problems, decide among potential solutions, design improved systems, and implement those systems successfully. This is still the only textbook covering the basic techniques of systems analysis targeted to the librarian or information professional, despite the fact that these skills become ever more important. The fact that the need is not otherwise met is shown by the number of requests for permission to reprint the first edition we received after it had gone out of print.

The authors have been reluctant to encourage this because they were aware of the shortcomings inherent in a first effort, exacerbated by the passage of time. In updating the materials for the new edition, the authors have drawn heavily on the suggestions and criticisms (for the most part constructive) which readers have submitted over the years. We would especially like to thank Dr. Anthony Debons for his careful and constructive critique.

Based on these suggestions and criticisms, as well as our own experience in using the text in classes each year, we have clarified several sections, rewritten and expanded the section on cost analysis, and included many additional examples. Also new to this edition is the inclusion of many sample problems which illustrate specific points and techniques along with their solutions.

Because the software engineering field is moving toward object-oriented programming, and the software systems analysis field is following closely toward object-oriented analysis and design, we have included a chapter on these techniques. Only time will show whether these techniques are appropriate for more generalized systems analysis, and what specific techniques and tools will become the standard for the field, but information workers will need to become familiar with the concepts and terminology.

Finally, as in previous editions, we must give credit and appreciation to our families, who have been tested as only the families of book authors are. Their support and forbearance was called upon and graciously given. However, in the end, much of what is clear and readable in this work is due to the efforts of editor Susie Sigman and the people of Libraries Unlimited, who have turned our prose into the best it could be, despite the efforts of the authors to insist on archaic, capricious, and eccentric literary styles.

Chapter 1

UNDERSTANDING SYSTEMS ANALYSIS

The Purpose of Systems Analysis

Certain terms evoke emotional responses in people, beyond what their actual definitions would seem to imply. Systems analysis is one of these terms. Depending upon preconceived ideas or past experiences, people may respond with either fear or relief at the prospect of being involved in a systems analysis project. Yet systems analysis is neither a threat nor a panacea; it is simply a tool which is valuable under many circumstances for identifying and solving problems. For example, a director of a university library may discover the shelves in disarray, or a school librarian may find that many students are graduating without returning materials to the library. These are commonplace problems facing library administrators. The usual response is to issue emotional memos, harass the staff, and invoke draconian measures. These actions are easy to implement, bring momentary satisfaction, and may even yield temporary improvement but seldom result in long-term resolutions of the problems. It is in cases like these (as well as more complex situations, e.g., the automation of an entire library system) that systems analysis proves useful. Systems analysis requires a great deal of time and effort and is not guaranteed to work, but it provides one of the few proven ways to make effective and lasting changes in an organization. *Systems analysis is a means of viewing circumstances realistically and designing practical solutions.*

1

Semprevivo (1982, 8) defines systems analysis as "the process of studying the network of interactions within an organization and assisting in the development of new and improved methods for performing necessary work." The pragmatism of this statement combines the critical elements of study and action. The statement has relevance to many environments beyond the narrow view of business as a commercial endeavor; a library, in fact, is a business that gathers resources, selects personnel, and conducts activities to meet its objectives. The ways a library keeps score (e.g., books circulated, reference questions answered, or collection size) may differ from the business technique (profit), but the goals of staying in business, remaining morally and ethically comfortable, and getting as high a score (profits, positive evaluations) as possible, are common to both.

Systems analysis, nevertheless, remains merely a technique—a means to an end. It is based on applying rational and logical methods. It is useful but has limitations. There are circumstances, especially those which involve largely emotional or social issues, where systems analysis is perhaps less useful than other tools. This is not meant to imply that systems analysis is ineffective in dealing with personnel (or personal) matters, nor that systems analysis should or can ignore human factors, only that the outcome of the analysis will be a rational recommendation. There are times, however, when it is better, or necessary, to make irrational decisions; one can, for example, apply systems analysis to the choice of a mate, but the authors are unaware of any systems analysts who have done so with success.

Systems analysis is a process that can be used effectively in an infinite number of environments, including the business world, the area of information studies, and the library world. The same basic elements of systems analysis apply to the different settings, and people in different environments may share the same misunderstandings of the meaning and purpose of systems analysis.

What Is a System?

It is easiest to understand the term *systems analysis* by clearly defining each of its component parts. First, it must be made clear that in systems analysis, a system is not simply a computer, nor is it a computer and a set of software, even though the word *system* is often used in conjunction with computers in other contexts. The concept of a system in systems analysis is a much broader one, and one that implies many elements that may or may not include computers.

Semprevivo (1982, 6) defines a system as "a series of interrelated elements that perform some business activity, business function, or business operation." This definition can be further refined by adding another phrase to define a system as a "series of interrelated elements *which can be considered complete* that perform some business activity, business function, or business." This supplies a description that includes several essential factors.

First, the interrelatedness of these elements is important; otherwise; the separate elements do not comprise a system. A lever, a parrot, a rope, and a magnifying glass would probably not be considered a system. Neither would the sun, an anvil, and a pea. Suppose, however, that they are connected in a Rube Goldberg invention where the sun rising above the horizon causes the magnifying glass to burn through the rope suspending the anvil over one end of a perfectly balanced lever, causing the anvil to fall and hurl the pea at the parrot, thus making it squawk. We then can see the relatedness of these elements in this primitive alarm-clock system.

Second, the system can be considered complete in the sense that it offers logical boundaries. Because any study of a system must set limits in order to begin discussing that system, it is important that these boundaries *can* be defined. A system must submit itself to a conceptualization as being self-sufficient, although in reality it is part of a greater whole. In the example above, the sun is part of the solar system, which is part of the structure we call the Milky Way galaxy. Nonetheless, the Milky Way is not part of the alarm clock.

Third, the elements must combine to meet some purpose if the system is to be productive. Certainly, purposeless systems exist, but *intentionally* purposeless systems are seldom found in libraries. Although the parrot alarm clock is primitive (and will not function on cloudy days), an intent—to awaken a sleeper—is clearly present. If a tree falls in a forest, and no one is there to hear it, it may or may not make a sound, but it certainly is not part of the lumber supply system.

Capron (1990, 285) defines a system as "an organized set of related components established to accomplish a certain task." Resources may include people, procedures, funding, and equipment. Again, the system must have a purpose. The concept of a system may be most easily grasped by using the analogy of an ecosystem such as a swamp. It can be conceived as a self-sufficient system; it has a series of interrelated elements, such as plants, water, soil, and animal life, acting upon each other in a natural life cycle; it has boundaries easily defined by the ecologist; and it serves a useful purpose in nature. (See figure 1-1.)

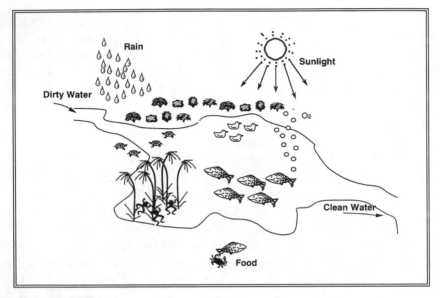

Fig. 1-1.

The example meets the criteria of a useful system:

- It is open, accepting input (dirty water, sunlight) and producing output (clean water, oxygen).

- It is stable within a given time frame and can absorb change while maintaining its integrity.

- It is part of a larger system and comprises subsystems.

It is easy to view the swamp as an isolated system. But take away the highlands upstream (or denude them of vegetation), and the system will be overwhelmed with silt. Raise the level of the land downstream and the swamp will be inundated. Add pesticides to the surrounding land and necessary components (e.g., the fish) will be killed. Thus, we must be able to conceptually isolate the system, while still understanding its relation to the larger world.

Similarly, a cataloging department in a library can be defined as a system because it includes a series of interrelated elements such as people, procedures, and equipment. It can be conceptualized as being self-contained or complete, (although it receives materials and information from beyond the system and sends out materials that have been processed); and it performs a function useful to the library. (See figure 1-2.)

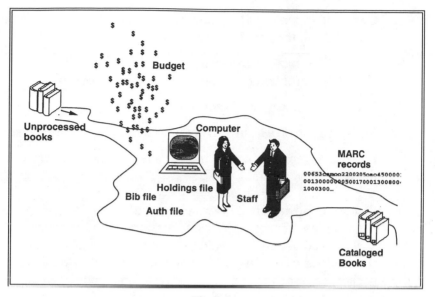

Fig. 1-2.

In this much-simplified illustration, the department receives unprocessed books and sends out bibliographic records and cataloged books. If too many books arrive for the department to handle, a backlog will develop that may eventually cause the system to fail. If the library administration decides to outsource its cataloging, there is no work for the librarians to do, output falls to zero, and the department effectively dies. If the staff is cut, there may not be sufficient people to do the work, and output may slow to a trickle.

What Is Analysis?

Analysis is the study of a problem *prior to taking action.* Analysts assume that the study will be honest, and that the purpose is not just to describe or to meet an externally imposed requirement but to precede and guide useful action. Analysis is not a process that affects only one person. De Marco (1979, 14–15), for example, speaks of hands-on users, responsible users, system owners, and analysts. A synthesis of several ways to look at the people involved might include the following:

1. Evaluator—the person within a system who asks, prior to the analysis, "Is improvement worthwhile?"; during analysis, "Does the study meet specifications?"; and after implementation, "Is the system satisfactory now?"

2. Client—the person who wants to have the analysis conducted and to whom the analyst reports.

3. Analyst/Designer—the person who does the work, which involves at least one problem (analysis) and a solution (design).

4. Manager—the person responsible for the system.

5. Staff—the person who uses the system (i.e., the "hands-on" person).

6. End-user—the person who receives the products or services of the system.

To illustrate these interlocking roles, consider the following case. One major university library, for various reasons, found it necessary to change its automated acquisition system from one vendor to another. A member of the staff, assisted by a committee, was charged with determining the best choice among the competing acquisitions products in the marketplace. She assumed the role of the analyst/designer. The head librarian, who was responsible for all library operations and authorized all contracts, was the client. Clearly the manager of the system was the head circulation librarian; the student assistants who worked at the circulation desk charging and discharging books formed the corps of operators; and the library patrons were the end-users. Eventually the decisions were made. The systems librarian evaluated both the original plan and the results of selecting the new vendor.

A single person can assume most of these roles, if necessary, with one exception: the analyst/designer and the evaluator should not be the same person. For example, in a self-analysis the client could be the manager and the operator at the same time. Or, in another situation, the manager could serve as evaluator. These and other combinations are valid as long as the person designing the system is not also in the position of evaluating its effectiveness. Few analysts are capable of being objective when evaluating the results of months of their own work. There is a tendency either to dwell on or defend all the mistakes made. Since neither is productive, it is better to let an objective evaluator judge the final results.

Analyze the following situation and try to determine what roles the participants would fill:

A medical center has, as part of its operation, a special library. The chief operating executive (COE) of the center becomes concerned about the costs of providing research assistance to health practitioners. She asks the head librarian to seek more efficient ways of providing services and to provide her with a plan for a more cost-effective operation. The head librarian, in turn, arranges for a librarian with a business background to meet with the COE, who instructs that librarian to prepare an analysis of the library's operations for her. In order to do this, the librarian is authorized to take work time to talk with the other librarians (including the head librarian), library assistants, and clerks, as well as the doctors and nurses who use the library. After the report is submitted to the COE, it is to be passed on to the accounting department, which is to determine whether it will be effective and should be implemented.

This example, taken from an actual case, illustrates that while real life is often less neat than textbook examples, the functions described above generally hold true. The medical center was unaware that it was conducting a systems analysis; the COE only wanted a report on how to do things better. No matter what it was called, however, what was needed was a systems analysis, and the result would be more likely to succeed if the tools of systems analysis were employed.

The analyst here is obviously the librarian selected to make the study. There is clearly a client, but is it the head librarian or the COE? Probably the COE is the client in this case, since the report is submitted to her; the head librarian is the manager. The other library employees are the staff, and the library clientele are the end-users. The evaluator role is more problematic. Evaluation for effectiveness is to be done by the accounting department, but departments do not evaluate things: people do. For an effective evaluation, a person must be designated as the individual within the accounting department responsible for the evaluation. A second difficulty with the evaluation is that there is no provision for evaluation of the implementation and no clear provision for post-implementation evaluation. These ambiguities should be cleared up before the analysis begins.

Reasons for Analyzing a System

There are a number of circumstances that may lead to initiating a systems analysis; not all of them are valid. Valid reasons for beginning a systems analysis include the following:

- Implementation of a new technique or new technology: Staff members may need to keep abreast of new developments, emerging trends, and evolving technology. When the Internet offered greatly increased access to information, public libraries were faced with multiple decisions related to staff development, acquisition of equipment, free versus fee access, and the introduction of patrons to Internet use.

- External environmental changes: New requirements or regulations outside the system may necessitate changes. As CD-ROM technology emerged, one major supplier of cataloging records changed its billing procedures. Instead of charging for sets of catalog cards and tapes purchased (with free searching), the supplier began to charge for the online time or number of searches. Libraries had to change the organization of their workflow in order to minimize online costs.

- Interest in improving a current system: (This is the soundest reason for conducting a systems analysis; it is also the most uncommon.) A system may be working quite well to the general satisfaction of staff members and end-users, but there is a desire on the part of the evaluator, manager, and/or staff to make the system work even better. An academic library administrator noted that when the online public access catalog system was not operational, students left the library rather than use the microfiche backup system. Although there were no complaints from the students or staff, the administrator considered the situation unacceptable. He initiated a systems analysis to determine if there was a more user-friendly alternative to the microfiche.

- Problems with a system: (This is the most common motivation for undertaking a systems analysis, but the most unconducive to good work.) General dissatisfaction among workers within a system or among end-users, or a crisis situation creating a demand for a systems analysis. A sit-in by disgruntled patrons unhappy about having to wait to use the available public access catalog prompted one library administrator to rapidly reassess the use of the public workstations and the staff workstations.

There are a number of negative, but not uncommon, reasons for undertaking a systems analysis. These include the following:

- Justification for a decision: A systems analysis may be requested after a decision has already been reached, in an effort to justify the decision (the systems analyst called to carry out a study under this condition faces unseen hazards).

- Fulfilling a grant requirement: Applications for funding may specify that a study must have been done, or that one is planned (since the grant proposal developers will have preconceived ideas about the desirability and design of the project, the systems analyst may encounter related difficulties in conducting an objective study).

Effective systems analysts must be aware of the positive and negative reasons that an analysis may be requested, discern the stated and the real motives of the client, and be prepared to deal sensitively with both.

Qualifications of the Systems Analyst

Systems analysts must be able to function well in a divergent array of tasks. *Ideal* analysts should:

1. be problem-solvers (i.e., be able to identify the problem(s) in a system and able to recommend solutions).

2. be familiar with a wide range of technology that may include, but not be limited to, computers and networking.

3. serve as a link between implementation of a new system and users of the old system, making the transition as smooth as possible.

4. feel at ease with people and be able to recognize their real, their perceived, and their expressed needs.

5. be able to find the underlying logic in a situation and to develop logical plans for correcting the problem.

6. be able to communicate well, to help other people articulate their needs, and to present the design effectively.

7. be expert in everything (i.e., be able to make a quick study of an unfamiliar field).

8. be able to deal with ambiguity, uncertainty, and adversity, while aware that the analyst's own role in the organization may be misunderstood, that there is no guarantee the finished design will be implemented in whole or in part, and that the recommended solutions may not always work.

In reality, of course, few individuals excel in all these areas, but most have strengths in some of them and function reasonably well in the others. The wide range of skills and experience points out the desirability of relying on several team members in systems analysis, so that the strengths of each member can contribute to the effectiveness of the whole.

In general, effective systems analysts must be able to operate not only with algorithms (clear-cut statements of procedures and predictable outcomes) but also with heuristics (general rules of thumb). Many people, especially those who are most attracted to computer processing, feel uncomfortable with the heuristic aspect of systems analysis. For example, one circulation policy might state, "Books are loaned for one month, unless they are reference or two-week books, or unless the patron presents a faculty borrowers' card, in which case reference books circulate overnight, and two-week books circulate for one month, except for the two-week books with green labels, which are two-week books, even for faculty." This is a complicated policy (although much simpler than many actual circulation policies), but it is essentially rational (although perhaps not reasonable). Following such a rule is much less disturbing than trusting the outcome of the analysts' work—and perhaps their careers—to such guidelines as: "Weeding 10 percent of the collection will increase circulation by 10 percent; weeding 20 percent of the collection will increase circulation by 20 percent . . . " The latter guideline, proven by experience, is only a heuristic. There is no certainty that circulation will increase after the collection is weeded, and obviously, weeding all the books in the collection will result in no circulation at all, not the doubled circulation that the model predicts!

It should also be noted that the title *systems analyst* is often misused to describe other responsibilities. For example, the person who responds to an advertisement for a systems analyst may discover that the library is actually interested in hiring a chief programmer. The title may also be assigned to librarians, network coordinators, or database administrators. Individuals in these positions may function at times as systems analysts, but a systems analyst is the person charged with the specific tasks of investigating problems, designing solutions, and sometimes overseeing the implementation of the design.

Librarians As Systems Analysts

By nature and training, professional librarians bring to systems analysis many of the needed traits and skills. Librarians often have an interest in providing logical order to a disorderly environment, but are also service-oriented, gaining satisfaction from helping others find solutions to their problems (e.g., meeting information needs). Communication skills are necessary if librarians are to help patrons articulate their needs. The research skills and strategies of librarians enable them to easily retrieve background information. In short, good librarians are well equipped to be good systems analysts.

Problems in Systems Analysis

Knowledgeable systems analysts are prepared for difficulties that may exist in the system being studied and for the pitfalls inherent to systems analysis itself.

- Analysts should not fall into the trap of believing that systems are simple. Systems are complicated; failing to recognize their complexity is often the first mistake of an outsider. Even if a system's complexity is recognized, a perfect and unambiguous description is virtually impossible. As a result, most analysts rely on visual tools to communicate the complexity in simple terms but sacrifice the richness inherent in narrative descriptions. For example, analysts studying a cataloging department may start with a notebook full of descriptions, interviews, diaries, and documentation. The product may be two or three (or twenty or thirty) pages of dataflow diagrams that are easy to understand but do not fully capture the reality of the system.

- Analysts may find that while they are completing the analysis and design of a system, the client is busy redefining the problem. The final product then addresses a problem that no longer exists in the mind of the client. This is especially prevalent in lengthy projects. Often an attempt is made to agree upon the exact system being analyzed and redesigned, to "freeze" the specifications. Changes in specifications, however, are not only caused by the whims of clients. Genuine changes in needs, or changes in externally imposed requirements, must also be taken into account. If a system is designed based on the cataloging function of a commercial vendor, and the vendor decides to eliminate cataloging as one of its products, freezing the specifications would not make any difference.

- Analysts are often presented with a set of problems to solve and systems to analyze, only to discover after weeks of work, the client had an entirely different issue in mind. Clients may not know what they want, much less what they really need. Vague statements such as "our use of CD-ROMs needs to be improved" must be clarified before extensive effort is made to solve the "problem."

- Analysts might not be given enough time for finding a solution, and quality suffers. The reasons for the time limitation may be valid, or the analysts themselves may become impatient to find a quick solution. Whatever the cause, rushing a systems analysis project usually results in a systems design that requires constant modification after implementation and massive amounts of long-term maintenance.

- Demands for improvement usually occur during times of fiscal constraint. Systems analysts are expected to redesign the system to yield the same (or improved) results using fewer resources rather than using more. This is often complicated by the fact that personnel cuts, which would be impossible in line-units such as circulation, are perceived as being easy in "nonproducing" units such as the systems office.

- People within a system may not react rationally to the presence of systems analysts. They may feel threatened by a study of the system and become antagonistic. This seems especially true for those who witnessed widespread downsizing and outsourcing during the 1990s, when systems analysts were called in to study the organization in order to determine which employees could be eliminated or shifted to contract work. Others may have witnessed the misapplication of systems analysis during the Vietnam conflict that resulted in the cynical inflation of "body counts."

- The results of analysis may be unequal. Optimizing an overall system may be perceived as improving the situation for one group by causing problems for another.

- There is little external ego reward for analysts. Clients will receive credit for improving a system, but the systems analyst will probably be held responsible for any failures.

- Politics are part of every system. Some areas are not safe to change because they are under the protection of someone in power. These areas are often within invisible boundaries that the staff is reluctant to mention, but danger awaits the systems analyst who fails to perceive and take into account the political reality of the situation.

System Life Cycle

Most systems undergo a life cycle of eight years or less, depending on how fast related technology and inquiry are developing. On the average, information systems seem to follow a five-year cycle. As shown in the graph below (see figure 1-3), the period that follows analysis and design is one of growing satisfaction as users become familiar with new equipment, techniques, or procedures. As time goes on, however, newer technology becomes available, new needs emerge within the system, and the maintenance of the system begins to create problems. As a result, user satisfaction begins to decline until it reaches the original level. At this point, a new analysis and design is required.

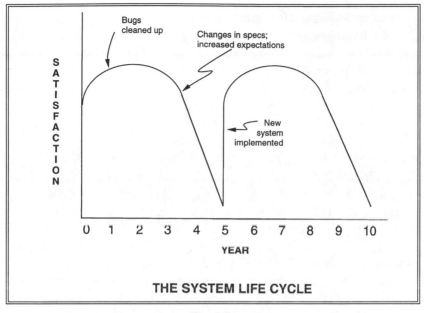

Fig. 1-3.

Knowing that initial enthusiasm will peak and then drop should not be used as a reason to avoid making changes at all. For example, if a library installs an online public access catalog (OPAC), the normal life cycle will go into effect. Users will (probably) be delighted with the increased information capabilities of an automated system, at least until newer technology begins to offer even greater advantages. The alternative, in this example, was to stay with a manual card catalog system. The drop in satisfaction with the card catalog would not be noticeable, because enthusiasm for using the card catalog was never very high.

Relationship Between Systems Analysis and Computers

A prevalent misconception is that systems analysis must involve computer technology and that systems analysts must be programmers with technical knowledge of computers. In cases where the use of computer technology within a system is under consideration, systems analysis can be an important factor in determining the feasibility and facilitating a smooth implementation of a computer system; in these cases, understanding of computers is extremely beneficial, if not crucial. Unfortunately, an understanding of computers is not a sufficient measure of the ability to function as systems analysts. Often in systems offices, the analysts are promoted from the ranks of the programmers; this can be as ineffective as promoting good teachers to become mediocre administrators. The qualifications for the two groups are not identical.

Systems analysis is, however, even more critical in a noncomputer setting. In these environments, error trapping is less precise. Instead of a system crash, people may adjust to ongoing problems and snags that remain unidentified but that prevent the system from functioning well. Such adjustments may take place at a cost of great loss of efficiency or increase in expense. For example, in a card-based library environment, filers can interfile cards with widely varying entries into a single file and can easily create several subfiles of erroneous entries. A catalog could contain whole sections of **New York (City)** and **New York (N.Y.)**, or **United States—History—Civil War** filed both as a chronological and a topical subdivision. In a computerized file, such an authority problem would probably be quickly perceived (and corrected). If problems of this nature are identified and corrected, there is one less error to correct during automation.

Some systems analysis approaches are designed specifically for computer applications. One of these, object-oriented analysis (OOA), was developed in response to needs created by newer programming languages. As programmers started to use object-oriented programming in the late 1960s, they needed object-oriented design resulting from object-oriented analysis in order to understand the systems for which the programming was planned. OOA, according to its proponents, incorporates systems analysis strategies and tools (Coad and Yourdon 1990, 18) but rather than using a process orientation, relies on an object-oriented approach—one that lends itself well to computer programming. Some analysts, though, find that the method is useful for software preparation, but not management. The authors' views on this subject are given more fully in Chapter 9.

A field related to both object-oriented analysis and to structured analysis is computer-assisted software engineering (CASE). Emerging as early as the 1950s, CASE uses structured analysis as a basis for its tools and techniques and forms a basis for OOA. Even in systems not requiring computers, CASE software provides useful tools for analysts in systems analysis, design, and implementation.

The misconception that systems analysis is only useful in a computerized environment and that it is only suitable for large systems is common. Wise analysts, and librarians, know that systems analysis can identify even small, but persistent, problems in noncomputerized environments and help to eliminate them. The growing power of microcomputers offers the opportunity for automating even the smallest businesses. Although these endeavors will undoubtedly be using software programs, it does not necessarily follow that they require programming. The role of the analyst in this case may be to select well-designed, cost-effective commercial software. The same sound principles of systems analysis should apply to situations involving programming, commercial software, or no computer applications at all.

Case Study—Fort Memorial Library

Nancy Malone was nervous. She had been hired, fresh out of library school, by Miskatonic University's Fort Memorial Library: a medium-sized library (about a million volumes) in a medium-sized university. She had her MLS, she had an appointment as a Librarian III (tenure track), and she also had an appointment to meet with Eli Tebbits, the dean of libraries.

She had met Dean Tebbits, during the interviewing process when he had struck her as being a kindly, if less than forceful, traditional librarian. Now he was in control of her immediate future, and she was less sure of his kindliness.

"Hrmph," began Dr. Tebbits. "I see you have taken all those computer courses in library school," dismissing 15 credits with a careless wave of his hand over the transcript on the desk before him. "We had a consultant in here last year, evaluating the serials collection. She put a recommendation in her report that we computerize our serials department. Personally, I think she was trying to drum up another consultancy, but the head of technical services insists that she had a point. I'd like you to look at our system and see what you think."

Nancy glanced down at her toes, thinking fast. "Well," she began, "I'm flattered that you think I can do the job, but I'm not sure..."

Tebbits broke in truculently, "Your transcript says you've had systems analysis. That ought to qualify you. After all, you took reference and that qualified you to be a reference librarian. If you need any help, we have a systems analyst assigned to us by the computer center. But he's working on a plan to install an integrated library system and doesn't have time to look closely at the serials department all by itself."

By this time Nancy was decidedly uneasy. Suddenly Dean Tebbits seemed to notice her concern and said absently, "Well, you can let me know if you're willing to do it later. Let's let the personnel librarian show you around now, and you can come back and see me tomorrow."

He buzzed for his secretary who led the bemused Nancy out of the dean's office.

Discussion Questions

- Why do you suppose that Nancy Malone was selected to head this project?

- Nancy seemed to have some concerns about her qualifications. Would you be concerned if you were in her position?

- List some reasons why taking on the job would be a good idea. In what ways might it backfire?

- Another person is doing a general systems analysis for the library as a whole. Does this duplication of effort seem reasonable to you? What other aspects of the general situation would you view with concern or interest?

References

Capron, H. L. 1990. *Computers: Tools for an Information Age*. 2d ed. New York: Benjamin/Cummings.

Coad, Peter, and Edward Yourdon. 1990. *Object-Oriented Analysis*. Englewood Cliffs, N.J.: Yourdon Press.

DeMarco, Tom. 1979. *Structured Analysis and System Specification*. Englewood Cliffs, N.J.: Prentice-Hall.

Semprevivo, Philip C. 1982. *Systems Analysis: Definition, Process, and Design*. 2d ed. Chicago: Science Research Associates.

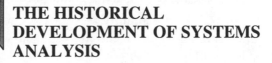

Chapter 2

THE HISTORICAL DEVELOPMENT OF SYSTEMS ANALYSIS

Introduction

Attempts have been made to show that systems analysis is as old as human endeavor. Van Court Hare (1967, 1) claims links as far back as Cheops Pyramid and the Phoenician astronomers. Another recent text has attempted to show that the builders of British megalithic monoliths employed systems thought. The authors prefer to search for the historical roots of systems analysis through an investigation into the post-industrial revolution development of business practices in general and industrial engineering in particular.

Although the industrial revolution occurred just prior to 1800, there was a lag in application of logical and humane processes for the next eight decades. As late as 1880, complex industrial operations were conducted in a manner that seems primitive by modern standards. According to Turner, Mize, and Case (1986, 13), very little planning and organization were involved; supervisors were given verbal instructions on work to be carried out by a poorly trained crew of workers. The objective of the supervisor was to get the maximum amount of work from his men. If any improvements in efficiency were developed, they were through the efforts of individual workers trying to find an easier way to accomplish their tasks. Coordination or analysis of the factory (system) was nonexistent.

Pioneers in Systems Analysis

Frederick W. Taylor is recognized as the leader of scientific management, a forerunner of systems analysis. In his work at manufacturing and steel companies, he developed the major concept of objectively analyzing current methods of operations for the purpose of improvement.

Taylor identified management's responsibilities: to select and train appropriate personnel, to analyze tasks scientifically, to collaborate with workers, and to divide work into logical subsystems—these concepts are still valid. (Taylor 1919, 36).

Though Taylor recognized the significance of the concepts he had developed and inspired a significant number of followers, his efforts to convince the larger community of fellow engineers and even his own managers was initially unsuccessful, especially in the eastern industrial states. The developing automobile industries, however, were quicker to grasp the concepts that eventually influenced American industry as a whole (Dale 1973, 124-28).

Other pioneers extended the work of Taylor, most notably Frank B. Gilbreth and his wife Lillian, whose primary contribution was in the area of work-motion studies. Although later criticism implied that work-motion studies were designed to create human automatons, the Gilbreth work should be viewed in the context of the poorly organized work stations of that time. For example, the operation that first drew Gilbreth's attention to the need for work-motion studies was the work of a bricklayer who had to walk away from his work and bend down to pick up each brick, then twirl the brick to place the right side up and bend over again to lay the brick. Not only was the work much slower and inefficient, the physical demands on the worker were much greater than would be required if logical and orderly processes were used. Like Taylor, Gilbreth's methods required the objective study and analysis that would later become a critical part of systems analysis (Yost 1949, 223).

Henry L. Gantt, who was associated with Taylor at Bethlehem Steel (Spriegel 1955, 25), developed the Gantt chart to plan and check the progress of multiple work activities within a system. Gantt charts are horizontal bar charts with a separate bar for each activity. The anticipated duration of the activity is shown by the length of the bar. A simplified example is shown in figure 2-1. Further discussion of the chart can be found in Chapter 13.

Couger (1974, 46) has identified specific periods in the evolution of systems analysis techniques, beginning with the period prior to 1920, when process flowcharts were used to show the flow of materials. From 1920 to 1950, general flowcharts and block diagrams began to emerge. These were combined in the 1950s to form information process charts (IPCs).

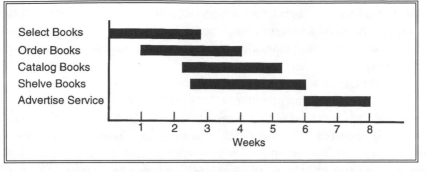

Fig. 2-1.

By this time, it was obvious that traditional project control based on Gantt charts and hard work was not sufficient. The large projects undertaken by both military and private industries needed better ways to ensure that resources were allocated to the appropriate subprojects, rather than being awarded to the person or department with the most power or persuasive methods. Specifically, during Lockheed's effort to deliver the Polaris missile for the Navy in 1957, the company realized that control and coordination of the project were beyond the tools available at the time. This realization led to the development of PERT (Program Evaluation Review Technique). PERT was used primarily to ensure the timely delivery of the product, with cost as a secondary factor. Concurrently, UNIVAC was implementing a major computer system for the DuPont Corporation. Faced with much the same problems as Lockheed, but with the added concern for cost, UNIVAC developed CPM (Critical Path Methodology).

Despite the fact that they were developed by different agencies working for different clients, the early forms of CPM and PERT had more similarities than differences. Both were types of network diagrams—they showed *relationships* and *dependencies* of time and effort by connecting nodes (events) with arrows (activities). Perhaps the most striking difference as originally conceived is that PERT was event-oriented (with nodes labeled), while CPM was activity-oriented (with arrows labeled). In modern usage, the two are often combined in a single effort, referred to simply as CPM. A more complete discussion of the two methodologies is included in Chapter 13.

Another of the streams that converged to yield systems analysis is cybernetics. First developed in the 1940s by Norbert Wiener, cybernetics was conceived as a general study of control and communication systems. Unlike most of the other fields that contributed to the development of systems analysis, cybernetics was academic in nature. It thus drew on physics, psychology, sociology, mathematics, and other university-based disciplines (Whitten, Bentley, and Ho 1986, 717). It was intended to cover both mechanical and biological systems. In addition to the idea that both living and nonliving system components could be analyzed in a rational way, cybernetics also emphasized the role of self-regulation and adaptation in systems (Wiener 1948). These two concepts are central to modern structured systems analysis and design.

Beyond these conceptual contributions, Wiener emphasized that systems could be described with mathematical models. Such models could be rigorously tested and thus proven to match reality. While cybernetics had an undeniable influence on systems analysis, it had an even greater influence on the nascent field of artificial intelligence, where much of its teaching was absorbed wholesale (Ashby 1963, 2-6).

On a practical note, it was Wiener who popularized the idea of the "black box" as a technique for analysts, which is a method of describing a component of a system solely in terms of its inputs and/or outputs, without dwelling on how the one is turned into the other. This was a common approach in electronics (where often a box literally had input and output terminals, and the engineer was unaware of the contents of this box), but Wiener extended the idea to nonelectrical areas (George 1977, 1-8).

Operations research, a related field, emerged at the beginning of World War II to facilitate the development of military weaponry. "Blackett's Circus"—British scientists working under the direction of P. M. S. Blackett—proved the effectiveness of bringing a variety of scientific disciplines to address operational problems (Leimkuhler 1968, 82). Operations research usually involves modeling a system so that variables may be manipulated in the model rather than through real-life implementations. This manipulation frequently takes the form of advanced statistical analysis and computer simulation. Such advanced techniques are necessary because operations research, by definition, deals with the real world (with the allocation of scarce resources, for example). This emphasis on solving real-world problems also forced operations research to pay particular attention to determining and defining these problems. In many ways the development of network techniques (CPM and PERT), described above, was due to the application of operations research to management functions. This stress on thoroughly understanding the problem before attempting to analyze or solve it has been incorporated into structured systems analysis. The techniques and results of operations research are exceptionally useful in systems analysis efforts, as well as in the traditional production optimization where they are conventionally applied.

Operations research, though fine for winning a war —a situation with few constraints on activities and a generally agreed-upon goal —has limitations when applied in other environments. Systems analysis evolved from earlier efforts to offer a unique way to improve or redesign a system. The earliest form of systems analysis involved seven steps:

1. Problem recognition

2. Feasibility study

3. Analysis

4. Design

5. Implementation

6. Testing

7. Maintenance

Inherent problems exist in this sequence of steps, however. First is the assumption that the problem is obvious. In fact, the real problem in a system can be identified only after careful study; unless a thorough study is the initial step, the systems analyst may be faced with an array of perceived problems. Second, there is no allocation for gathering the data to serve as a basis for analysis. This sequence also implies autocracy: analysts see, understand, and implement without acknowledging human factors or politics. Finally, proceeding directly from design to implementation without testing almost guarantees that implementation will be an ongoing effort to correct flaws that could have shown up sooner if testing had been carried out at an earlier stage.

Structured analysis, as developed by Tom DeMarco, avoids the dangers of the preceding process. Semprevivo (1982, 19) identifies the logical steps of structured analysis as problem definition, data collection and analysis, analysis of systems alternatives, determination of feasibility, development of the systems proposal, pilot or prototype systems development, systems design, program development, systems implementation, systems review, and evaluation. DeMarco has identified the benefits of structured analysis. These include avoiding delays in systems completion, avoiding delays in implementation once a system is delivered, avoiding systems that produce useless or irrelevant output, eliminating time wasted in programming, and eliminating wasted time in retraining workers (DeMarco 1979, 25). To these may be added the benefit of eliminating time wasted using the system.

Steps in Modern Systems Analysis

Each of the steps listed below is covered in detail in the following chapters. They are brought together here so that readers may get a feel for the way the individual steps fit together as a system.

1.   Problem definition. The first step in conducting a systems analysis using the structured analysis approach is problem definition. It is critical to differentiate between the real and the perceived problem in a system. Those responsible for the system may recognize that there is a problem because of symptoms they observe (e.g., piles of sawdust-like material may begin to appear on shelves), but without a formal problem definition process they may be misled into purely superficial action (increasing janitorial services) rather than dealing with the real problem (insect infestation). Without a valid problem definition, the subsequent steps in systems analysis will be futile. The task of the systems analyst is to conduct a preliminary study and analysis to accurately define the problem.

2.   Data collection and analysis. This involves determining what the systems analyst needs, deciding the best way to get the information, gathering the data, and analyzing the data as a basis for the next steps of the process. Means of gathering data include observation, interviews, surveys, and other tools. (Tools for data collection are discussed in Chapter 5.) Data collection and analysis may, together with the first step problem definition, become a looping process: analysis of the data may give evidence that the real problem has not been identified; when a different problem is identified, further data collection and analysis may be required for confirmation and refinement.

3.   Analysis of alternatives. It is most effective to begin with a large number of alternatives. If a team of systems analysts is involved, brainstorming is a traditional and effective way to develop the first list of alternatives. The results are then narrowed to three or four possible alternatives. Usually these alternatives represent 1) a basic improvement in the current system, with minimum investment of resources; 2) substantial changes in the current system; and 3) the design of an ideal system, given unlimited resources.

4. Feasibility determination. After a set of possible alternatives is developed, each is analyzed to determine the tangible and intangible costs and to examine the benefits. Costs are broken down into categories of immediate, projected, and ongoing.

5. System proposal. This is the first official document of the systems analysis project. It is a formal statement of the proposed solution and the system's general specifications; both the client and the manager sign the agreement. Later, if changes are made to the proposal, they are specified in writing and again, signed by the client and the manager. Despite only a single signature appearing on the document, the system proposal and subsequent modifications are often approved at meetings between representatives of the client and the systems analyst. For further documentation, the analyst may wish to take notes on such meetings' discussions and participants.

6. System design. The system design is a clear statement of the new system; it is the master plan. It includes both the logical design (*what* the system is to do) and the physical design (*how* the system is to do it). The design is the proposal in fruition: general proposal statements are replaced with specific statements of action. For example, a general proposal statement—"a user interface"—may be replaced with many pages of actual forms, screens, and other tools. Thus, one phrase generates detailed listings of inputs, processes, files, and outputs, as well as specific materials needed to implement the design.

7. Pilot study. A pilot test of a prototype of the new system should be conducted to determine how well it works, using quantifiable standards to test the system's effectiveness. If the system is a large and expensive one, or if it is a turnkey system, it may be more difficult to conduct a pilot test. Alternative methods are to test one component of the system, especially the most questionable part, or to test the system in a smaller subsystem, for example in a single branch or department. System design and pilot study become another looping process if a pilot study reveals problems; the system design should be revised and retested until the test brings satisfactory results.

8. Implementation. The system is installed, staff training is completed, and documentation is prepared for system maintenance.

9.   System review and evaluation. The system is subjected to acceptance testing on the behalf of the client. User satisfaction is determined.

A related process, the systems development life cycle (SDLC), is an
approach used by companies to develop information systems. SDLC consists of five steps: preliminary investigation; systems analysis; systems
design; systems development; and systems implementation and evaluation (Shelly 1991, 1.12).

Caveat

Systems analysis and design is a valuable—perhaps critical—weapon
in the arsenal of librarians. It is not, however, a panacea or a magic bullet.
When it is applied with cynicism or indifference, it can produce gro-
tesquely distorted results, as even the proponents of its techniques will admit. For examples of these disasters (beyond the illustrations interspersed
throughout this text), the interested reader is referred to Hoos's *Systems
Analysis in Public Policy: A Critique* (1983). Perhaps even more dangerous than cynicism is worship. There are situations, especially those without well-described and quantifiable goals, where application of systems
analysis is attempted only by those who feel its techniques are revealed
truth. Such distortion serves neither systems analysts nor clients. This
quasi-religious application has been justly criticized by Lilienfeld (1978).
(The authors often resort to Lilienfeld and Hoos during the initial eupho-
ria that attends beginning a new project.)

Case Study—Fort Memorial Library

After a night of soul searching, Nancy decided to take on the systems
analysis effort. When she told Dean Tebbits the next morning, he seemed
unsurprised. In fact, he handed her a list of four people who were to be on
her team, including a representative of the university's computing center.

Flattered to be a team leader on her second day on the job, Nancy
called a meeting for that afternoon to discuss the task before them. The
meeting was set for 1:30 in the library conference room, and by 1:28 three
people, in addition to Nancy, had gathered around the table. She started by
asking them to introduce themselves.

Sue Schriver began by saying that she was a "junior systems analyst" from the university's computer center. Her primary task in the past had been maintenance of the university's payroll and accounting programs. She had requested another position because she was tired of writing COBOL code.

Benjamin Root was obviously a fragile person. He had been a reference librarian for the past eight years. He had no idea why his superior had picked him for this assignment, except that she was always assigning the unpleasant tasks to him. Benjamin made it clear that any assignment was better than being stuck at the reference desk with "the crazies and the smellies."

Rachael Bai was on loan from the Asian collection. She was a quiet, soft-spoken (indeed almost silent) woman. Chinese was her first language, and although competent enough in English, she was not confident in her speech. She did point out, however, that her superior had asked her to keep her eyes open for ideas that could be applied in their department.

At 1:50 Maria Escontrias arrived at the meeting. She explained that she had been at a meeting of the Concerned Staff's Ergonomics Task Force, which was more important. She announced that her position on the systems project was to be an advocate for the staff, to ensure that management didn't take advantage of them. (Later Nancy discreetly checked with Dean Tebbits and discovered, as she had suspected, that this role was a self-assigned one.)

Nancy then explained her background, apologized for her lack of experience, and outlined the purpose of their group. Then she threw the meeting open for comments and suggestions. Ben Root began by saying that the effort was a waste of time because no one ever paid attention to reports anyway. Sue Schriver pointed out that there was no real need to have an analysis group, since the application was trivial, and a program could be written in a few days. Maria Escontrias said the members of this team were intended to be puppets in a management plan to reduce staff levels in the serials department. Rachael Bai said nothing. Eventually the meeting broke up dispiritedly.

Discussion Questions

- Why do you think *these* people were selected to be in the systems analysis group?

- Suggest some techniques Nancy might use to get her team to pull together. Do you think Nancy handled things well? What, in your opinion, did she do right? Wrong?

- How might she have structured the meeting in order to produce useful suggestions for the conduct of the analysis?

- Do you think this group is representative of interdepartmental groups, committees, and task forces in libraries? How does it compare with your own experience as a group participant? As a group leader?

- What problems can you anticipate from these individuals? How might Nancy use them to her best advantage?

References

Ashby, W. Ross. 1963. *An Introduction to Cybernetics.* New York: John Wiley.

Couger, J. Daniel. 1974. "Evolution of Business System Analysis Techniques." Edited by J. Daniel Couger and Robert W. Knapp. In *System Analysis Techniques.* New York: John Wiley.

Dale, Ernest. 1973. *Management: Theory and Practice.* 3rd ed. New York: McGraw-Hill.

DeMarco, Tom. 1979. *Structured Analysis and System Specification.* Englewood Cliffs, N. J.: Prentice-Hall.

George, F. H. 1977. *The Foundations of Cybernetics.* London: Gordon and Breach.

Hare, Van Court, Jr. 1967. *Systems Analysis: A Diagnostic Approach.* New York: Harcourt, Brace & World.

Hoos, Ida R. 1983. *Systems Analysis in Public Policy: A Critique.* Rev. ed. Berkeley: University of California Press.

Leimkuhler, F. F. 1968. "Operations Research." In *Encyclopedia of Library and Information Science.* Edited by Allen Kent, et al. New York: Marcell Dekker.

Lilienfeld, Robert. 1978. *The Rise of Systems Theory: An Ideological Analysis.* New York: John Wiley.

Semprevivo, Philip C. 1982. *Systems Analysis: Definition, Process, and Design.* 2d ed. Chicago: Science Research Associates.

Shelly, Gary B., Thomas J. Cashman, Judy Adamski, and Joseph J. Adamski. 1991. *Systems Analysis and Design.* Boston: Boyd and Fraser.

Spriegel, William R. 1955. *Industrial Management.* 5th ed. New York: John Wiley.

Taylor, F. W. 1919. *Principles of Scientific Management.* New York: Harper.

Turner, Wayne C., Joe H. Mize, and Kenneth E. Case. 1986. *Introduction to Industrial and Systems Engineering.* 2d ed. Englewood Cliffs, N.J.: Prentice-Hall.

Wiener, Norbert. 1948. *Cybernetics.* New York: John Wiley.

Whitten, Jeffrey L., Lonnie D. Bentley, and Thomas I. M. Ho. 1986. *Systems Analysis & Design Methods.* St. Louis: Times/Mirror/Mossby College.

Yost, Edna. 1949. *Frank and Lillian Gilbreth: Partners for Life.* New Brunswick, N.J.: Rutgers University Press.

Chapter 3

THE HUMAN ELEMENT

Introduction

Many interpersonal factors affect systems analysis. Concerns such as real and perceived problems, interviews, and other areas that involve the human aspect have been touched on briefly. Because of the critical nature of the topic, however, this chapter will deal more formally with the major elements that determine the way systems analysts function and the elements that prevent systems analysts from functioning effectively. Because systems analysis is a rational, logical process, unwary systems analysts may underestimate the irrational, illogical, and emotional elements that may exist within a system.

Organizational Commitment

Systems analysis has inherent risks: there is no guarantee that solutions can be found, or, if they are found, that they will be successful. In an atmosphere of uncertainty, wise analysts try to ensure that the chances of success are as high as possible. A basic means of increasing the chance of success is to ensure commitment to the project by all those who will be affected. Since this is critical, special attention must be given to gaining, maintaining, documenting, and publicizing commitment from (and to) all levels. While the organizational structure of libraries is typically rather flat, many levels may exist in an organization. Still, most organizations are like the military: they include officers and enlisted personnel, or, in civilian terms, managers and workers.

Management Level

The most obvious level of organizational commitment needed for a successful project is the upper level, because it is the management level that can ensure funding, allocation of staff time, and cooperation of staff members. In order to obtain this commitment, systems analysts must:

- be prepared to give an honest assessment of the amount of time and effort that will be required by the study. Sometimes, in an effort to sell the systems approach, analysts tend to understate the amount of work involved. The negative consequences of underestimating (or concealing the truth) are inevitable when the actual study is carried out.

- be prepared to explain the concept of underlying problems because analysis identifies but does not solve existing problems. The people who are working within the system will be those who will actually solve the problems; they should be aware of this fact.

- show management *why* they should use systems analysis to help solve their problems and how *they* can solve their own problems by using systems analysis. Good analysts have faith in the techniques of systems analysis—but not blind faith. The reasons for using systems analysis are rational and can be explained rationally. Analysts can assume that rationality is a common trait of people at the management level. Businesses led by irrational management soon cease to exist; unfortunately, the same is not always true of libraries. If management is to make a commitment to a long and arduous effort, they will expect to understand why systems analysis, rather than their own (or the analysts') intuitive feelings, should guide them in the solution of problems. To make a true commitment to the systems analysis effort, they must have a sense of owning this effort. They will receive much of the credit for its success (and may even share part of the blame for any failure)!

At several points in the systems analysis process, there are opportunities for management to sign documentation to show acceptance of and agreement with the analysts' work on the description of the existing system, and on the proposal of a new system design, for example. Astute analysts make sure they obtain these signatures to document the commitment of management at each stage of the systems analysis. This "signing off" is a way to emphasize to the client that the analyst is serious and that the analyst is working to create a solution that is truly the client's solution. Such documentation also gives proof that the client was kept informed and was satisfied at each stage; otherwise, it is easy to treat the analysts as unwelcome, external intruders if any problems arise at a later point. Including the practice of signing or initialing reports in the process from the very beginning can make it a nonthreatening routine. However, if things begin to deteriorate and the client is only then confronted with such a procedure, it can be exceptionally counterproductive.

Maintaining Commitment

Once the initial commitment has been made by management, systems analysts must work to maintain this commitment. Management must be kept informed and interested, but must not be bothered or harassed. In some organizations, management itself will institute a method for keeping track of the project's progress. Such methods are, however, designed to further management's goals, which, while probably not in conflict with the analysis project, may not be optimal from the analysts' viewpoint. Systems analysts may want to create additional means of communication.

Providing honest and brief reports is generally the key to maintaining commitment from management. The reports may be verbal or written but should be short—less than 15 minutes for verbal, or 3 pages for written—and submitted about once a week, assuming the project is progressing satisfactorily. The object of the reports is threefold: to keep management informed without worrying them; to enable management to speak confidently about the project's progress; and to ensure that management receives more reports that are positive than they receive requests for additional resources or reports describing crises. Reports should not hide problems, though; management can accept problems more readily than surprises. Difficulties have a tendency to escalate; four reports indicating an increasing problem will maintain commitment better than three positive reports followed by one that reports a crisis. A sample project report is included in Appendix A.

Lower Administrative Levels

Gaining and maintaining commitment from levels below management are equally important, but often more difficult: these are the workers who experience the disruption of the analysis process, who will bear the brunt of changes made, and whose positions may be jeopardized. On a practical note, commitment from this level is essential because these are the people who can make the new system run smoothly or can sabotage it— perhaps even unknowingly.

In order to obtain commitment from lower administrative levels, systems analysts must:

- be honest with each person or group within the system. This means being honest enough to admit a lack of knowledge in some areas.

- avoid making promises that cannot be kept. It is comforting for workers to hear that no jobs will be eliminated by changing to a new system, but credibility and commitment are the first casualties when it becomes obvious that staff reduction is indeed planned.

- point out how the new system will help the individuals do their jobs better. This is much more effective than explaining how much money the new system will save the organization.

- respond to the emotions that people invest in their work. Most people define a large part of themselves in terms of what they do. They think their jobs are important, and they try to do them well. Approaching systems analysis as a purely logical, fact-based endeavor may give the impression that systems analysts are uncaring and a threat. System analysts should *never* give the impression that a job is pointless, unimportant, or unnecessary (even when it is).

Maintaining Commitment

Commitment from the lower levels within the organization can be maintained during the project through a combination of honesty, communication, and effectiveness. Honesty can be demonstrated by keeping (or not making) promises, by performing tasks and delivering modules by the established deadline, and by fairly representing lower-level workers to administrators. Communication is best established directly by talking with the people being analyzed, drinking coffee with them, and asking them for help when appropriate.

Once analysis and design has commenced, the walkthrough is a primary tool in ensuring commitment. This technique is borrowed from software engineering, which borrowed it (and developed it as an analog) from theatrical technique. In its original form, a walkthrough is a type of rehearsal where actors, having read their parts enough to feel comfortable with them, finally begin to move across the stage, feeling out the motions they will use as the performance is refined. In systems analysis walkthroughs, the analyst, having studied the system sufficiently to be comfortable with it (or having created enough of the system to be able to describe it), reviews the system with the person from whom the information was obtained or for whom the system was designed. In other words, once a worker explains exactly how his or her part of the system functions, and the analyst has formed an understanding, this information is passed *back* to the worker. Throughout this recital, the analyst ensures that his or her understanding matches the user's. There is no more effective way to prove an understanding of what someone has said than by paraphrasing it. If the analyst can give a succinct, organized, and accurate restatement of a worker's explanation, that analyst has gone far toward gaining the trust and commitment of the employee.

The walkthrough serves several other functions. Its primary purpose, of course, is to ensure that the analyst understands that specific part of the system and has not missed any facets. It is also an excellent opportunity to engage in public relations, allowing the analyst to demonstrate that the worker is actively contributing to the project and has a stake in its success.

Interest may be shown through communication, but effectiveness must be demonstrated. While it is not possible in every project, some obvious improvement in operations made early in the project will go far toward proving to workers that the analysts are on their side. In one project, for example, the analyst noted that redundant and confusing temporary cards were being filed into the shelflist. Though a change here would be a small part of the overall new design, it was obvious that a recommendation *would* be made later to stop filing these cards. In fact, the problems caused by this practice were so obvious that the analyst convinced management to eliminate the step immediately, to the great relief and satisfaction of the library staff. From that point on, there was no doubt on the part of the workers that the analyst was competent and helpful, and there was no doubt in the mind of the analyst that he had the staff's support.

Ethics of Systems Analysis

The systems analyst must be aware of and concerned with the obvious and subtle questions of morality involved in systems analysis. The excuses of "only following orders" or "just doing my job" are offensive and dishonest and simply unacceptable. Systems analysts must come to grips with situations that the process may present and be prepared to defend their actions, if only to themselves. An exhaustive list of potential moral dilemmas is impossible, but some examples include:

- Making recommendations that will result in loss of jobs. Generally, projects involving computers will create more jobs at a higher level, in the long run. However, people buy groceries and pay their bills in the short run. Automating operations may result in job loss for those who will have the most difficulty finding new jobs. Providing retraining of those individuals is an alternative that *might* resolve the problem of eliminating unskilled jobs, but there is no guarantee that all workers will be able to assume a higher level of tasks.

- Designing a project that promotes economy through such avenues as stealing data or taking advantage of contract loopholes. For example, cataloging records might be downloaded from a remote database by "printing" a screen image into a program that reconstitutes the MARC record rather than ordering and paying for those records. If the library's contract does not specifically prohibit this practice, it may not be illegal and would certainly reduce costs to the library. These cost reductions, however, would be realized by increasing the costs to all the other libraries using the database, since the vendor would be forced to raise rates to make up the lost revenue.

- Hiring nonprofessionals to perform professional tasks, knowing that those individuals lack the breadth of knowledge necessary to move up a career ladder. Eventually, such people become frustrated with their inability to advance—the best may go back to school on their own (perhaps with organizational support or help), but others will swell the ranks of disgruntled employees and become disgruntled former employees.

- Covering up or not reporting issues that will cause difficulty in the future. For example, an online catalog could be created that functions satisfactorily with the library's existing records, but which will fail when the library expands or when older records are converted to a machine-readable form. During the interim between system implementation and system failure, which may be years, the analysts have time to find other positions.

- Using knowledge gained from one organization to aid a competitor. Fortunately, this is seldom a problem when systems analysis is being applied to libraries, since libraries are rarely in competition with each other. A situation, however, may arise in which system vendors are changed, raising the question about the extent to which analysts can pass on their knowledge about the operation of the old system to the new vendor. In some cases a nondisclosure agreement specifies what is legal; still, it cannot cover what is legal but unethical.

- Manipulating the results of analysis to agree with the results the client wants. This is frequently requested of analysts, particularly when the organization wants to buy a specific system or to justify a grant. Simple codes of ethics can be designed to prohibit specific actions, but when the analysts must choose between supporting management and being replaced, criteria for ethical behavior often seem less clearly defined.

When the results of analysis lead to a path difficult for analysts, they can compromise and accept the personal dissatisfaction that follows, violate their integrity and produce dishonest design, or resign from the project. Dror (1985, 323) has stated, "When the goals and values of a particular client contradict basic beliefs of the analyst, the analyst should resign rather than help in the realization of goals and values with which he or she intensely and fundamentally disagrees." Most analysts can agree with this statement. The difficulty is deciding what is an intense and fundamental disagreement, and what is only a momentary qualm. No simple answers for these kinds of moral issues exist. One thing is clear: refusal to acknowledge a moral issue is not a defense. Systems analysts must be prepared to make conscious decisions in consonance with their values. If their values conflict sharply with those of the client, analysts must remember that they work for the organization but must live with themselves.

Case Study—Fort Memorial Library

We join Nancy several days later. She had several additional meetings with her team and eventually has gotten them to, provisionally at least, pull together on the project.

Now she must do the same thing with the Serials Department. Nancy started by asking the head of serials to call a general meeting of the serials department so that she can explain the purpose of systems analysis and what it can accomplish. Nancy prepared for the meeting by reviewing her notes from the systems analysis class she took in library school and rereading her textbook. By the time she finished, she once again felt confident.

She walked into the meeting to find her staff seated at one end of a table and the department personnel arranged in rows at the other side.

"To begin with," she started after introducing the team members, "we can only help you identify problems and solutions. In the end, it will be up to you to actually change the system. You are the most important part of the system, and you are in a position to improve it."

From there she went on to give a general description of how systems analysis and design works and what steps would be followed. As she spoke, she began to become more at ease. "My goodness," she thought to herself, "I really believe this!" She finished up with an animated description of several other systems efforts (culled largely from her reading and notes) where the efficiency of systems was vastly improved.

"Now," she finished briskly, "what questions do you have?"

After being caught up in her own eloquence, she was surprised to come back to earth and look into the poker-faced group before her. A weighty silence fell.

"Surely," she said, a little desperately, "there must be some questions." One older woman raised her hand. "Who loses their jobs?" she asked.

Nancy could see that Maria Escontrias was opening her mouth to reply. She knew that if Maria came out with a ringing "No jobs will be lost!" cry, it could backfire and be worse than saying nothing. In desperation she opened her mouth to speak.

Discussion Questions

- What do you think Nancy will say?

- Conventional systems analysis wisdom says that Nancy is right and Maria is wrong. Do you agree? If not, how would you seek to come through on your promise that "no jobs will be lost?"

- Why do you think the department appeared unmoved by Nancy's oratory? Should Nancy be worried by this reception or not?

References

Dror, Yehezkel. 1985. "Public Policymaking Reexamined." Quoted in *Handbook of Systems Analysis*. Edited by Hugh J. Miser and Edward S. Quade. New York: North-Holland.

Chapter 4

IDENTIFYING AND DEFINING PROBLEMS

Introduction

In a small Catholic university for women, books were disappearing from the shelves at an alarming rate of 10 percent per year. After each set of examinations, stacks of books were found in the dormitory halls; even worse, library staff members found numerous books discarded in dumpsters near the library. Since the books had not been properly charged before removal from the library, the director of the library concluded that the students were untrustworthy (or, as she put it, "a bunch of thieving weasels") and asked a systems analyst to take on the task of selecting a security system for the library. She felt such a system was necessary even though its cost would be more than twice the library's annual book budget.

Before accepting the director's problem definition and solution, the systems analyst began to look more closely at the types of materials being stolen. He discovered, through observation and informal interviews, that the materials fell into three categories: reference books, art books, and volumes from the set *Fathers of the Church*. He also learned that all of these books shared a common factor: students needed them for required courses, but none of them could be borrowed.

Based on his findings, the systems analyst recommended that all noncirculating books be placed on overnight reserve to allow students increased access to the books. Despite misgivings, the director agreed to a test of the analyst's suggestion before committing the library to purchasing a theft detection system, but only if losses were closely monitored. The book losses immediately dropped to less than one percent a year. This simple solution to a real problem rather than an expensive effort to solve a perceived problem was the result of accurate problem definition.

Identifying Problems

This case study points to the necessity of conducting an objective, preliminary study of the system in order to accurately identify the problem, or set of problems, actually present. It is not uncommon for the client and others within the system to be unable to make this identification; the old problem of not being able to see the forest for the trees is particularly operative in systems. Also, the personal biases of staff members, the involvement of staff members in only portions of the system (without full knowledge of the operations of the rest of the system), and a lack of analytical skills contribute to the difficulty of making a logical assessment.

In addition, not all hindrances within a system are actual problems that merit systems analysis. A policy that is a disadvantage for one section of the library may be an advantage for the library (or society) as a whole. First then, the term *problem* itself needs to be clearly defined. If a problem is *an undesirable condition or situation that prevents an organization from fully meeting its goals*, then what could otherwise be considered a problem may in fact be a desirable condition that should not be eliminated. A federal requirement to make a facility barrier-free for physically handicapped people may involve a major investment of existing financial resources, cause major disruption for a period of weeks or months, and (as in the case of lowering elevator buttons) actually result in a disadvantage for nonhandicapped staff and library users. But society (or the government) has decided that the result is an advantage, not a problem. It would be foolish to conduct a systems analysis that would determine no modifications are necessary.

Finally, it is impossible to understand, much less define, a problem unless its environment is determined. In other words, a situation cannot be identified as solvable unless it is put into context meeting four criteria: there must be a choice of alternatives, a decision maker, doubt about the best alternative, and an identifiable environment.

Suppose, for example, that you are on a flight from Honolulu to Hilo, Hawaii, when the wings of your aging airplane peel off. This is not, in systems analysis terms, a problem. You and the pilot will descend toward the ocean at an acceleration of 32 feet per second squared. *For it to be a problem, there must be a choice of alternatives.*

Suppose a less drastic disaster overtakes you. Rather than the wings falling off, the top of the fuselage peels off and falls into the sea. As a passenger, you are not in a position to make a decision. You will continue to Hilo, return to Honolulu, or ditch in the ocean, depending on the laws of physics and the ability of the pilot. The pilot, faced with alternatives at 25,000 feet, does have a problem. *For there to be a problem, there must be a decision-maker.*

If the aircraft is at the end of the runway when the top peels off, the pilot has no problem because there is no doubt about the correct action to take. She does not shout, "Go for it!" and rev the engines for takeoff; she shuts down the engine and radios for help. *For there to be a problem, there must be doubt about which is the best alternative.*

Finally, if the fuselage disintegrates in the repair shop, there is a different problem than if it happens on the runway or at an altitude of 25,000 feet. If the fuselage fails when stressed beyond its design strength in a test facility, no problem is present at all. *For there to be a problem, there must be an identifiable environment to determine its character.*

These criteria can be applied to less dramatic, but equally valid, library situations. If a library closes because its sponsoring institution is closing, no real problem is involved, because no decision made within the library will affect the outcome, and a problem implies a choice of alternatives. Of course, alternative *ways* to shut down are available, and the decision of which to choose constitutes a problem; this is amenable to systems analysis.

Similarly, no matter how much a cataloger may dislike the idea of contracting with an external vendor for cataloging services, if the library's administration dictates that all cataloging will be outsourced, whether to outsource or not is not a problem for the catalogers, because they are not in a position to make a decision. Systems analysis will, however, help the cataloger with the problem of whether to seek a position in a different library.

Another example is that a library would like to start a preschool summer program but lacks the funds to do so, the decision to use money from a federal grant appropriated specifically for adult literacy or to use scarce local funds does not constitute a problem because defrauding the government is not a viable option. If, on the other hand, the decision is whether to use *local* funds for adult literacy or for preschool programs, the best alternative is not obvious, and systems analysis techniques may be usefully employed.

Finally, a simple statement such as "We have no programs for preschoolers" does not constitute a problem. The environment must be understood. Is this a university library? If so, it probably has no need for such a program. But, if that library wishes to be involved in an employee day care center, a problem may exist. Such a statement would probably indicate a problem for a public library, but perhaps not if the library was located in a retirement community.

Sources of Problems

Initial investigation of the problem, or problems, within a system can be facilitated by examining the most prevalent areas in problem identification (Semprevivo 1982, 126-33):

1.   Response time: A system is failing to provide information, services, or products to users in time for the output to be useful. Example: An interlibrary loan system may be retrieving the desired materials from another information center but has such a backlog of requests that the materials arrive too late for patron use.

2.   Throughput: A bottleneck in the system prevents the rest of the process from being effective. Example: Materials are being discharged in a timely fashion, but insufficient shelving staff results in a growing number of items that need to be shelved. Note that throughput is always limited by the least efficient part of the system.

3.   Economy: The system is meeting the needs of its users, but the process is too expensive. The cost per unit of individual steps within a system often reveals startling figures. Example: Cataloging of materials requires a lengthy use of staff time; the work is done well, but it is too costly. In one university library it was determined that each book cost $80 to put on the shelf (exclusive of the purchase price).

4.   Validity: Data is inaccurate or irrelevant. Example: Catalogers retrieving cataloging records are transposing digits (inaccurate) or entering a Library of Congress control number instead of an OCLC item number (irrelevant).

5.   Reliability: The system does not produce consistent results in identical situations. Example: The same query entered into an online system at different times retrieves different citations.

6.   Security: The system lacks security to protect property, data, or human rights. Example: A circulation system allows a student helper to determine who has borrowed materials on transvestitism.

7. Quality of information: The system is not providing users with information that is timely, useful, relevant, organized in a logical manner, and in as complete a form as needed. Example: An information retrieval system provides a bibliography of articles but it lists only the eight most recently published articles and lists them in order by date of acquisition by the library.

8. Efficiency: The system fails to balance the elements listed above, and as a result, all parts of the system cannot be optimized. Example: A library has established procedures to ensure reliability but has slowed the response time to an unacceptable rate.

Real systems often have several (or even many) of these problems. Consider the situation below, which was the first substantial case of one of the authors:

> Paul, the owner of an auto parts store, complained that his sales were down and profits were plummeting. In spite of this, the secretary was obviously overworked. Paul wanted to automate in order to simplify the secretary's job and to reverse his negative profit trend.
>
> The budding analyst was late for his first appointment because he had difficulty finding a parking place near the store, which was located in the downtown area. Later, he realized that he had to allow extra time in order to find a parking space, and he had to carry change to feed the meter whenever he visited the store. During the next few days, he managed to interview the owner (who also staffed the desk), the secretary (who also provided bookkeeping), the delivery driver, and the stock clerk. He observed the mix of professionals and amateurs who made up the clientele, and he looked at the financial records of the shop. He discovered that:
>
> - walk-in trade was diminishing;
> - professional accounts showed a slight increase; and
> - the number of unpaid accounts was increasing.
>
> Further observation and interviewing over the next week revealed separate policies for the two types of customers. Professionals received a 30% discount, were billed later, and were not charged for deliveries. Retail customers had to visit the store to get parts, were not extended

> credit, and received no discount. He also noted that the secretary/bookkeeper kept a record of customers who had not made payment, but the owner/counter clerk did not have that information available at the point of sale.
>
> The owner said that the profits had been declining for several years, and he blamed the change on the growth of malls. As president of the Downtown Businessmen's Association, he was committed to supporting downtown trade and couldn't consider a change of location.

Readers might wish to enumerate the problems that can be identified in this operation. What recommendations should be made? Would installing a computer resolve the problem(s)? Would automation decrease the problem(s)? A discussion of the author's actual solution is provided in Appendix B.

Taxonomy of Problems

The scope of the problem-solving effort will directly affect the scope of the solution, the cost of the solution, and the effectiveness of the solution. Systems analysts must be aware of the range of the problem and determine how far-reaching the solutions need to be. Properly selecting the problems to attack increases the success rate. Semprevivo (1982, 134-38) has identified four levels of problems in a system:

1. Organization-wide: If the system being addressed is an entire, large organization, analysis will require a) coordination of all departments; b) a larger staff; c) increased time; d) more money; and e) more compromises within the organization. There is an increase in the likelihood of political agreements that will need to be made between departments. Changes can be made that will profoundly affect the organization if the new system works. A successful conclusion to an organization-wide problem can be a great coup for systems analysts. However, the risks are much greater because of the complexity of the problem and the greater investments involved. The results of any failure will also be massive. Performing a management audit and reorganization for a library system is an example of an organization-wide effort.

2. Functional (Departmental): The analyst will work with lower level management within one department. The input from and output to other departments can be shown on charts as a "black box"—in existence but not under consideration. The process is less complex, with better chance for agreement within the single department. Concomitant with the size of the system, the impact of changes and the risk of failure will be less. The cataloging department of a large library is an example of a functional system.

3. Operation: The analyst will work with an operation that may be interdepartmental but will not involve all the operations of each function. For example, management of serials within a library may involve the orders department, processing department, and circulation department, but serials management represents only a portion of the operations of those departments. Analysis of an operation involves more coordination and can require more time than anticipated. The results, however, can be dramatic since they are evident in more than one department.

4. Activity: The procedure within a single function is studied. This is a process that is easier and less expensive, with less chance of major failure because of its limited scope. However, even a completely successful analysis, design, and implementation may do little to affect the overall operation of the library. The process of reshelving books after they are discharged is an example of an activity. Conducting systems analysis at the activity level can sometimes be analogous to selecting the perfect bucket with which to bail water, while not doing anything to plug the hole in the boat.

Wise analysts will ascertain the level of problem being addressed; this knowledge can help forearm them. (See figure 4-1.) Analysts cannot expect far-reaching results and great recognition if an outstanding solution is found for problems at the activity level. The potential for great success and the risk of major disaster is greatest at the organizational level. The height of the expectations of the client are directly proportional to the breadth of the system being analyzed. For example, a mediocre solution for an organization-wide problem will bring dissatisfaction with the analysts. Knowledgeable analysts should be able to assess the scope of the task and their own ability to deal with the problems.

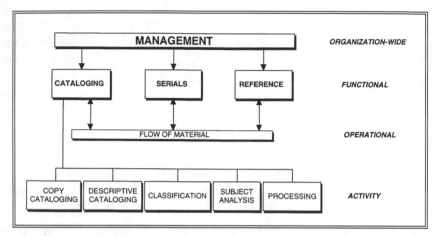

Fig. 4-1.

Even the most experienced analysts are sometimes surprised when a problem they thought was clearly limited to an activity or department suddenly expands like a striking cobra into an organizational or operational one. In one case, for example, a request was made to analyze a university archive. During the course of the investigation, the problems became obvious. First, reproduction of documents was complicated by lack of a copy machine in the archives area. Second, the lack of a special-purpose software package meant that the archivist, unable to adapt the university's integrated library package to the needs of his environment, was forced to maintain a cumbersome paper system. Initially, the solutions seemed obvious. Copy machines and specialist software for archives are readily available. Less than $2,000 would have doubled the service the archive could provide. Unfortunately, as the investigation deepened, it became obvious that the archive fell under the control of the library, which would not permit what they saw as a "rival catalog" within the organization. Further, copy machine allocation was controlled at the university level, which had its own team of specialists who determined placement. Rather than a small departmental analysis, where decisions and approvals could be made with the stroke of a pen, the boundaries of the system had greatly expanded and along with them the difficulty and expense.

In such a case only two things are really possible for analysts to do. They can include the necessary wider-scale negotiation and analysis as part of their proposal, allowing the client to make use of it as part of an effort to influence higher authority. In the example above, for example, the proposal could be used as a supporting document when appealing to the copier committee for permission to purchase a machine. The other alternative would be for analysts to provide the best solution possible within the constraints of the wider system. Analysts confronted with the problem above might propose a more efficient paper system, with the specialized software package mentioned as an unselected alternative, along with a explanation of its rejection. The client can then make what use of that portion of the proposal he feels will best support his operation. In no case should analysts take it upon themselves to actively work outside the system as defined by the client. To do so could endanger the client's position within the organization.

Case Study—Fort Memorial Library

As the first step in the analysis proper, Nancy made an appointment with the head of serials, Margie Norris. When she arrived she discovered that the three professional librarians in the department were all waiting for her. She began by thanking Margie for suggesting that analysis be done for the department.

"That's not exactly the way it happened," broke in Ms. Norris. "When Readers' Services got a consultant in to evaluate the collection, they asked her to blame us for their problems, and she obliged. I couldn't defend myself, so I suggested the dean get in an outside expert. I don't see that we really have any problems. Sure, things are a little slow, but no worse than anywhere else."

"That's right," said the head of the check-in section. "I think the whole thing was caused by a combination of unreasonable expectations for the time it takes to get a journal from the mail room to the stacks, coupled with a little jealousy over the number of clerks we have. There are 10 of them, and in this library clerks are power: the more you have the more resources you can demand."

"Well," said the serials cataloger, "they can't complain about the speed with which I work. I get all my cataloging done by noon, so I can help check in periodicals all afternoon."

"And," cut in the acquisitions librarian, "we do all the ordering and processing for anything belonging to a series. Naturally that takes time, especially with the monograph department constantly ordering serials and not telling us. We must spend three or four hours a day just looking over the incoming books to see if any of them are really serials."

"So you see," finished the department head, "all you have to do is suggest that we be given a little more money."

"And a few more clerks," interjected the check-in librarian.

"And everything will be fine," said Margie. She smiled at Nancy encouragingly.

"But we definitely need more clerks. You could get them from the circulation department." added the check-in librarian.

Nancy felt a little like Alice in Wonderland. This certainly wasn't the way serials was taught in library school. Or systems analysis, for that matter. She longed to tell them so, but these were people she would have to work with long after her temporary assignment was finished. Yet, she would also have to work with Reader's Services.

Discussion Questions

• The serials department has stated their proposed solution to the problems. How should Nancy respond to this proposal?

• Are you suspicious of any areas in the operations of Miskatonic University's serials department? List them.

• The head of the check-in section seems very concerned with getting more clerical help. What should or shouldn't Nancy say to her?

• What problems might Nancy anticipate in conducting a systems analysis for the serials department? What experiences have you had that parallel Nancy's? What happened in *those* situations?

References

Semprevivo, Philip C. 1982. *Systems Analysis: Definition, Process, and Design*. 2d ed. Chicago: Science Research Associates.

Chapter 5

COLLECTING DATA

Introduction

Although the tools of data collection are discussed in this chapter, in actuality, data collection using these tools is an iterative process and should be conducted throughout the systems analysis. Systems analysts should be alert to emerging information and employ data collection strategies at any point in the process where further data is needed. System analysts have a wide repertoire of data collection methods to draw on. These fall into four major categories: conducting interviews, administering questionnaires, conducting observations, and reading existing documentation. Each method has its special benefits and limitations; each should be used in conjunction with the others when appropriate and practical in order to extract all the data necessary to proceed to the next step in the systems analysis process. This chapter attempts to introduce the basic methodologies and their applications but is necessarily superficial. It is strongly recommended that budding analysts complete a course in research methods in the social sciences. While practicing systems analysts can seldom achieve the rigor of their academic counterparts, better investigations lead to better systems.

Conducting Interviews

Interviews serve a dual purpose: they are useful in gathering data and they afford the systems analyst an opportunity to discover and overcome resistance to change in the present system. The drawback to conducting interviews is the time required for both the analyst and the person being interviewed. For maximum effectiveness, a wide range of interviewees should be included in the interview process. Any change in the system will affect the client, managers at several levels, staff members, end-users, and gate-keepers (those outside the formal line of command who control access to information through an organization, such as secretaries, assistants). Their roles in the current system should be explored prior to designing a new system. The astute interviewer will tailor the interview according to the person or group being interviewed.

In order for an interview to elicit useful data, the interviewer must have a clear understanding of what information must be gathered. This includes what is being done in the current system; what problems are being encountered in the present system; and what the requirements are for the new system. One paradigm that can be used to structure requirements breaks them into:

1.   Mandatory: Requirements essential for the user to function effectively. "If I don't have this, I can't do my job!" "The circ. system has to be able to tell us who has a book checked out."

2.   Flexible: Requirements for which the user can accept alternatives. "We can use magnetic strips or barcodes."

3.   Deferrable: Requirements for the indeterminate future. "Eventually this will have to link to our anticipated online catalog."

4.   Desirable: Things the user wants, which are not essential to the system, and for which the user is willing to pay. "Of course all the hardware will have to be beige in order to coordinate with our décor."

Note, that when the final list of requirements is determined, it becomes the list of specifications for the new system. It is important that the user recognizes the difference between a "wish list" and actual requirements. Confusing the two will result in unrealistic expectations for the new system. Often, interviews will elicit conflicting requirements. This is only to be expected, and part of the analyst's job is to reconcile these conflicts. Individuals being interviewed, however, do not know of the conflict. It is reasonable for them to expect a seemingly minor request to be fulfilled; therefore, it is important to inform them that not all requirements will be realized.

Successful interviewers need to be aware of several factors that might affect the outcome and eventual value of the interview. First, it is important to realize that the interview*ee* may assume knowledge on the part of the interview*er* which simply is not there. The person interviewed might consider some facts not worth mentioning because she or he considers them to be common knowledge or too basic to mention. Often these factors are crucial to the system. Analysts must never try to cover up their ignorance; if something seems to be missing, it probably is. It is also important to listen for inputs and outputs which are similar when conducting interviews with various people. These may be couched in different terms (one person may mention "authority control" and another "standardization of terminology" for example), but if the analyst recognizes them as essentially the same, it is often possible to simplify the design by using a single procedure for both.

Second, it is important to determine and verify use requirements with each level and its auditors, both fiscal and legal. The information should be checked for accuracy, completeness, and priority. Operators within a system may underestimate or overestimate the importance of a particular requirement because they may not know the impact of the requirement on other parts of the system.

A conscious effort must be made to dismantle barriers to communication:

- A manager should not be present during interviews. The person being interviewed will be inhibited and tend to give answers that will be pleasing to the manager instead of a candid assessment of the current system.

- Interviewers should control their personal emotion or biases. If the person being interviewed senses frustration, anger, or lack of respect, the interview will become detrimental to the outcome of the process, as well as a solicitation of inaccurate data.

- The setting for the interview should be controlled. A quiet and comfortable location is essential, with a sufficient amount of time set aside. The timing of the interview is also important: the middle of the week has been established as the ideal time to gather data through interviews (people are neither tired from the previous weekend nor distracted by looking forward to the next one).

- Interviews should be designed to acknowledge and focus on the interviewee's past experience. An employee in a new job will not be able to give the best information about the system.

- Interviews should acknowledge the interviewee's negative response to the prospect of a change in the system. Most people find change to be stressful, even if the change will result in improvements to the system. If the person being interviewed has any doubts about job security or the new skills that may be required in a new system, the problem is compounded. Interviews provide a setting for interviewers to recognize anxiety and, when appropriate, to provide reassurance.

- System staff members, or end-users, may come to an interview with preconceived, unrealistic notions, the most common of which is that a computer can solve all problems.

- Interviewers must guard against "wishful listening," hearing what they want to hear. The data gathered must be objective and accurate, or else the data collection process becomes flawed and will have a negative effect on the system design.

- Interviews should be carefully structured, with those being interviewed understanding the purpose of the interview, the value of the information they will provide, and the time they will have to expend in the interview. Unprepared interviewees will be understandably resentful of the time they are "wasting" and will feel threatened by the interview.

Types of Interviews

There are numerous types of interviews. One is a structured, or standardized, interview involving the use of a list of questions that remain unchanged throughout the interview cycle. If multiple interviewers are to be involved, they are trained in order to ensure the consistency of the interview. Alteration in the questions or variation in the styles of the interviewers will result in data that cannot be accurately assessed.

One type of question that can be included in a structured interview is the fixed response question. This requires a response that has to fit within pre-established boundaries, although some flexibility can be added by including an "other" response.

Example:

When I am unable to locate a particular title in my school library, I usually

_____ask the librarian for help.

_____go to the public library.

_____stop looking.

_____other:

The fixed response question is useful in gathering information that is uniform, information that results in responses easily coded for analysis. The disadvantages of this type of question, are that: 1) interviewees are able to give a response to cover up ignorance even if they do not really know the answer; 2) interviewees may be irritated if the correct answer is not included in the responses; and 3) the data produced from this method may be superficial. However, the response may be "Would you repeat the question?" If so, the question is probably stated poorly, or it might be better addressed through a questionnaire.

Another type of structured interview question is the open-ended question. This type of question allows the interviewees to provide information in their own words rather than choosing a response from a list.

Example:

> If you are not able to find the title you need in this library, what do you do?

The data collected through the use of open-ended questions 1) is flexible and has more depth; 2) allows the interviewer to make sure that the response is being interpreted correctly; 3) gives a better indication of the level of knowledge of the interviewee; and 4) can suggest further questions to elicit more information. However, interviews involving open-ended questions are extremely lengthy to conduct and may result in uneven application by different interviewers and with different interviewees. The resulting data is also difficult to code for statistical analysis.

A third type of question is the funnel question, which is designed to lead the interviewee from the general to the specific. The first question can determine which set of questions should follow with the implication that either set of questions is acceptable.

Example:

> 1. Have you ever used OCLC to retrieve cataloging records?
>   Yes _____ No _____

If the answer is no, the interviewer would skip to the next section.

If the answer is yes, the interviewer would continue with the next question.

> 2. Did you find OCLC search keys difficult to learn?
>   Yes _____ No _____

Criteria for Evaluating Interview Questions

Given the investment of time required for interviews for both the interviewer and interviewee, it is important to ensure that the questions are well designed. Some key tests to apply are the following:

- Is the question related to the analysis? Asking interviewees about their marital status gathers irrelevant information, (unless, of course, the system will use the information).

- Is this an appropriate type of question for the data needed? If the object is to determine color preference, it is easier for the interviewee to answer the question "What is your favorite color?" rather than "Is your favorite color blue, red, purple, orange, or other?"

- Is the question clear and unambiguous? Using the term *online*, for example, may be interpreted by one respondent as referring to accessing DIALOG and by another as using a local area network or public access catalog.

- Is this a leading question that will solicit only one response? There is only one answer to the question, "You don't like working with the existing database program, do you?"

- Does the question ask for information the interviewees may not have? Asking someone whether the library should use TCP/IP or X25 protocol will be confusing to many.

- Does the question require an answer that reveals sensitive or personal information? (These can be asked at the end of an interview in a carefully worded manner.) Asking workers whether their department is overstaffed will create anxiety.

- Is the question loaded with social desirability? "Do you believe in equal pay for equal work?" has only one socially correct response, but the response may not reflect the true opinion of the respondent.

A short interview schedule (script) is given below. Readers may wish to consider the quality of the questions in light of the criteria given above.

1. Have you used the library computers to access the World Wide Web? (If the answer is yes, continue. If the answer is no, thank the interviewee and go on to the next interview.)

2. How often do you use the library's computers for World Wide Web browsing?

3. Do you use the Web for pleasure or for research?

4. How did you learn to use the World Wide Web?

5. What are your favorite Web sites?

6. Do you think pornography should be available at Web sites accessible from library computers?

7. If not, how do you think this should be prevented?

Preparing for an Interview

Interviewers should be professional before, during, and after an interview to ensure they receive useful information and continued cooperation from the interviewee. Cardinal rules include:

- Be prepared. Know the interviewees and their function within the system.

- Be tactful. Remarks such as "We're interviewing the less important people today" do not build rapport with interviewees.

- Be reassuring, if possible, but not misleading. The interviewer can make it clear that the purpose of the study is not to eliminate positions within the system, *unless* a real possibility exists that staff reduction will result from the new system design.

- Be polite. A letter of thanks is a courteous follow-up.

- Be exact. Match your vocabulary to that of the person being interviewed.

- Listen carefully, but do not get involved in the responses. Interviewees may try to get a commitment to their position or to gain support for their complaints about the system. Getting caught up in political issues never helps.

- Make a record of the interview. Taking notes during a structured interview is generally appropriate. Three choices are available for unstructured interviews: 1) take no notes at all; 2) write notes during the interview; or 3) tape-record responses. (Interviews should never be recorded without the knowledge of the interviewee.) The last two choices may be intimidating to interviewees. However, taking no notes will result in less useful data unless the information is recorded immediately after the interview is completed. A practical compromise is to take brief notes during the interview and to expand them immediately afterward.

- Be aware that in a few instances the analyst might have to resort to "force," to ask the manager for assistance if someone refuses an interview. If the person is the best source of the information needed, in the end, the interviewer may have to settle for a hostile witness.

Interviewing is not an easy skill to acquire; indeed entire academic courses are devoted to interview and questionnaire construction and analysis. Analysts who expect to make extensive use of these tools would be well advised to seek instruction through a social science research course. A badly botched series of interviews can easily compromise the entire analysis and design project.

In a well-conducted interview, the interviewee has been informed that an interview is to take place and what topics it will cover. A mutually agreeable time has been selected, and a meeting arranged at the interviewee's workplace or on neutral territory (not in the supervisor's office). When the interviewee arrives, he or she is welcomed by the interviewer. If time allows, coffee or tea might be provided. The interviewer repeats the purpose and scope of the project and interview and answers any questions the interviewee might have. The interviewer confirms consent if the interview is to be recorded. When both participants are at ease, the interview proper begins. Since most systems analysis interviews are informal, the interviewer pays particular attention to the *way* questions are answered, and expands or adds questions to bring out as much useful information as possible. The optimal interview proceeds like a friendly, although somewhat formal and structured, conversation. Of course, it is the interviewer's responsibility to keep the conversation on topic. When the interview is concluded (when the entire interview schedule has been covered) the interviewee is offered a chance to add any useful information that he or she feels the interviewer might find interesting or useful. The interviewer then thanks the interviewee and retires to expand the notes and prepare for the next interview.

It probably does not surprise readers that this ideal is not universally achieved. The authors have observed many less-than-ideal interviews. Examples of these include the time when extreme shyness over a minor speech impediment was misinterpreted by the interviewer as hostility toward the entire systems analysis project. In another case, a response by an interviewee produced an openly stated condemnation based on the interviewer's religious belief. A third example is the time the interviewer became confused about the interviewee's position title and asked a high administrator the questions intended for clerical workers. That case was doubly embarrassing for the interviewer, because the administrator realized what was happening and played along, giving true but misleading answers such as "Oh, I have no idea how many hours I work in a week, I just come and go whenever I like." Finally, one interview became so informal and friendly that, while intended to elicit details of an automated authority module for a cataloging system, it was actually devoted to a spirited debate on unidentified flying objects.

It is easy to feel petty pleasure when contemplating these gaffes (and one of the authors must own up to being guilty of the last example), but it is much harder to recognize them when they are developing. The ability to do just that, and then to successfully conclude the interview, is a mark of the true professional.

Administering Questionnaires

From the above discussion it is obvious that using interviews to get information from hundreds of users scattered over the world would be an impossible task. Fortunately, another tool is available that is better suited for this purpose: the questionnaire. Questionnaires can be thought of as self-administered interviews.

Well-designed questionnaires are useful for the specific purpose of gathering a limited amount of information from a large number of people, with a number of advantages:

- They elicit data that is uniform and easy to tabulate.

- The anonymity of questionnaires encourages honesty.

- They are inexpensive to administer.

- Information can be gathered from respondents at a greater distance from the system.

Questionnaires, however, also offer distinct disadvantages compared to other methods of gathering data:

- The return rate is usually low. The average number of questionnaires returned by mail is only 30 percent.

- There is no opportunity to clarify ambiguous answers.

- The data from a closed question tends to be superficial; open-ended questions elicit less information because respondents must write their answers instead of discussing them.

Designing Questionnaires

A variety of questions is available to the designers of questionnaires.

- Agree/disagree
  Example: Fines are useful. A D

- Agree/disagree with a four- or five-point scale (strongly disagree to strongly agree). The argument of whether to use an odd or even number of answers is still unsettled; generally, though, the authors believe it is wise to use an even number of answers to prevent respondents from simply selecting the safe "middle ground." After all, few issues elicit no opinion at all.
  Example: Fines are useful. SA A D SD

- Multiple answers
  Example: Fines are useful to

(Check all that apply.)

_____ encourage prompt return.

_____ discourage theft.

_____ generate income.

_____ teach discipline.

- Several options with prioritization
  Example: Rank in order of importance (1 is highest, 4 is lowest)

_____ Community outreach

_____ Story hours

_____ Telephone reference

_____ Multiple copies of romance novels

- Open-ended questions
  Example: How can our library improve its services?

- Others, such as psychological tests. These are rarely used in systems analysis except at the organization-wide level. Wise analysts will seek expert assistance if their use seems justified.

As an exercise, consider the following two questions asked on recent (separate) questionnaires. Identify the problems:

> Many rules in AACR2 are vague and subject to local and subjective interpretations. This diminishes the degree of consistency from one library to another, which has a negative effect on the preparation of national and union catalogs. A D

> Economic and social freedom is worth far more to women than acceptance of the ideal of femininity which has been set up by men. A D

The first is an example of a portmanteau question. It is actually seeking information on at least three separate issues: Are many rules in AACR2 vague?; Does this diminish the degree of consistency?; and Will it have a negative impact on preparation of union catalogs? What if you agree with the first and last statements but disagree on the second as being the cause? Should you agree with the whole or not? This is a good example of where a funneling question would have helped.

The second case, given to female graduate students, is both a portmanteau question (Is freedom worth more...? and Was the ideal of femininity established by men?) and a question that is heavy with social desirability. The use of the word *freedom* and the phrase *which has been set up by men* show which response the researcher believed was correct. A more experienced researcher would have been more subtle, perhaps by presenting the subject with a situation in which the student would have to decide between femininity and freedom, and then asking which she would choose.

The target audience of questionnaires usually should be the users or operators of a system. Less frequently, questionnaires are sent to managers and clients, but usually as a supplement to interviewing. If analysts determine that it is appropriate to survey the end-users of a system, and if the group contains more than 400 people, it is practical to survey a sample of the group. In this case, it is important to ensure that the sample is a true one. For example, the nonusers of a system sometimes must be surveyed if the sample is to be considered truly representative and reveal deterrents to use.

Two aspects of the sample are especially important if the sample data is to accurately represent the population from which it is drawn: randomization and size. In order for a sample to be random, each individual in the population must have an equal chance of being selected. The best way to ensure this is to use a random event—a coin toss or a random number table—to select the sample. (Random number tables can be found at the back of almost every statistics textbook.) While some variation from this ideal is permissible (e.g., the use of systematic sample—taking every *n*th person or card), accidental or self-selected samples will almost certainly lead to improper conclusions. Examples of automatically biased samples include those based on piles of questionnaires left on a table for users to fill out, those selecting only interested users for interviews, or those asking for volunteers. Such techniques, though making data collection easy, immediately determine that the data is not representative, because these techniques exclude those who do not like to fill out questionnaires, are not interested, or are too shy to volunteer.

The size of the sample is also important. Figure 5-1, based on a formula presented in *Educational and Psychological Measurement* (Krejcie and Morgan 1970, 30: 507-610), shows the relationship of population size to sample size, if the data is to be representative. Note that for small groups (less than 400), a very large proportion of the population must be reached in order for the sample to be valid. In such cases it would be wise to interview or send questionnaires to the entire population. However, a sample of 400 is sufficient if the total population is close to a million, assuming a .05 confidence interval. Larger sample sizes are necessary to produce a .01 confidence interval. While this chart is useful, a short Java applet and HTML document is included as Appendix C, which produces proper sample sizes for any population size input when viewed with an appropriate Internet browser (such as Netscape 3.x).

As an example of a situation where a random sample would be appropriate, consider a small university library serving a population of 15,000 that has recently changed its OPAC from an in-house only, text-based interface to a Web-accessible graphical user interface (GUI). The library wishes to determine whether their current users like the change, as well as to find out whether the extensive media campaign that accompanied the unveiling of the new system was effective in reaching people who had previously avoided the library and its catalog.

A random sample would be appropriate in this case. More obvious techniques, such as questionnaires placed beside the OPAC terminals, would yield biased data and could actually be used to intentionally skew the results, in fact, if a group wished to fill out multiple reports. The most direct way would be to take a list of all potential clients (in this case, students and faculty) and number them. Then a table of random numbers could be consulted, and 400 unique numbers obtained. These, matched to the list, would identify people to be contacted with a survey.

Population size	Sample for .05 confidence	Sample for .01 confidence
10	10	10
50	44	50
100	80	99
150	108	149
200	132	198
350	183	343
400	196	391
450	207	438
500	217	485
750	254	718
1,000	278	954
2,000	322	1,785
3,000	341	2,541
4,000	351	3,223
5,000	357	3,842
7,500	365	5,165
10,000	370	6,239
25,000	378	9,972
50,000	381	12,456
75,000	381	13,583
1,000,000	384	16,317

Fig. 5-1.

The analyst should make it as easy as possible to complete and return the survey; certainly a stamped return envelope or self-mailer should be attached. Assured anonymity typically is offered to increase the return rate. Because the percentage of items returned has a large effect on the reliability of the results, rewards are considered ethical: certificates for food, copier cards, and even cash, often accompany surveys. A good rate of return is important; the authors are reluctant to make decisions based on a less-than-50-percent return and feel steadily more confident as the rate approaches 100 percent.

Action Logs

A valuable method of data collection that may be overlooked in the library setting is the practice of keeping logs of actions and interactions. For example, a reference librarian's log of the questions (or categories of questions) asked and their outcomes provides a useful source of information. An analysis of the log could provide some insights.

- Are many of the questions directional? Improved signage and posted directories could free the librarian for reference questions.

- Are patrons frequently asking for help in using the workstations? More detailed instructions posted by the workstations, or in-service training for new patrons might be effective.

- Is the information requested not available in the library? Documentation is useful in justifying increased funding for materials, interlibrary loans, or online access to information.

- Did the librarian fail to direct the patron to useful information? Additional training may be needed, especially for recently hired personnel.

Because keeping a log may appear to be an added task in a busy situation, it is important to follow some basic rules:

- Be sure that those involved understand that the initial investment of time can result in long-term resolution of problems.

- If resistance to log-keeping is encountered, consider conducting a pilot test of the practice. If the log-keepers discover that the benefits outweigh the inconvenience, they will be encouraged to continue.

- Ensure that logs are reviewed and action is taken on a timely basis. If keeping a log becomes an empty exercise, the log-keepers are justified in becoming cynical and resentful. For example, in one school district, elementary teachers were required annually to create a pie graph showing how much time they spent teaching each subject area. After several years of no response to the reports, the teachers in one school began copying the district sample annually; no one at the district level noticed!

Conducting Observations

Gathering data through observation has a better potential of determining reality than do interviews or questionnaires. This method is much more difficult to conduct than it might first appear and has inherent disadvantages. First, observers may be biased or may misinterpret the actions of those being observed. When an observer sees a cataloger lean back and close her eyes for five minutes, it is difficult to tell from observation alone whether she is sleeping or contemplating the application of an obscure cataloging rule. The observer may see a subject make a series of keystrokes but may not know what was entered or why. One way to offset this problem is to use the technique of protocol analysis. The subject performs the task as if simple observation is taking place, but maintains a running verbal commentary on what they are doing and why. This technique is an extremely powerful one for investigating technical tasks that require analysis and decision-making, but only when trust and rapport has been established between the observer and the subject. Second, those being studied may well become nervous and modify their behavior, behaving as they think they should rather than as they usually do. This tendency can be offset by conducting an observation over a long period of time, allowing the observer to become just a part of the surroundings. Finally, observation under any circumstance is very time consuming.

Several methods may be considered when conducting observations:

- Self-observation can be used (such as with the use of a diary or log (although these may be inaccurate). However, logs are also time consuming for the self-observer and do not address the problem of bias.

- Unobtrusive observation—when those observed are unaware—may be useful. For example, noting the number of people in a queue waiting to use a terminal does not violate any principles of privacy but provides information about the number of terminals needed. However, observing individuals at work without their knowledge would be unethical spying. Many businesses, when providing telephone customer service, make a practice of alerting the caller that the call may be monitored for quality control. Since both the customer and the customer service representative are aware that a supervisor may listen, intervene, or make suggestions to the employee, the process is both practical and ethical.

- Indirect observation can be carried out by gathering clues from inanimate objects. Scuffed wax in front of a terminal is a clue to the frequency of use. A turnstile at the library entrance gives an accurate count of the number of people entering the library during a given period of time. Indirect observation, when feasible, can be more accurate than other means of observation.

- Current technology has made direct, but invisible, observation possible. Gathering data by computer is a simple matter but raises ethical questions. Recording the number of "hits" on a Web site provides useful information to the company represented by the site but does not invade the privacy of those accessing the site. However, analyzing the accessors' interests and depositing information "cookies" in the users' computers without their knowledge or consent raises concerns about invasion of privacy.

- Observations may be carried out for a long period of time or at random times. In the latter instance, especially, observers must avoid making judgments on actions that may not be representative of the usual procedures. A decision based on observations conducted only on a Friday night or just before school assignments are due may lead to systems that are unrealistic at other times.

A typical case where observation provided the best data-gathering techniques occurred during one analysis, when it became necessary to determine whether online catalog users were primarily using keyword searches, or whether authority-controlled searches were more common. The authority-control subsystem, where terminology was recorded in a standardized (authorized) format with elaborate *see* and *see also* references to broader and narrower terms used up vast amounts of storage space for its indexes and was expensive and time consuming to maintain. It was possible that little effective use was made of this capability, and it could thus be deemphasized or eliminated. Several possible methods of gaining this data were considered: logs kept by librarians in their searches, observations of patron searches, post-search interviews with patrons, etc. In the end it was decided to take advantage of the system itself. A short macro routine was written to count the types of searches completed, and the number of failed searches attempted (the number of searches which produced no hits). From this it was ascertained that while keyboard searches were more common, authority-controlled searches succeeded much more often. This data, added to information obtained from patron interviews, justified a large-scale education campaign for both new and experienced searchers.

Using Existing Documentation

Written guidelines and procedures for a system would seem to be a logical, if boring, source of information for analysts. Too often, though, manuals are poorly written and, worse, do not reflect what is actually happening. Instead, the documentation shows what someone thought the old system was *supposed* to do and, therefore, may help to identify the problems of the old system. Observation has shown that people rarely follow written documentation. Knowing how the system was intended to function may be useful, but discovering how the system actually is working is best accomplished through observation, interviews, or questionnaires.

An additional type of documentation that may be useful is the documentation of system inputs and outputs—what are traditionally referred to as "statistics." Generally these are counts of some sort: the number of reference questions asked, the number of books circulated, the percentage of books lost in a year. Such documentation can be a valuable resource in spotting problems and potential solutions, but analysts must be careful not to become overly dependent on them. Such measures are often manipulated (consciously or unconsciously) by their creators.

Evaluation of the Usefulness of the Data Collection

Before proceeding to the analysis of the data, analysts should ask two key questions: "What else do we need to look for?"and "What did we miss?" The process of analyzing the data, discussed in the next chapter, will reveal gaps in the information that is needed, but it is better to gather as much useful data as possible in the data collection stage to make best use of the analysts' and the information providers' time.

Practice in Selecting Data Collection Methods

Determine which method is most appropriate for each of the following situations. Refer to Appendix B for actual solutions found in analysis projects.

1. The theft rate at a self-storage facility is much higher than average.

2. The new director of the educational services section of a library software company discovers that a large number of training sessions is pending. These had been assigned to a group of contracted trainers but had not been completed.

3. The absentee rate of a department in a college library is much higher than the other departments.

4.   A large collection of uncataloged books has hampered library operations.

5.   Students are complaining that not enough online public access catalog workstations are available in an elementary school library. The librarians think the problem is caused by students browsing with no real search in mind.

Case Study—Fort Memorial Library

Nancy has brought her team into the serials department to conduct interviews with the staff. She has Sue Schriver (the COBOL programmer) and Ben Root (the reference librarian) talk with the check-in clerks. They are determining how the current system, based on visual Kardex cards, actually works. Meanwhile, she is interviewing Margie Norris, the serials head.

But Margie can't understand the *point* of it all. "After all," she keeps saying, "I spent *months* writing a procedure manual that covers every possible situation arising within the department. All you have to do is read the manual, and you'll know *everything* that goes on here. *No one* would do *anything* without following the manual."

She has given Nancy all three loose-leaf volumes of the manual. Nancy has read it, and Sue and Ben are using questions derived from it to find out what the clerks actually do.

They are discovering that the clerks don't refer to the manual at all. They can't find anything in it since it isn't properly indexed, and in any case, it bears little relationship to the actual day-to-day running of the department. The rules really needed for checking in serials are passed down by word-of-mouth from one clerk to another. The average periodical takes a week to be checked in and forwarded to the reference staff. No two clerks do their jobs exactly the same way, and none of them do it exactly the way the manual says it should be done.

Discussion Questions

• Nancy is using Sue and Ben as interviewers. Were these wise choices? Discuss the pros and cons of each of Nancy's staff for this task.

• Do you think this is a situation where a formal or an informal interview would be appropriate? Nancy's staff does not seem to be working from a list of questions. Is this a good idea? What questions would you want to ask?

- Nancy is getting into a ticklish situation: Margie thinks the procedure manual is being followed, but Ben and Sue are discovering that it is not. What problems might this discovery cause? How can Nancy ethically deal with these problems?

References

Krejcie, Robert V., and Daryle W. Morgan. 1970. "Determining Sample Size for Research Activities." *Educational and Psychological Measurement* 30: 507-610.

Chapter 6

ANALYZING AND DISPLAYING DATA IN FLOWCHARTS

Standardization of Communication

As can be seen from discussions in previous chapters, obtaining enough correct data is anything but easy. Yet, after all that work, data is useless unless it can be recorded and shared with the client, and it is meaningless for the purpose of analysis unless it has passed the test of validation with the client or users. The problem is that systems are large: they cover space, they involve people, and they are made up of solid objects. Even if the analysts believe they understand the system, that understanding must be passed on to the client. Analysts are in the position of an architect who wishes to show a client what a building will look like when it is finished and how it will blend into the existing landscape. In fact, they use the same tool; they build a model. Once data has been displayed in a logical and accessible format, it becomes a model of the system, and it can serve a number of purposes.

First, properly recorded data improves communication between the analyst and the users by ensuring that terminology is used in the same way by both. The term *erase*, for example, can mean several different things depending on whether it is used by a programmer, a computer operator, or a secretary. Standardizing terminology limits the number of potential ambiguities and misunderstandings. Good recording standards also ensure consistency in the reporting of data gathered at different times during the analysis and design process, and save time by allowing a single manner of reporting to a variety of users.

Second, clearly recorded data improves communication between the analyst and the system vendors. The specifications of the system are easier to define when the processes or data flows involved have been clearly identified. Use of well-constructed and standardized tools helps prevent important but subtle operations from being overlooked and allows the library and the vendor to gain the same view of the system.

The display of data can also promote good management of the systems analysis effort. Rigorous use of standardized tools pinpoints vague terminology or unclear procedures. Vagueness is often a result of the analyst's or the client's reluctance to admit that they do not understand what is happening, and modern tools such as data flow diagrams reduce the possibility of accidental or intentional obfuscation that will create problems during the implementation of the new design. Ultimately, the data, displayed in a standard form, will document the results of the analysis and design effort. Because future professionals may be expected to be familiar with the standard recording techniques, using such tools will ensure that the reasons for decisions will be understood. Future efforts to improve the system will thus have a clearly defined foundation for a new design.

The systems analyst has a useful array of methods for recording and displaying data, some of which are more appropriate at different stages in the systems analysis process. In the analysis stage, the most appropriate techniques to employ are flowcharts, data flow diagrams, and data dictionaries. Data flow diagrams and data dictionaries are also especially useful in the design stage. Implementation may call for data flow diagrams, flowcharts, data dictionaries, and a combination or choice of structured English or decision tables and trees. These last, structured English and decision tables and trees, will be discussed in Chapter 8, and data flow diagrams in Chapter 7. At all stages well-written narrative text will also be needed.

Recording Data in Flowcharts

The flowchart is a traditional method of showing the step-by-step operations that take place as part of a procedure. In other words, flowcharts document the flow of control within a system. Thus, flowcharts are best used to document instructions, decisions, and alternate actions. This is accomplished by assuming the viewpoint of one person or group within the system.

Flowcharts have numerous advantages that have ensured their survival over some 50 years. Probably the largest advantage is that almost everyone is familiar with flowcharts. Thus, they are relatively nonthreatening and can be comforting in a stressful situation. Another advantage is that they are ubiquitous. An American National Standard (ANSI-IEEE 5807-1985) specifies the symbols and techniques of flowcharting in the United States, and similar formal or informal standards are in use throughout the world. This leads to extreme portability of flowchart documentation. The logic described in a flowchart created in Istanbul can be easily understood in Tokyo, even if the specific words are not.

The graphic nature of flowcharts enhances this portability and understandability. They consist largely of easily comprehended pictures (of Hollerith cards, of pieces of paper, of computer tapes, etc.). These are augmented by logical symbols that are used to express acts and decisions. The combination of easily comprehended symbols and a relatively small set of logical operations make flowcharts especially well suited for recording the logical flow of very low-level processes within a system.

Finally, because flowcharts track the step-by-step operations and decisions within a process, they are easily translated into program code or policies and procedures. In many cases this is simply a matter of translating the symbolic and abbreviated language of the diagram into structured English or a programming language on a "one box on the chart equals one line of instructions" basis.

Despite these advantages, flowcharts are not in high favor with today's systems analysts (Martin and McClure 1985, 160-63). Perhaps their largest disadvantage is that they do not lend themselves well to a top-down approach. Many people have tried to create rules for drawing sets of flowcharts that would clearly, evenly, and accurately decompose broad system flowcharts into sets of specific detailed ones. Despite these attempts to create levels of flowchart detail, flowcharts simply do not break down from the general to the specific, and this decomposition is the essence of a structured approach.

The graphic aspects of flowcharts, listed above as an advantage, can also be a disadvantage. It is altogether too easy to become tied up in the symbology. For example, the ANSI symbol for magnetic storage is a picture of a computer drum, a device that has not been used for decades (see figure 6-1),

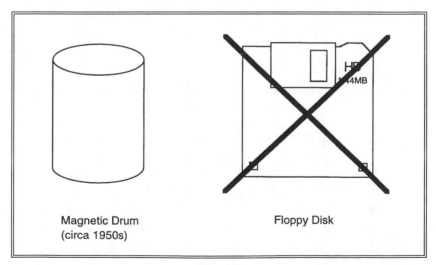

Magnetic Drum
(circa 1950s)

Floppy Disk

Fig. 6-1.

but there is no symbol for floppy disks. How then should such disks be represented? Should the analyst create a custom symbol, thus sacrificing standardization, or should the magnetic drum symbol be used, which might necessitate explaining the usage to the client? While a seemingly small point, such adaptations can easily detract from the communication between analyst and client. The symbology has a less obvious disadvantage as well. Once it has been shown that a file is on a reel of tape, there is a tendency to continue to think of it as a tape file, and a concomitant reluctance to consider that a CD-ROM or a card file might be more appropriate. Thus, flowchart symbology tends to emphasize the physical structure of a system; yet one of the analyst's most difficult tasks is to free the client from thinking in such physical terms.

Also, flowcharts, because they are not easily decomposed, quickly become very complex. Most individuals have difficulty following a multipage flowchart, but few systems can be adequately represented on a single page. This problem is worsened by the fact that operations of very different levels of complexity are usually shown on a single flowchart with no indication that different levels of complexity are being represented. A part of a flowchart for a technical services department shows this rather well (see figure 6-2).

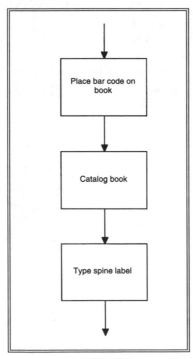

Fig. 6-2.

Placing bar codes and typing spine labels are relatively simple clerical operations, but cataloging books is a complex intellectual operation. Despite this massive difference, the flowchart treats them all equally.

Yet another difficulty with flowcharts is their inability to represent concurrent operations. Because they are designed to be followed step by step (i.e., to document the flow of logic from the standpoint of the user), they are not suitable, for example, for showing that while a letter of acceptance is being typed by one person, a query is being answered by another.

Finally, perhaps the largest disadvantage of flowcharts is that, once they are drawn and presented, the analyst and the client tend to believe they understand the actual system, even when they do not. Flowcharts lend themselves well to intentional or unintentional obfuscation. It is all too easy to look at a pretty flowchart, drawn with a graphics tool and printed on a laser printer, and feel satisfied no matter what the reality of the situation. Analysts should keep in mind the words attributed to Neils Bohr: "Never speak more clearly than you think."

The disadvantages of flowcharts do not mean they are useless—quite the opposite. Flowcharts, properly used for the proper purpose and in the proper place, are extremely functional. Their proper purpose is to document in an easily followed, step-by-step fashion *what someone should do*, and their proper place is *at the low-level procedural steps in a system.*

Creating a Flowchart

The first step in creating a flowchart is to investigate the system. It is impossible to draw a flowchart if the analyst does not know what is being diagrammed. Once a general understanding of the system has been accomplished, the analyst can determine the five to ten major steps in the process, list them, and put them into logical order. The flowchart itself may then be drawn, representing repeated steps with logic loops. It is then checked for accuracy and usefulness. Does it record the process as the analyst understands it? Is it detailed enough to be useful, but not so detailed as to be confusing? If the flowchart does not work, the investigation must be repeated, the steps broken down again, or the logic re-analyzed, as appropriate. Once the flowchart meets with the analyst's approval, it must be shown to the client, who also checks it for accuracy and level of detail. If it does not meet with the client's approval, corrective measures must be taken. This process itself may be shown as a flowchart (see figure 6-3).

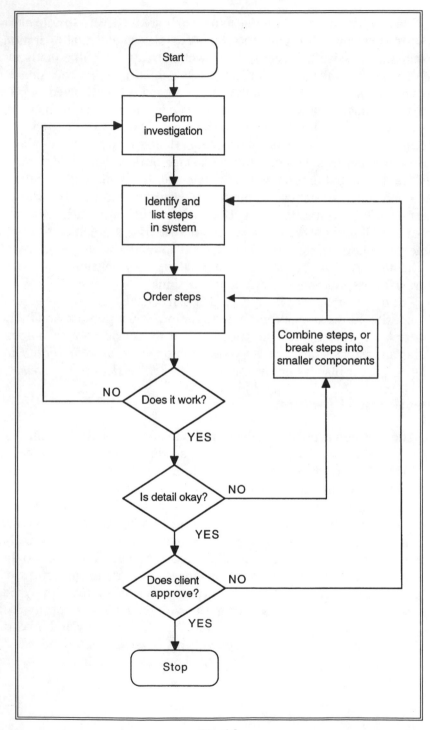

Fig. 6-3.

The chart in figure 6-3 illustrates some of the strengths and weaknesses of flowcharts. It is clearer and more graphic than the narrative explanation that precedes it, but its clarity is misleading. It exhibits the drawback related to various levels of complexity being shown as equal in complexity: the processes "perform investigation" and "order steps" are shown as identical boxes although they are clearly tasks of differing complexity. It also illustrates the problem of "I drew it so I understand it." If the client does not approve the chart (last step), do analysts always return to listing the steps, or would redoing the investigation be the appropriate response? The chart is graphically clear, but the best action is not.

Compare the difficulties of figure 6-3 with the flowchart in figure 6-4.

This chart is simple and easy to follow. Each step is of approximately the same level of complexity, and clear and unambiguous decisions are shown. Such a flowchart could be followed by either a person or a machine.

Flowchart Symbols

As explained above, flowchart symbols are covered by ANSI-IEEE standard 5807-1985. A chart of the most common symbols and their meanings is shown in figure 6-5. Note that in some cases a nonstandard symbol (e.g., the off-page connector) is more common than the ANSI-ISO prescribed symbol. It is recommended that these symbols be used and that analysts resist adding local symbols for things such as floppy disks. Should it prove necessary to create such a symbol, take care that it matches the style of the other symbols as much as possible.

Flowchart Conventions

A number of general rules govern the construction of flowcharts:

1. A flowchart is designed to be read first from top to bottom and then from left to right. Theoretically, arrows to show direction of the logic flow need only be used when this top-to-bottom, left-to-right convention is violated (in practice, arrows are nearly always used, as in figure 6-6).

Text continues on page 77

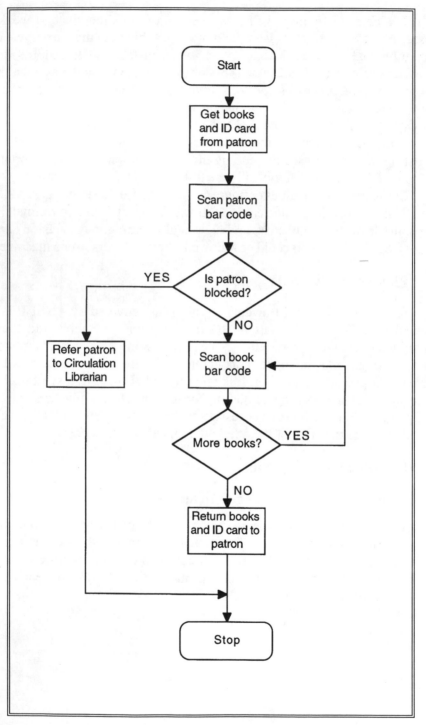

Fig. 6-4.

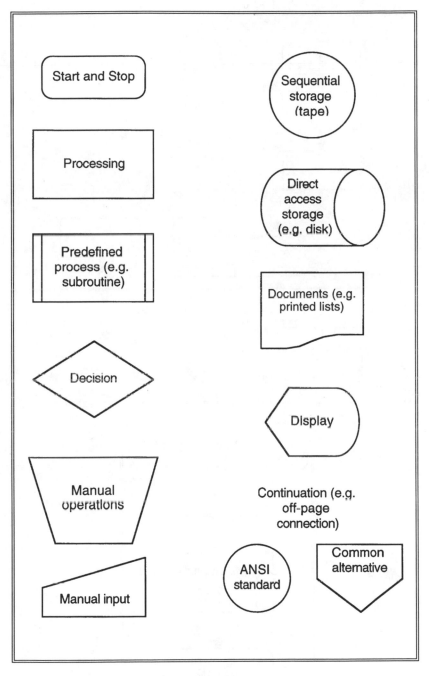

Fig. 6-5.

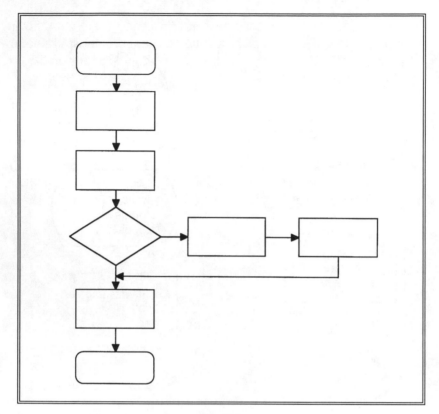

Fig. 6-6.

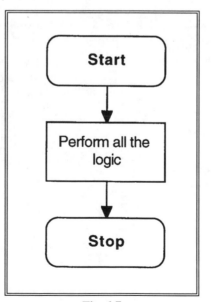

Fig. 6-7.

2. The start and stop of each chart is clearly indicated with the appropriate symbol. All paths through the diagram must ultimately begin at "Start" and eventually reach "Stop" (see figure 6-7).

3. Optimal flowcharts record from five to ten separate processes; the ideal number is seven processes. Analysts often deviate from this ideal, especially when recording process flow in large software modules.

4. A flowchart is neat, clear, and legible. The person drawing the chart should use a template rather than working freehand. Templates are readily available at stationery and computer stores; there are also several excellent flowcharting programs available for both IBM and Macintosh personal computers. The diagrams in this chapter, for example, were made using *MacFlow*, *MacDraw II, and Flowcharter.*

5. For the sake of simplicity, off-page connectors are avoided, if possible. As their name implies, off-page connectors are used when a flowchart becomes too large too fit on a single page. A connector with a unique identifier inside it is placed with the point out where the line is to leave one page, and a similarly marked symbol is placed on the next page where the line is to enter (see figure 6-8). While sometimes necessary, off-page connectors make a diagram more difficult to use and to understand. Excessive need for off-page connectors is a sign that the overall system was not decomposed sufficiently before flowcharting was done. In these cases, another tool (e.g., data flow diagrams) might be more appropriate at the higher levels.

6. A flowchart displays, if possible, a consistent level of detail. Each process should have about the same complexity.

7. Lines are not crossed unless the process cannot be accurately depicted otherwise. When lines must be crossed, a "wicket" is often used to make it clear that no connection is implied (see figure 6-9).

8. If an action is repeated, it is shown as a loop. For example, if the action to be recorded is "First get the top worksheet, tear it up, then get the second worksheet and tear it up, and then get the third worksheet and tear it up, and so on until all the worksheets are torn up," a logic loop as shown in figure 6-10 may be used.

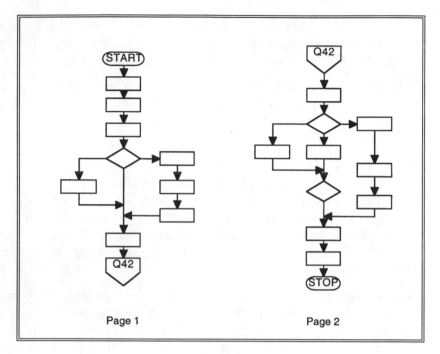

Fig. 6-8.

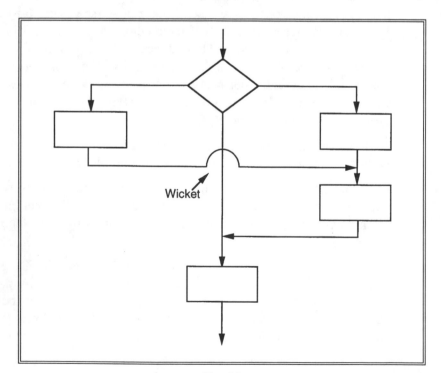

Fig. 6-9.

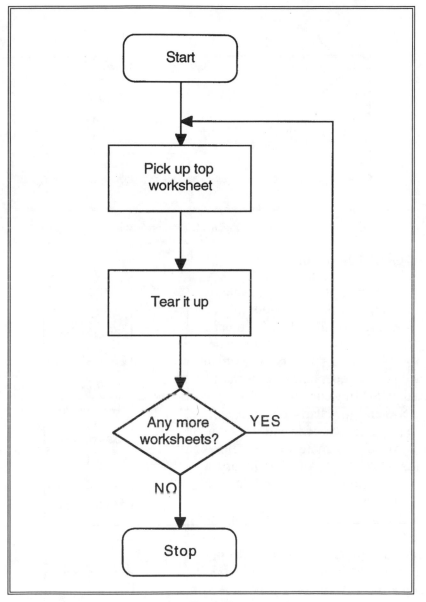

Fig. 6-10.

9. A decision symbol generally has two or three lines emerging from it: one line for a "yes" decision, the other for a "no" decision, or one for "greater than," one for "less than," and one for "equal to," or three other possibilities (see figure 6-11). While the ANSI-IEEE standard has a convention for describing more than three options, it is seldom encountered.

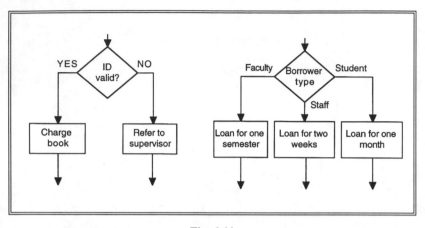

Fig. 6-11.

Types of Flowcharts

In an attempt to make flowcharts fit the top-down, structured model, several levels of flowchart have been suggested. For example, texts often describe three levels of charts: system flowcharts, generalized flowcharts, and detailed flowcharts.

System flowcharts are large, simple representations of an entire system, used to put the more detailed flowcharts into context. An entire library at the system flowchart level might look like figure 6-12.

Generalized flowcharts break the system-level flowcharts into functional components. They show the operation at the departmental or workgroup level. Their primary purpose is to allow the analyst to investigate alternate arrangements of processes within departments and to put the detailed flowcharts into context. A generalized flowchart for a cataloging department might look like the one shown in figure 6-13.

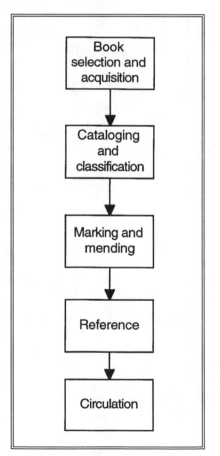

Fig. 6-12.

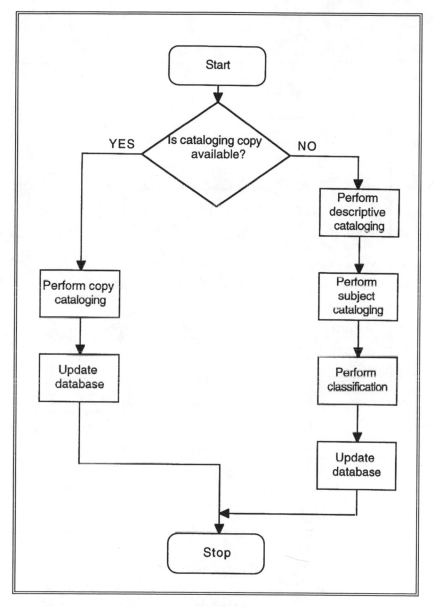

Fig. 6-13.

Detailed flowcharts are process-specific and show the flow of documents and logic. This is the level at which flowcharts are most useful, and the only level at which the authors suggest they be used. A detailed flowchart for a weeding process is illustrated in figure 6-14.

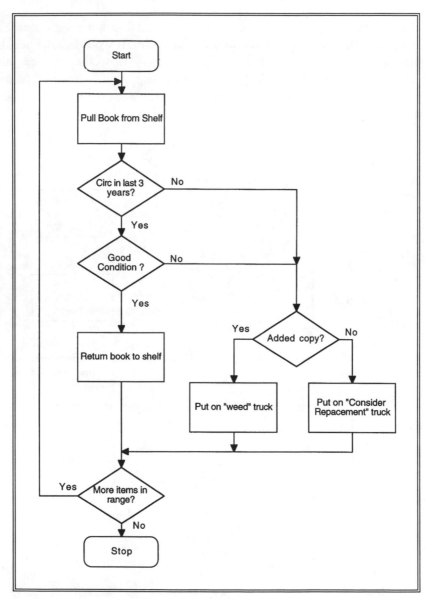

Fig. 6-14.

Illustrative Examples

Despite the apparent simplicity and ease of creating flowcharts, many people have difficulty at first in creating good, clear, logical, accurate flowcharts at an appropriate level of detail. Creating bad flowcharts, however, is not difficult, as the examples below illustrate.

In figure 6-15, the level of complexity is suitable and even necessary for documenting the logic of a computer program; it would, however, be confusing in a management report. Thus a "good" flowchart for one purpose can be a "bad" one in another context. The authors have often observed this level of flowchart used during presentations to management and users. In some cases, this may be attributed to an attempt to present all available information; in others, as part of an intentional effort to "blind them with science." In any case, it is not appropriate.

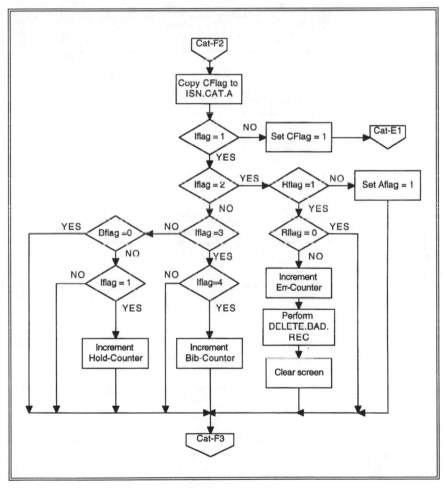

Fig. 6-15.

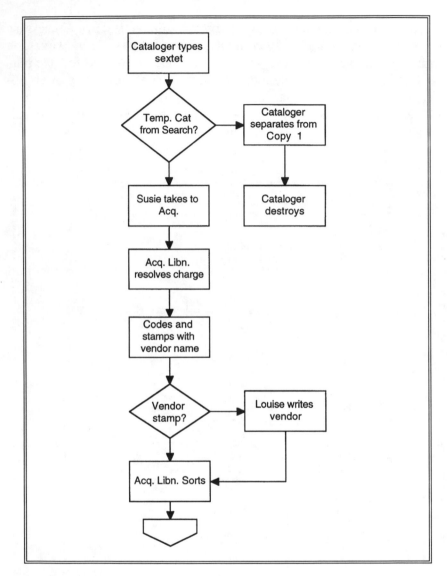

Fig. 6-16.

In figure 6-16 (drawn from an actual flowchart), however, complexity is not an issue, but the chart is so poorly labeled that the logic is hard to follow. Neither the meaning of "cataloger destroys" nor the fact that this step is really a dead end is clear. Such a flowchart is often the result when a person who really does not accept the utility of documentation is asked to perform the documentation process. It is perfunctory, hard to understand, incomplete, quite possibly wrong, and certainly useless. Flowcharts, like all tools, can only do a good job when the person using them understands and appreciates them.

Modified from the State of Hawaii Department of Education
Annual & Financial Report, 1991-1992

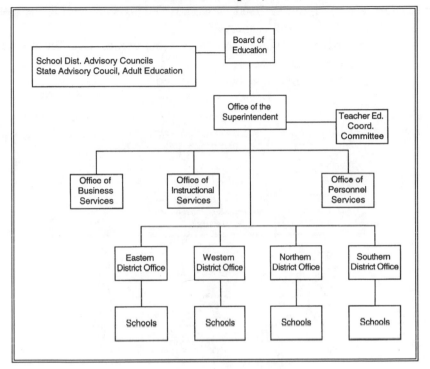

Fig. 6-17.

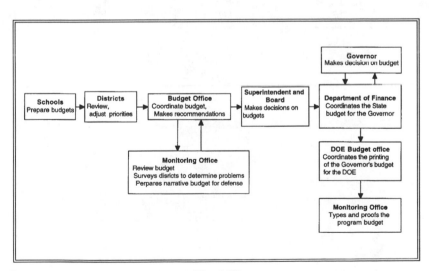

Fig. 6-18.

Figure 6-17 shows a chart that is *not* a flowchart, but an organiza-tional table or hierarchy, while figure 6-18 is an example of a Visual Table of Contents (VTOC) rather than a flowchart. VTOCs are useful manage-ment tools but not in systems analysis.

Although it is important to follow conventions to avoid confusion, the intent of a flowchart is to clearly show steps to be followed, not to show that the conventions have been followed.

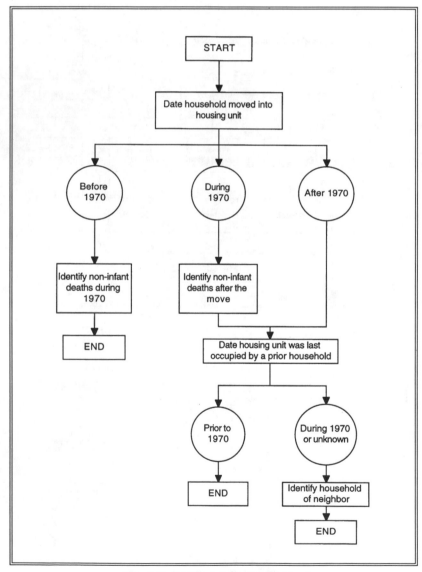

(From United States Census Bureau)
Fig. 6-19.

In figure 6-19 (drawn after an instruction for census takers), the decision diamonds are not represented as diamonds, but their meaning is clear. Obviously, a trained analyst would prepare such a flowchart using proper ANSI standard symbols, but confronted by a user-drawn flowchart such as this, or if the user has strong objection to the use of correct symbology, most analysts would agree that communication in a flowchart is more important than aesthetics or "proper" symbols. Analysts should make an attempt to explain the rationale behind standard usage but the use of should remember that proper function of the chart is more important than its outward form.

It is easy to point fingers at bad examples, but it is harder to design a good flowchart. Well-designed flowcharts can be a useful means of communication with a client and can enhance other forms of arrayed data, but their creation is usually the result of long practice. As long as analysts are aware of the advantages and disadvantages of flowcharting, it can be an effective tool.

Practice in Drawing Flowcharts

Consider the following situation. Draw a flowchart describing it. A suggested answer appears in Appendix B.

As part of a retrospective conversion project, inputters are instructed to access a CD-ROM database by searching for a Library of Congress Control Number (LCCN). They go through the shelf list, card by card. If a record cannot be found, they put the card aside (reject it). If a record *is* found, they check the author, title, publisher, and date of publication against the record on the screen. If all agree, they add the barcode for the book and the library's call number and download it to a floppy disk; at that point they are finished with that record (it is converted). If they find a close record (one that almost matches the criteria listed above), they modify it to match the card they have in their hands, add the local data (barcode and call number), and download the record to the floppy. They are then done with that record and can get the next card.

Analysis of Data

It usually becomes evident, as flowcharts or other data representations are designed, that the processes of recording and analyzing data are intertwined. It is impossible to analyze the data without first recording it, but recording the data involves analysis. As charts and other arrays are checked against reality with the user—and revised accordingly—the analysis is further corrected and refined.

Case Study—Fort Memorial Library

Weeks pass. At last the system has been investigated. After interviews, re-interviews, observations, and long, weary hours with the serials department's procedure manual, a set of flowcharts, data flow diagrams, and a data dictionary have been prepared. As a last step, Nancy writes a narrative description of the overall process. She arranges a meeting with the dean of libraries and Margie Norris.

But a nagging worry is still in her mind. She has noticed that Margie, the department head, has been unusually agreeable over the past few meetings. Indeed, she hasn't found a single problem during any of the structured walkthroughs. "We're good," thinks Nancy, "but we're not *that* good."

The next day she calls the team together and puts that thought into words.

"She's stonewalling us," mutters Ben Root.

"It's a guerrilla tactic," agrees Maria.

"We know more about that system than anybody else in the library, and we are right about what is happening. We must be sure that we are allowed to improve it," says Rachel, quietly but firmly.

Soon the team begins to form a strategy. The team reaches a consensus: Nancy should talk to Dean Tebbits about their concerns—before the meeting. Nancy isn't so sure that a meeting is a good idea.

Discussion Questions

- The group seems to have coalesced. Why might this have happened?

- Is Nancy correct to be concerned at a lack of criticism from the department head? What are some of the reasons why this might be happening?

- Nancy doesn't seem to have been keeping Dean Tebbits up to date on the project. Is this a bad thing? If so, how can she correct her error at this late stage?

- The team wants Nancy to prepare the dean for their meeting. Is Nancy correct in being reluctant to do so? What alternatives does she have, and what are the possible outcomes?

References

American National Standards Institute. 1991. *American National Standard for Information Processing—Documentation Symbols and Conventions for Data, Program and System Flowcharts, Program Network Charts and System Resources Charts.* New York: American National Standards Institute.

Martin, James, and Carma McClure. 1985. *Diagramming Techniques for Analysts and Programmers.* Englewood Cliffs, N.J.: Prentice-Hall.

Chapter 7

DESIGNING DATA FLOW DIAGRAMS

Introduction

As its name suggests, a data flow diagram (DFD) focuses on the *flow of data* through a system rather than the flow of logic emphasized in flowcharts. In contrast to flowcharts, they are more useful in analyzing a system, rather than illustrating it; they assume the viewpoint of the data itself rather than that of an operator or end-user in the process.

Data flow diagrams overcome many of the disadvantages flowcharts present when describing higher-level systems. Because they display the flow of data rather than logic, DFDs are well suited to display clearly the parallel processes of systems. This is a major advantage for DFDs and is extremely useful for analyzing the overall system: though people usually perform only one task at a time, there are usually several people operating concurrently at any given time as far as the entire system is considered. Also, DFDs were specifically designed to allow a top-down, structured approach, to allow clear breakdowns into increasingly specific diagrams. This ability to decompose systems neatly and accurately makes them particularly useful in the analysis stage and allows the analyst to identify and concentrate on processes that are poorly understood or illogically created. Graphically, DFDs are more advantageous than flowcharts because they do not describe physical hardware in terms of pictures. They are essentially hardwareless, and thus help keep analysis and design from bogging down under premature hardware concerns. Finally, when properly used, they are much harder to create incorrectly, or, at least, incorrectly created DFDs are easier to detect and correct than bad flowcharts. They lend themselves to probing questions on the part of both the analyst and the client; perhaps this is why it is almost impossible to create an inaccurate DFD (accidentally or purposely) if *either* participant takes a serious view of the task.

91

However, data flow diagrams do have some disadvantages. They are often unfamiliar to clients, necessitating a certain amount of selling by the analyst, and they do not translate directly into procedures or program code as do flowcharts.

Data Flow Diagram Conventions

Compared to flowcharts, fewer general rules govern the design of a DFD, but these are more rigid:

1. Only four symbols are used.

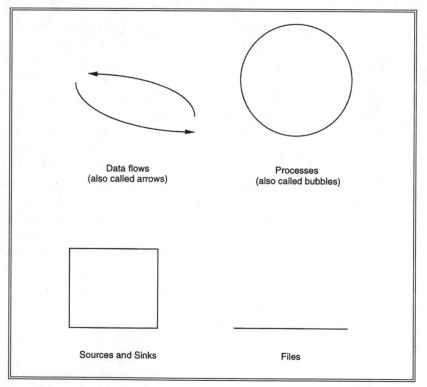

Fig. 7-1.

There are two basic styles of symbols used on DFDs. *Your-don*-style DFDs (named after the consulting, education, and publishing firm that created and popularized them) uses circles, squares, rectangles, and straight and curved lines as shown in figure 7-1. *Gane and Sarson* DFDs, described in detail in their book (Gane and Sarson 1979) replace circles with round-cornered rectangles and straight lines with open-ended rectangles, as shown in figure 7-2.

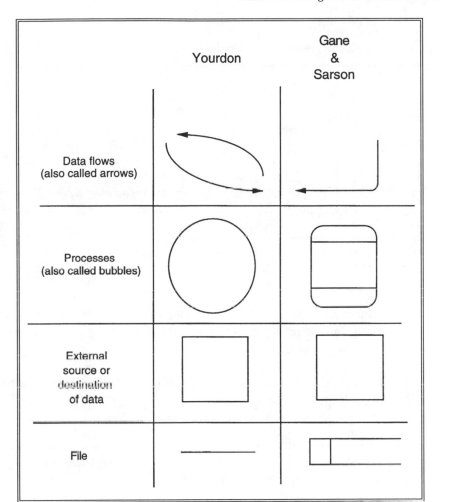

Fig. 7-2.

Semantically, these styles are the same. It is simpler for most computer software and printers to draw neat, round-cornered rectangles than attractive circles; the Yourdon requirement that data flows be shown as curved lines is also a problem for many computers. However, most DFDs are created using paper and pencil, and *Yourdon*-style symbols are particularly suited for this. Many analysts use both styles at each different stage in the documentation process, (though obviously not on the same diagram). The authors use *Yourdon*-style bubbles, arrows, and boxes, but *Gane and Sarson*-style file symbols.

2.   Data flow names are hyphenated (see figure 7-3).

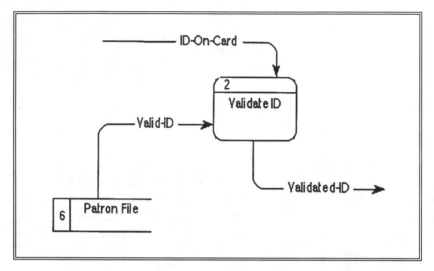

Fig. 7-3.

This is a throwback to the conventions of the COBOL programming language, it helps ensure that two similarly named data flows will not be confused.

3.   Data flow names are unique. The same name is never used for two different streams of data, and the *same* stream of data must always use the same name whenever it appears.

4.   DFDs do not normally document logic. Logic takes place inside the processes and is detailed elsewhere; hence there are few, if any, loops shown explicitly in a DFD.

Uses of Symbols

Tasks are accomplished inside circles (called processes or bubbles). A circle's function is to take the data flows coming into it and turn them into the data flows going out. One of the primary rules of DFDs is that processes must be able to build their outputs using only their inputs (plus constants). All data flows must be named. Process names ordinarily take the form of verb phrases such as "validate ID," "assign call number," and "transmit order." If a process cannot be given a name in the form of a verb phrase, it probably is not a process at all. However, this rule is often bent at higher levels in the diagram in order to use terms the client can easily identify. Care should be taken to ensure that processes actually accomplish something. Those who are accustomed to following the flow of control in flowcharts should avoid attempting to use the same technique in DFDs by using processes instead of decision boxes.

Arrows, or data flows, are quantities of real data that are passed from one process to another. Generally, this flow does not consist of physical items but, in some cases, it can be a combination of data and a physical carrier. Because data flows are *things*, their names generally take the form of nouns or noun phrases. "ID-number," "book order," and "invoice" are all valid data flow names. If it is not possible to give a noun or noun phrase to a data flow, the analyst should suspect that no data is actually flowing. Analysts should be able to state specifically *what* is flowing in each data flow.

Files are places where data is temporarily stored. They are generally used as interfaces between processes, with data flows going into and out of them. Dead-end files should be suspect. If data flows into a file but never flows out, the analyst must question the file's usefulness. Of course it may be an archival file, or a file used only by some other system, but such occurrences are rare.

Sources and sinks (same symbol) are optional. They are, by definition, outside the system. They are used to show the source of a data flow that is entering a system (when that source is not obvious), or to show where a data flow goes once it leaves the system (if that is not obvious). Sources and sinks (also referred to as data stores) are not required but may make the diagram more understandable.

Levels of Data Flow Diagrams

DFDs are created as sets. This is consistent with their inherent top-down nature. At the top is the broadest diagram, the one that serves to put the rest into context. This level is the *context*, or *top*, level diagram (see figure 7-4).

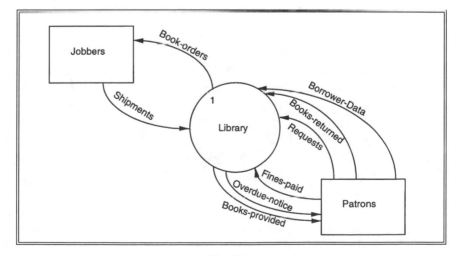

Fig. 7-4.

Under the context level falls one or more *middle* level diagrams (see figure 7-5). These represent successive decompositions of the context level.

The *functional-primitive*, or *bottom*, level of a system shows processes in terms of their most elementary components (see figure 7-6). At this point, the process can be described by a narrative paragraph, a decision table or tree, or a few lines of computer code. Note the use of data flows labeled "rejects" in this diagram. Often, though something must be done with exceptions, stopping to deal with them in the heat of analysis would interrupt the momentum of the project. Under such circumstances it is permissible to mark such exceptions as "rejects," and then come back and deal with the specifics later. It *is* necessary to come back and deal with them, however.

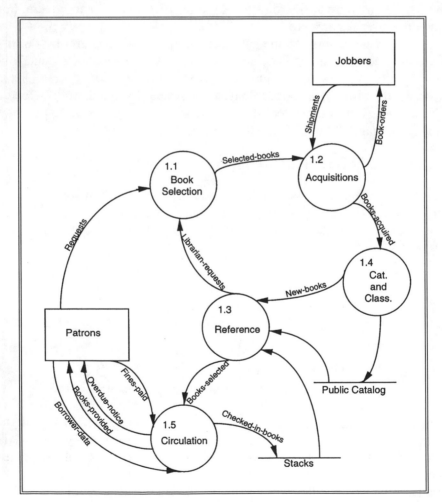

Fig. 7-5.

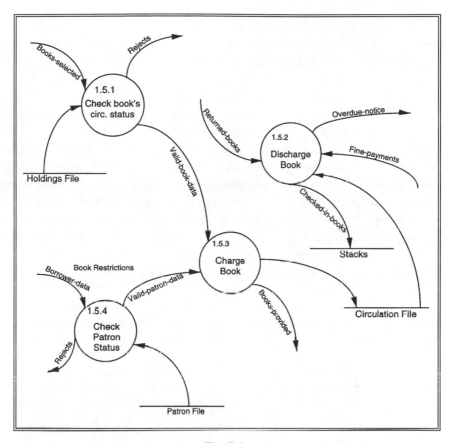

Fig. 7-6.

Note that the relationships between the diagrams are made explicit by use of a numbering standard. As each decomposition takes place, new processes are numbered by concatenating a sequential number to the string that represents the process being decomposed. The placement of the numbers within a diagram is not meaningful (i.e., numbers do not necessarily increase from left to right or from top to bottom).

Designing a Data Flow Diagram

It is important to realize that when used as an analysis tool, a data flow diagram should always reflect what is actually taking place within the system at that level, not what *should* be occurring or what operators may perceive is occurring. The "correct" procedure will be established as part of the design stage of the project. Analysis documents reality. Analysts usually start by drawing the first middle level just below the context level, and then work down to the functional-primitive level, and finish with the context level.

The technique most commonly used in describing a system is first to discover and name what processes are taking place. *This is a different order than will be used to create the new system!* For example, one process might be "send the order lists to the local libraries." The user's terminology should be utilized as much as possible in order to establish a meaningful name that is understood by those working with the system. Next, the inputs and outputs to the process should be identified. Look closely to be sure that outputs actually go somewhere and that all inputs are used to create an output. Because the old system is probably inefficient, there will quite likely be data flowing into processes that does not flow out. It is essential to examine such inputs, because either they are unnecessary or they point to an output that the analyst has not yet identified. What do you suppose happens to the "Fine-payments" data flow going into process 1.5.2 of figure 7-6? Finally, any files used should be shown. Files need not be shown until they are used as an interface between two processes. From that point they should be shown whenever they are accessed.

Once the diagram is complete, it should be discussed with the client. This is best accomplished as a structured walkthrough. In a walkthrough, each level of the DFD is presented to the client. A typical dialogue might be:

> **Analyst:** Now at this point, you've received the lists from the printers, and you're ready to send them out to the libraries. You take the mailing list and type labels for each library and put them on envelopes, and then stuff the order lists in the envelopes. Finally, you send them to the post office, right?

> **Client:** Well, you've left out the fact that we have to count how many we'll be sending out and get stamps from the business office. We don't stock the stamps in this department. They have to be requested each time on a QBX-135 form.

> **Analyst:** I must have missed that when we went over the process the first time. Let's pencil it in like this. Now, is that more correct?

The information derived from the client is then used to create a more accurate view of the system—one that the client recognizes as being exactly what happens. This is an iterative process, and one that involves much scratching out and starting over. The authors suggest that early DFDs should be done with pencil and paper; drawing software or special DFD software should be used for the final report only. Analysts tend to believe they are finished when the picture looks nice; pencil on paper encourages refinement.

The end product of the analysis will be a series of DFDs that break down the process into its smallest component but which can also be related to the overall picture at any time. In the end, a "pyramid" of DFDs will be produced, with each level made up of subunits of the one above. (See figure 7-7.) The drawings in this chapter were produced using either *MacDraw* or *DFD Editor*.

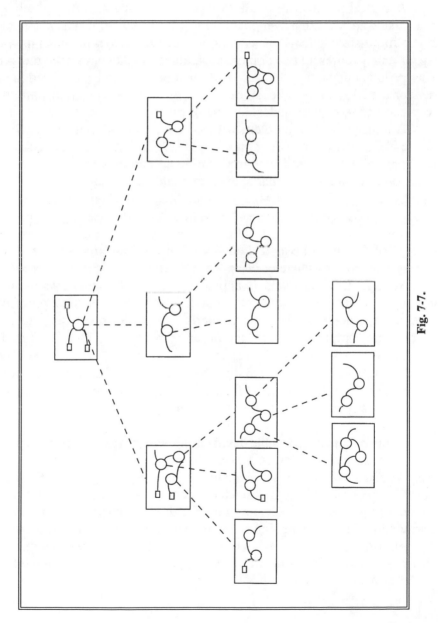

Fig. 7-7.

Typical Problems

Although it may not be intuitively obvious, one of the nicest things about DFDs is that inconsistencies exhibit themselves as problems. This encourages finding solutions to these problems rather than ignoring them or covering them up.

A typical problem is a data flow without a name. One of the basic rules listed above is that every data flow within a DFD must have a name. If it is impossible to name the data flow, it probably does not exist in reality, or it may represent two or more separate flows that have been merged. Any problem in naming the data flow must be analyzed and solved in order for the DFD to be valid, since problems with naming are usually the result of an incomplete understanding of the system.

Another common problem with DFDs created during the analysis phase is data flows appearing on a "child" DFD that are not reflected on the "parent" DFD. These are similar to dead-end processes or dangling connectors found in flowcharts. Such suddenly appearing data flows are usually a sign that management (generally consulted when creating upper-level DFDs) is not aware of what their subordinates (primarily consulted when creating lower-level DFDs) are actually doing. In short, any display of data must be logical and avoid mysterious processes or flows that appear from nowhere or disappear into limbo.

Strange files that suddenly appear, or into which data flows without any outward flow, are another problem. Files shown at the most primitive level must, in actuality, be in use as interfaces between processes; that is, a process may output data stored temporarily in a file and then input into a new process. It is often good practice, but not requisite, to label data flowing in and out of files. One exception is made to this: if the file is an archival one with data flowing in, the flow of data into that file must be labeled. Of course, any data flows that might otherwise be ambiguous should be labeled.

Many people have trouble determining which way the arrows should flow when accessing files. In a case where a user queries a database and then receives data, there is a tendency to show arrows going both directions. The operation becomes much clearer if it is understood that arrows show *changes* being made. Querying a file does not change the file, so the arrow should be shown pointing away from the file, in the direction the extracted data flows. Arrows should point toward a file only when that file changes because of the data (i.e., when records are added, deleted, or modified).

A final common problem is that of trying to specify control in the DFD. Flow of control can often be detected by observing circles with logic-testing or logic-questioning names: "Are all entries complete?," "Is it Tuesday?," or "Is the borrower flagged?" Such processes lead to difficulty, because no data flows out of them. Logic is accomplished *inside* processes; it is not a process in itself.

Data flow diagrams are not difficult to construct, but they are seldom completely correct on the first try. The designer must be prepared to revise them repeatedly . The process of revision, however, is also a process of more accurate detailing. The result is not just aesthetic; a good DFD is a valuable tool for examining what is actually taking place in a system.

Criteria for Evaluating a Data Flow Diagram

The process of evaluating a data flow diagram is more structured than that of evaluating a flowchart. The resulting display of a DFD demands a higher level of integrity. DeMarco identifies three tests to apply to DFDs (1979, 105-12).

1. Correctness. The designer must check with the user and refine the DFD to correct any earlier mistakes caused by poor communication. With the help of the user, the designer must determine if there are missing data flows, extraneous data flows, missing processes, deceptive labels, displays of control rather than data, or missing levels. The last error can be suspected if one circle decomposes into many processes at the next level down indicating a level is missing or the DFD is addressing the wrong level.

2. Usefulness. The DFD must not involve such complexity of interfacing that the diagram is difficult to understand. The name of each process must reflect reality, and partitioning must be even. Typically, the functional-primitive levels depicted should be reached in the same number of decompositions. For example, a process with 10 or 15 data flows going into and out of it implies that one step in the decomposition process may have been missed. A mid-level process that takes five lower-level diagrams to reach the functional-primitive, while others on the same diagram take only one more decomposition to reach bottom level, may indicate improper grouping farther up.

3. Bookkeeping. All data flows must have names, and the data that is flowing must be obvious. There should be no dead-end data files except for archival files, and the net inputs for a process on each level should be equal. Since data can neither be created nor destroyed, the system must be able to build outputs from the inputs and constants within the system.

In the event that a data flow diagram fails to meet these three criteria, the designers have three choices: 1) create a new DFD if the existing one is fatally flawed, 2) start at the level where the problems first appeared and work downward through logical decomposition to the lower levels, or 3) display the information in a different format. For example, if the process seems to involve complicated decisions, it may be necessary to break it down further with flowcharts, structured English, or decision tables and trees (which are all described in the Chapter 8). However, if one piece of data appears with several names, or if data is made up of other data, a data dictionary can add the necessary refinement of identification.

Examine the DFD fragment in figure 7-8; see how many errors you can spot.

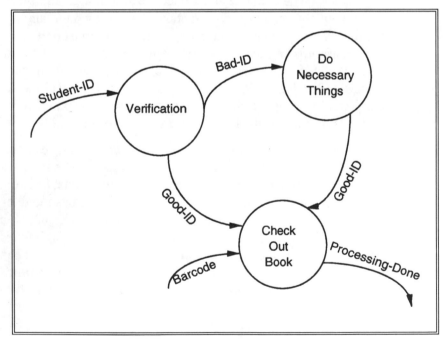

Fig. 7-8.

You should have caught at least five errors:

- Two data flows with the same name.

- Use of a noun "verification" instead of a verb "verify books" in a process name.

- Vague name for a process "do necessary things."

- Use of a verb form for a data flow name "processing done."

- Process that does something without the necessary tool "verification"—on what basis, probably a missing file.

Practice in Drawing DFDs

After discussion, observation, and investigation, the head of the serials receiving unit at a small university library came up with the following summary of her bailiwick:

> We get serials in three ways: direct from the publishers, through vendors, and as gifts. When they arrive, they are sorted out by title and entered into our Kardex file, on cards. We keep track of the volume, number, date, and copy numbers on each journal. The gifts go on red cards, the direct orders on blue cards, and the vendor-supplied journals on green cards (new subscriptions received since February go on yellow cards, because the manufacturer stopped making green ones). All three kinds of cards are interfiled in a single series. If we notice a journal between the last recorded issue and the one in-hand has not been received, we check in the one we have, leave a space for the missing issue, and fill out a "pink slip" for the secretary, who types up a claim letter (for gifts) or a claim card for publisher- and vendor-supplied journals. The pink slip is then filed. Once the issue has been checked in, the call number is written in it and it is sent to the Public Services Department.
>
> Oh, yes, in addition to checking in the journals, themselves, we provide answers to queries like: "Did we ever get the November 7, 1947, issue of *Life Magazine*?"

For this system: a) produce a context-level and one lower-level DFD and b) describe what additional data and clarifications the systems analyst would need from the serials department head. A suggested answer is found in Appendix B under "Chapter 7."

Data Dictionaries

A data dictionary is a repository of information about data. It may thus be considered to be an authority file for data. It consists primarily of definitions but may also include charts and diagrams. A data dictionary can be designed manually on index cards or with a computer using a database management program or even a word processor. For large-scale projects, elaborate (but costly) special-purpose data dictionary software is available. The primary purpose of the data dictionary is to define and keep track of terms used in DFDs. Thus, one entry is given for each data flow, one for each file, and one for each process *at the functional-primitive level.* There is also a special class called *data elements*, which are terms listed in other definitions but not in the DFDs themselves.

Data dictionaries lend rigor to DFDs. Without a data dictionary a DFD is only an artist's rendition of the system. With the addition of a data dictionary, the engineer's vision is added to that of the artist. The data dictionary ensures consistency of terminology throughout the system. When a question of what a process does arises, or what data actually flows in a data flow, the data dictionary should be consulted.

Sample Data Dictionary Templates

Perhaps the best technique for creating a data dictionary is to create a set of templates for each type of data: data flow, file, process, and data element. Then, the first time the item is used, a new definition should be added by filling in the appropriate template. The templates shown here were done with *4th Dimension*, but a word processor or even a typewriter would be sufficient.

Figure 7-9 is a template for a data flow entry. The "Data Flow Name" is the name used on the DFD to represent the data flow. The entry for "Aliases" is used when a data flow has more than one name. Normally, of course, this should not happen, but might occur in two instances. First, the data flow might be called two different names by two different users. For example, the same data flow called "order number" by the acquisitions department might be called the "accession number" by the cataloging department. It would be nice if the analyst could create harmony in such a case, but often it is better to simply acknowledge the duplicate name as an alias. Second, an alias might occur when the same data flow is assigned different names by the analyst, who realizes that fact late in the analysis project. In such a situation, one name should be selected to be the official data flow name, but because users may have been exposed to the other name in the analysis project, it should be recorded as an alias in case anyone refers to it by that name. The "Composition" section is the heart of the data dictionary entry. It is in this field where the data flow's composition is defined. This definition is made up of references to other (smaller) data flows and to data elements—bits of data that are not broken down any further. For example, an entry for a data flow called "Borrower-Info" might be:

Composition: Borrower-name + Student-ID-#+Borrower-status

This, in itself, is a kind of top-down partitioning of data. While many analysts opt for a narrative description of elements (especially if the system is not automated), more formal representations are available. Partitioning of a data flow is shown with the plus sign: The concept A equals B *and* C is A=[B+C]. The concept A equals B *or* C is shown as A = [B | C]. The concept A equals one or more Bs is shown as A = {B}, and the concept A always contains B and sometimes C is shown as A = {B + (C)}.

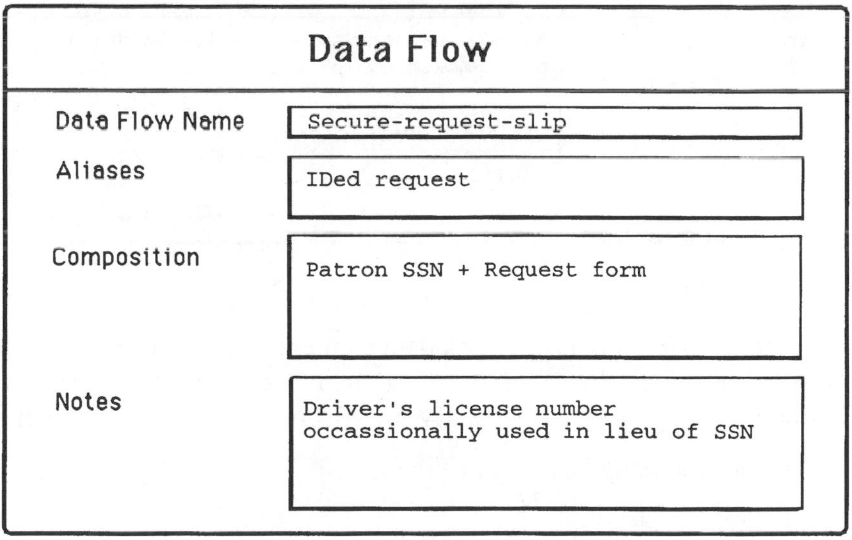

Data Flow

Data Flow Name	Secure-request-slip
Aliases	IDed request
Composition	Patron SSN + Request form
Notes	Driver's license number occassionally used in lieu of SSN

Fig. 7-9.

The items listed as definition of a data flow might be used as data flows themselves at a lower level, in which case they would have their own data dictionary entries (Student-ID might fit into this category); or they might be considered self-defining (such as Borrower-name), in which case they would not require an entry. Each identifiable piece of data that is not self-defining should have a data dictionary entry. Any term used in a data dictionary entry that is neither self-defining nor used as a data flow in its own right (Borrower-status might fit in this category) is a data element and should have its own data dictionary definition.

The final part of a data flow definition is space for notes. Any useful information, explanations, or instructions can be given here.

Data Element

Data Element Name	Patron-Status
Aliases	Patron Code
Codes/Meaning	1 Current valid patron 2 Expired patron account 3 Invalid - fine limit exceeded 4 Invalid - >5 "claimed returned"
Notes	Currently there is no code for "other" invalid cases ... this should be added during the next revision cycle.

Fig. 7-10.

Figure 7-10 is a template for a data element entry. It differs from the template for a data flow in that, rather than "Composition," a field for "Codes/Meaning" is given. An entry for "Borrower-status" might be:

Codes/meaning: 01 Full privileges
02 May not borrow
03 Two book maximum
04 Refer to supervisor

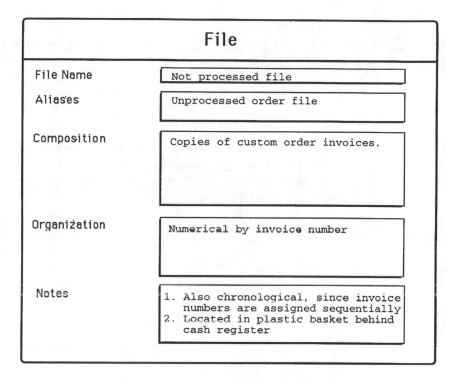

Fig. 7-11.

Figure 7-11 is a template for a file entry and includes the name, aliases, composition (defines what data is included in the file), organization, and notes fields. The composition field might be a template for a record in the file, or it might be a list of the elements to be included if (like "USMARC Authority Records,") the elements are well understood by the clientele. Under "Organization," the file's form (e.g., card, CD-ROM) and any access software required for its use might be listed.

```
                         Process

Process Name        ┌─────────────────────────────────────┐
                    │ Laminate board                      │
                    └─────────────────────────────────────┘
Process number      ┌─────────────────────────────────────┐
                    │ 2.2.3                               │
                    └─────────────────────────────────────┘
Process description ┌─────────────────────────────────────┐
                    │FOR each order form                  │
                    │   Check logo directions on order form│
                    │     IF specific logos requested     │
                    │        THEN follow direction on form│
                    │     ELSE select random logo from pool│
                    │   Place decal on board              │
                    │   Cover surfboard with fiber glass  │
                    │   Apply resin to board and allow to dry│
                    │   Add date of lamination to form    │
                    │   Initial order form                │
                    │                                     │
                    │                                     │
                    │                                     │
                    │                                     │
                    │                                     │
                    │                                     │
                    │                                     │
                    │                                     │
                    │                                     │
                    │                                     │
                    │                                     │
                    │                                     │
Notes               ├─────────────────────────────────────┤
                    │ Actual lamination is performed to   │
                    │ Spec. HSI 47.321                    │
                    │                                     │
                    │                                     │
                    └─────────────────────────────────────┘
```

Fig. 7-12.

Figure 7-12 is a template for a process, made only at the functional-primitive level. This is because the top-down decomposition of higher-level processes are self-defining. The purpose and use of the "Process Name" and the "Process Number" field is obvious, as is that of the "Notes" field. The "Process Description," however, is more complex. Several techniques are used to describe processes. One of the most useful is the flowchart, described in Chapter 6. Other techniques, such as structured English, decision tables, and decision trees, are described in Chapter

8. The process description must be a clear statement of what is accomplished in the process and how this occurs: how the process takes inputs and turns them into outputs. It is the process descriptions that become items in procedure manuals, specifications for system purchases, and steps for programmers to implement.

Data flow diagrams and data dictionaries are powerful tools for systems analysts. The considerable time spent in designing, checking, and redesigning the diagrams and dictionaries can make the subsequent steps of the process much faster and more effective. CASE (computer-aided systems engineering) software products can facilitate the development and evaluation of data flow dictionaries and diagrams by automating the verification of the diagrams. (Shelly et al. 1991, 4.27).

Case Study—Fort Memorial Library

Nancy was a little nervous about the fact that she was presenting the results of the analysis phase of the project to her boss, even though she had gone over all of the material with the head of serials. Somehow things were going too smoothly for her comfort, especially in light of the earlier conflicts with the serials department. Still, she had faith in the analysis—indeed some of the conclusions (e.g., that filing each part of an eight-part claim form in a separate file was unnecessary) were unassailable.

As Nancy entered the room, Margie was telling an anecdote about the mailroom cat while Dean Tebbits filled his pipe. They both looked up, and the dean waved her to a chair. "Now, what have you got for us, eh?" he asked. "Are all our problems behind us?"

"Well," Nancy began, "I don't know if they're behind us, but at least we know what they are. Margie and I have been going over the serials department's operation, and I think we've got a good idea of exactly what is happening throughout the process. Here is a set of data flow diagrams and flowcharts that show each of the department's processes in detail. If you'll look at the first one—the one labeled context—you'll see…"

Step by step, Nancy led them through the analysis. When she had finished (and even she was surprised at how lucid the walkthrough was), she looked up at the dean and said, "Now from this analysis I think you can see that the department, despite being made up of hard-working professionals, does have some problems. If you'll look at the next page, you'll see our summary of what should be done. If you think we're on the right track, we're prepared to begin designing an even better system."

"Wait just a minute," interjected Margie forcefully, "*I* don't agree with this analysis at all. It simply doesn't reflect reality. Your chart says that the check-in clerk takes the first journal and finds the Kardex cabinet it belongs in, but that isn't true. That's Murray, and I know he would follow the procedure manual, which clearly states that the serials are sorted first. The whole thing is nonsense. Why if you were to believe this, you'd think the system didn't work at all!"

"But," put in Nancy, equally forcefully, "the clerks don't sort the journals. Every step in this document has been confirmed by observation, as well as through interviews. We went over every step together in structured walkthroughs, and you had no objection then. *We* stand by the report without reservation." Margie was turning red. She opened her mouth, but the dean forestalled her.

"Now just a minute," he said. "I think…"

Discussion Questions

- In Chapter 6, Nancy's group said she should talk to the dean before the meeting. Assuming she did, what do you think he is about to say? Assuming she did not, what will he likely say?

- How would regular reports to the dean and Margie have helped Nancy in this situation?

- What will happen to Murray? What is Nancy's responsibility to him, if any?

References

DeMarco, Tom. 1979. *Structured Analysis and System Specification.* Englewood Cliffs, N.J.: Prentice-Hall.

Gane, Chris, and Trish Sarson. 1979. *Structured Systems Analysis: Tools and Techniques.* Englewood Cliffs, N.J.: Prentice-Hall.

Shelly, Gary B., Thomas J. Cashman, Judy Adamski, and Joseph J. Adamski. 1991. *Systems Analysis and Design.* Boston: Boyd and Fraser.

Chapter 8

USING OTHER ARRAY METHODS

Introduction

The final component of the structured system representation is the process descriptions. These form a part of the data dictionary and are the basis for documentation and specifications. One tool for specifying processes—the flowchart—has already been discussed. This chapter discusses the alternatives to flowcharts: structured English, decision tables, and decision trees.

Structured English

Flowcharts and structured English are the primary tools for specifying procedures. Structured English is especially useful for documenting procedures in a logical and clear fashion that is still reasonably close to normal narrative English text. The technique grew out of the concept of pseudocode used in programming. Often, programmers needed to write a detailed description of a program, step by step, but without the restriction of having to adhere to a specific programming language. Pseudocode was the answer to this problem (*code* is computer jargon for a "program"). For example, the phrase "Open the file" could be written in pseudocode and then translated into the necessary language-specific terminology once the program logic was worked out. System designers, often programmers themselves, were quick to see the attraction of pseudocode and to use it in the larger task of system design.

Structured English, in the most basic sense, is simply good, clear English usage. It does, however, have some generally accepted restrictions that serve to make it less graceful but more precise than typical English narrative. Structured English is characterized by certain constraints:

1. All sentences are written in the imperative voice. Each sentence tells the client (or computer, in the case of programs) to do something. An example is "Enter borrower number in field 14."

2. Only six types of words are used.

    a. Verbs: common unambiguous, transitive English verbs (e.g., *write, set, place, read*).

    b. Objects: nouns that have either been identified in the data dictionary (*files, data flow, data element*) or that are self-explanatory (*Social Security Number, client name*).

    c. Values: data element values or specific strings (e.g., *1, blocked patron*).

    d. Subordinating conjunctions: *if, while, until,* and other similar words. The number of conjunctions is usually strictly limited to those in a keyword list, although the actual contents of this list vary from site to site.

    e. Coordinating conjunctions and relational words: *and, or, greater than, equals,* and other similar words. These words should also be limited to and recorded in the keyword list.

    f. Adjectives and adverbs: these should be used sparingly and must be meaningful (e.g., *blue cards*). Vague words such as *good* or *adequate* may not be used.

3. A limited set of logical constructs should be employed. Usually there are three.

    a. Linear constructs: do one thing, then another, then another, and so on. Figure 8-1 shows this construct used in a flowchart.

    b. Looping constructs: do something while a certain condition exists, or do something until a certain condition exists. Figure 8-2 shows this construct used in a flowchart.

    c. Decision constructs: often called the IF/THEN/ELSE construct: if a certain condition exists, do something; otherwise, do something else. Figure 8-3 shows this construct used in a flowchart.

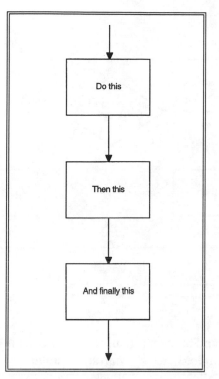

Fig. 8-1.

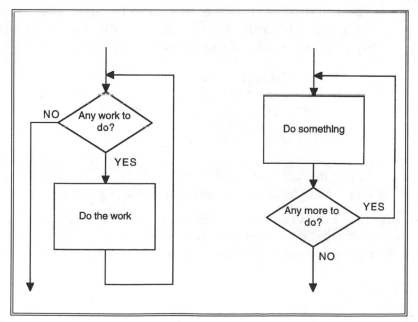

Fig. 8-2.

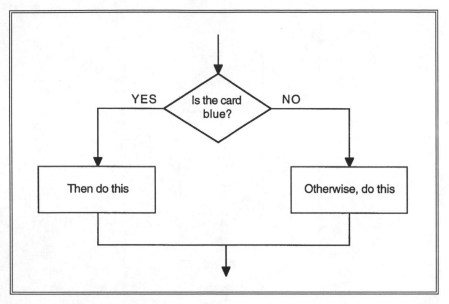

Fig. 8-3.

4.   Indents and brackets are used to make the logical structure clear. For example, here is a narrative statement: "First get the borrower applications and check them to see if they have a barcode number. If they do not, add one to the total of undone applications, and write the SSN on the input list. If a barcode is present, add one to the done list total, get the next one, and so on, until you're done," structured English would say:

> FOR EACH application
>   IF there is no barcode
>   INCREMENT undone-counter by 1
>   WRITE SSN to input-list
>   ELSE INCREMENT done-counter by 1.

5.   Within the constraints of the first three rules, the language should be as readable and understandable as possible.

Structured English is easy to use once the five rules used to clarify an obfuscated narrative are learned. For example, the following quote is an actual transcription of a process, as described by the clerk who performed it.

Eventually we go through and see if we should deal with the suspended ones. Until then, we just keep them in the upper left drawer of Polly's desk. What we do is look at them, one at a time, and see if they have the word *suspended* written in the block marked "status." Well, if it isn't, we just put the record back in the drawer, but if it is, then we look to see if they've checked anything out and how long it's been.

Actually it doesn't have to be something they've checked out. Any library use they've recorded could be a transaction—something like using a meeting room. Usually, though, it's a book they borrow. Lately, there have been more videos, I guess.

Now if it's more than 30 days ago they checked out the book or whatever they did, we do something; otherwise it's back in the drawer, back to the drawer. But, speaking of the ones older than 30 days, we change the *suspended* to *revoked*.

That's not a transaction to my way of thinking, but it goes in the transaction column, along with today's date. We also note the transaction (or whatever it is—the revoke) in the revocation log. Anyway, that's what we used to do before we got the copier. Now we just make a copy of the record and file it in the revocation file. Then we don't put the form back in the desk drawer, but we put it in the dead patron file.

  This process, after negotiation and clarification, was reduced to the following structured English form:

```
FOR EACH Patron-Record IN Account-File:
  IF Borrower-Status EQUALS Suspended
    AND Today's-date MINUS Transaction-date > 30
    THEN:
        Set Account-status to Revoked
        Set Transaction-date to Today's-date
        Copy Patron-record
        Place Copy in Revocation-file
        Place Patron-record in Dead-patron-file
    ELSE return record to Account-file
```

This form has the advantage that terms like "Polly's desk," which are limited to specific physical environments and times, are replaced by more general—and meaningful—terms such as "Account-File." It has the further advantage of allowing the reader to follow the process step by step without ambiguities. All terms in boldface, of course, should be defined in the data dictionary, and all the terms in uppercase are from a list of the reserved words. The remaining terms were supplied using the general rules for standard English given above.

Although structured English in its fully reserve-worded and indented form is excellent for systems analysts and designers (and knowledgeable managers), users sometimes object to the unusual appearance. Designers should try to remain true to "real" structured English, but sometimes accommodation must be made for timid or disapproving clients. In such cases, the designer may have to resort to "Fake Olde English Style." For example, with the loss of some clarity and rigor, the same procedure becomes:

> Go through the account file, one record at a time. For each patron, examine the borrower status to see if it is marked "suspended;" then check to see if the last transaction occurred more than 30 days prior to today's date. If not, go on to the next record. If it has been more than 30 days, do the following four things:
>
> 1. Change the account status to *revoked*.
> 2. Put today's date in the transaction date column.
> 3. Copy the record and put the copy in the revocation file.
> 4. Put the record itself in the dead patron file.

This style should be used only if necessary. Every effort should be made to get the clients to understand and appreciate structured English. Often, nontechnical users quickly appreciate the clarity and purity of structured English. It is condescending to assume that only the computer-literate or highly educated are capable of such appreciation.

Procedures are usually fairly easy to document by using structured English, but policies are often more effectively described through the use of decision tables or decision trees. Both provide a means of mapping certain input conditions to the proper output conditions; decision tables and trees can always be converted back and forth.

Since flowcharts and structured English are interchangeable, interested readers may wish to convert one or more of the sample flowcharts from Chapter 6 to structured English form. An example for figure 6-4 is given in Appendix B.

Decision Tables

Decision tables are made up of two parts: conditions, which describe the states of input variables, and actions, which describe policy alternatives to put into practice. A set of conditions with their resulting actions is called a *rule*. To illustrate a decision table, the following simplified borrowers' policy for a library is given:

Three types of borrowers exist: faculty, staff, and students.

Two types of books exist: regular and two-week.

Two states of overdue status exist: a patron either does or does not have overdue books.

Faculty can borrow any number of books for a full semester, regardless of their overdue status, except for two-week books, which can be checked out for only two weeks.

Staff may borrow any number of books for a full semester, unless they have overdues, in which case they cannot borrow. Two-week books may be borrowed for only two weeks.

Students may borrow books for one month, except for two-week books, which may only be borrowed for two weeks. They cannot borrow books if they have overdue books.

This is a gross oversimplification of a typical university library's borrowing policy, but it is nevertheless confusing. A decision table will definitely make this policy easier to understand and enforce.

The steps for constructing a decision table are:

1. List conditions and their associated values. For the above example, this would include:
    borrower type (faculty/student/staff)
    book type (regular/two-week)
    overdue status (yes/no)

2. Determine the number of rules. This will always be the number of values for each condition multiplied together. In the above example the number would be 3*2*2=12

3. List actions. In the example, these would include loan book for a semester, loan book for a month, loan book for two weeks, and do not loan book.

4. Create a rule matrix, with each condition listed along the left side and sufficient cells for each rule along the top. Figure 8-4 shows a blank matrix for how this example would appear.

	1	2	3	4	5	6	7	8	9	10	11	12
Borrower type												
Book type												
Overdue status												

Fig. 8-4.

5. Enter all possible permutations of values into the rule matrix. Use a systematic alternation of values across each row to ensure that all permutations are used. For the example (see figure 8-5), three types of borrowers are given, so the first row is divided into thirds (of four columns each). Because there are two types of books, *each* of the three groups is divided into two parts (of two columns each) for regular and two-week books. Finally, because two kinds of overdue status are given, each of the two book-type groups is divided into two parts (of one column each) one for those with overdue books and those without.

	1	2	3	4	5	6	7	8	9	10	11	12
Borrower type	F	F	F	F	Su	Su	Su	Su	Sf	Sf	Sf	Sf
Book type	R	R	T	T	R	R	T	T	R	R	T	T
Overdue Status	Y	N	Y	N	Y	N	Y	N	Y	N	Y	N

Notes F=Faculty
       Su=Student
       Sf=Staff
       R=Regular loan
       T=Two-week loan
       Y=Yes
       N=No

Fig. 8-5.

6. Record the appropriate action under each rule (see figure 8-6).

	1	2	3	4	5	6	7	8	9	10	11	12
Borrower type	F	F	F	F	Su	Su	Su	Su	Sf	Sf	Sf	Sf
Book type	R	R	T	T	R	R	T	T	R	R	T	T
Overdue Status	Y	N	Y	N	Y	N	Y	N	Y	N	Y	N
Loan for semester	X	X								X		
Loan for month						X						
Loan for two weeks			X	X				X				X
Don't loan books					X		X		X		X	

Notes F=Faculty
 Su=Student
 Sf=Staff
 R=Regular loan
 T=Two-week loan
 Y=Yes
 N=No
 X=Acceptable action

Fig. 8-6.

The table is now complete. A rule may be selected based on each and any of the conditions, and the acceptable action can be found at the bottom of the table.

One of the side benefits of decision tables and trees is that they help to clarify and validate policies. Once the table has been completed, analysts may find that some rules have no associated acceptable action. There are several reasons why this might occur. The simplest reason is that the combination is impossible. A circulation table which includes a condition for "media format" (book, tape, or sound disk) might also include a condition for "rewind status" (rewound or not rewound). Clearly there are no circumstances under which a book may be rewound, so the rule will never need to be invoked in this regard. Other reasons why there may not be an action for a rule include the possibility that the case has not yet come up, that the policy is ambiguous, or that the analyst simply does not understand what the policy says. In such cases, the analysts must seek clarification and correct the table, either by adding the appropriate action or by marking the rule as being impossible. When the table is in its final form, the impossible rules need not be shown.

Decision Trees

Decision trees are a graphic form of decision tables in which each condition is shown as a set of alternative paths. Analysts build a decision tree by using the same process as for a table: by listing the conditions and values and determining the possible results.

A base line is placed on the center of the left side of a sheet of paper. The name of the policy is written on this line. Individual branches are then drawn for each of the values of the first condition. Each of these branches is ended in a horizontal line, on which are written the conditions and values represented. Figure 8-7 illustrates a first-level chart for the borrower's policy example.

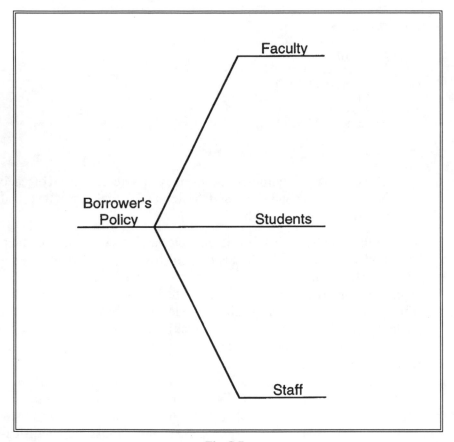

Fig. 8-7.

Each of these horizontal lines is broken down with branches for each of the second condition's values. These are again terminated in horizontal lines, on which are written the second condition's values. This breaking down of each value into the values of the next condition is continued until all conditions have been used (see figure 8-8).

An action, or set of actions, is then written at the end of each terminal branch (see figure 8-9).

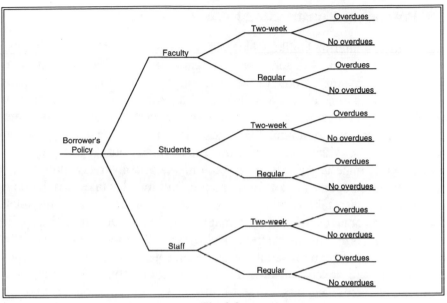

Fig. 8-8.

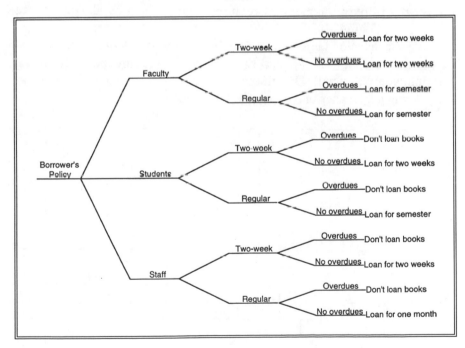

Fig. 8-9.

Practice in Constructing Decision Tables

Students entering Unlikely University can go into either the Alchemist or the Wizard track. In each case, applicants may be divided into men, women, and creatures. Some of the men and women who wish to be wizards already possess a two-year degree in legerdemain from community colleges, while others enter directly from secondary school. Creatures are never admitted to community colleges. Students take a total of seven courses. Female wizard applicants must take three courses in right-brain magic, while male applicants must take only two; conversely male applicants take three courses in left-brain magic, and females take two. Human wizards must also take two courses in brain stem magic. Creatures must take all seven courses in brain stem magic. All this is true unless the applicant already has a two-year degree, in which case their required courses are reduced by one in both the left and right brain categories (making a total of five rather than seven). Insofar as alchemists are concerned, men and women both take five courses in left-brain magic, and two courses in brain stem magic, but none in right-brain magic. No community college programs are offered in alchemy. Creatures who wish to be alchemists are awarded the degree after only five brain stem magic courses.

Write a decision table to illustrate this policy. If you decide to do a table you may use the skeleton below (but note that there are more cells in the grid than you will need). Do remember to label any "impossible" rules as such. A suggested answer is given in Appendix B.

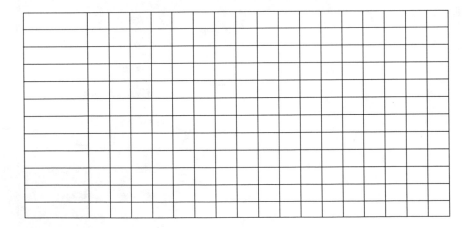

Selecting a Technique

It was noted earlier that structured English and flowcharts are best suited for procedures, while decision tables or decision trees are particularly well-suited to define policy. The choice will involve tradeoffs: varying degrees of clarity, ease of use, and aesthetics. For small policies, especially those that must be followed by human beings, decision trees may be easier to use. Decision tables are preferred for complex policies because the replication of conditions soon makes the tree too large to easily understand. Tables are also preferable when the procedure will be implemented as an expert system: tables are easily translated to the production rules often used in this type of software. In addition, tables reveal missing, ambiguous, or impossible rules. In contrast, it is fairly easy to omit a branch in a complex tree and have difficulty determining where the error was made. The same error in a decision table would result in a blank column—an obvious omission.

Other Tools

DFDs, data dictionaries, and process specifications (e.g., flowcharts, decision tables, decision trees, and structured English) are probably the most useful techniques for creating library and information systems. However, many other methodologies can be useful to systems analysts. This discussion of other methodologies is not an in-depth treatment, but it may help analysts decide whether or not one of them might be useful in a project, and it may direct analysts to further information. The intent of this discussion is also to reinforce the concept that all methodologies are simply aids to thinking clearly and to prevent useless biases toward one particular methodology.

Nassi-Schneiderman Charts

Nassi-Schneiderman charts were developed to replace flowcharts by providing a more structured method. They are particularly useful for detailing the logic flow to be input to programmers, because they enforce structured programming conventions: one entry point and one exit point; use of sequence, selection, and repetition constructs; and nesting of operations. A Nassi-Schneiderman chart takes the form of a box, generally no larger than a single page, broken up into operations. Because it is a part of the structured repertory, the individual operations shown may be broken down into separate subdiagrams. Figure 8-10 shows the IF/THEN/ELSE construct.

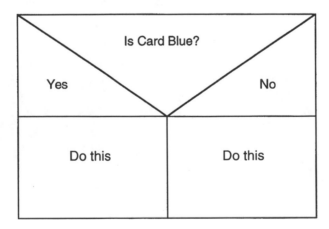

Fig. 8-10.

Figure 8-11 shows the WHILE and UNTIL constructs.

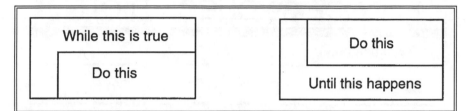

Fig. 8-11.

Figure 8-12 shows how multiple cases can be diagrammed easily. A flowchart representing this would be much more involved.

Color of card					
Red	Green	Blue	Goldenrod	Buff	Puce
Process for red cards	Process for green cards	Process for blue cards	Process for goldenrod cards	Process for buff cards	Process for puce cards

Fig. 8-12.

Nassi-Schneiderman charts are particularly useful for specifying detailed program logic. They can be used to replace other techniques in process specification within the data dictionary. Figure 8-13 shows a Nassi-Schneiderman diagram explaining how to compute the typical MOD-10 check digit used on library barcodes.

Warnier-Orr Diagrams

Warnier-Orr diagrams show relationships of data or program logic by means of vertical brackets. Since each bracket represents a breakdown of the item the bracket points to, the diagram is inherently structured as it is created. An example of a Warnier-Orr diagram is shown in Figure 8-14.

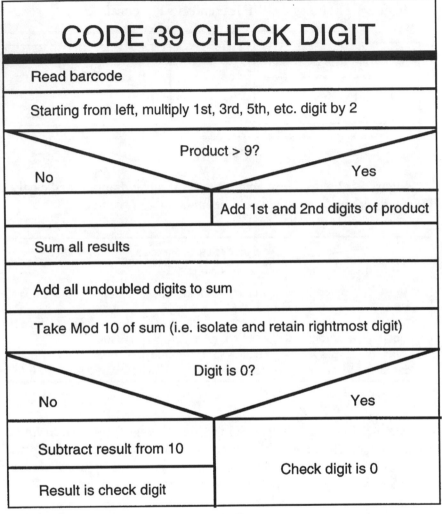

CODE 39 CHECK DIGIT

Read barcode

Starting from left, multiply 1st, 3rd, 5th, etc. digit by 2

Product > 9?

No   Yes

Add 1st and 2nd digits of product

Sum all results

Add all undoubled digits to sum

Take Mod 10 of sum (i.e. isolate and retain rightmost digit)

Digit is 0?

No   Yes

Subtract result from 10

Check digit is 0

Result is check digit

Fig. 8-13.

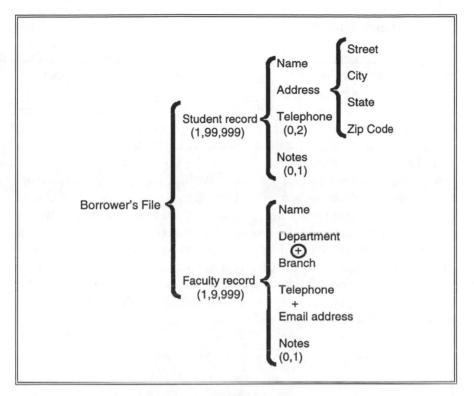

Fig. 8-14.

A Warnier-Orr chart is read from left to right and, within brackets, from top to bottom. Thus, the borrower's file is made up of student records and faculty records. Student records are made up of a name, address, telephone number, and any other information. ("Notes"). Several other conventions are followed. Numbers in parentheses below an entry show the number of occurrences: (1) means that there is one item of the entry; (1,250) means there are between 1 and 250 of this item; and (0,1) means the item is not mandatory (i.e., it may or may not be present). A plus inside a circle indicates that the elements above and below are exclusive: that one or the other occurs but not both. Without the circle, the plus indicates that one or both may be present.

The same representation may be used to show program relationships. Warnier-Orr diagrams are especially useful in showing data hierarchy rather than program structure, although they may be used to illustrate the overall relationship of routines within a program.

Structure Charts

Structure charts show the relationships of routines to programs. They are very useful for documenting detailed program listings because they decompose the process visually; hence, they are appropriate for specifying functional-primitives in the data dictionary. A structure chart is a tree diagram of the operation of a program. Each element is shown as a box or module. These are linked with arrows showing control of the modules, with the direction of the arrows showing the flow of data and/or control. Data flows are named next to the arrow. While modules can call or invoke several child modules, only one top-level or root module can exist. If a decision structure determines which of several alternative modules will be invoked, a diamond (called a *transaction center*) is placed in the ceiling module, and the alternative data flows are linked to the diamond. When a lower-level module finishes its operation, control is passed back up to the module that invoked it. In this way, the entire diagram begins and ends at the root module. Figure 8-15 shows an example of a structure chart with no decision structure.

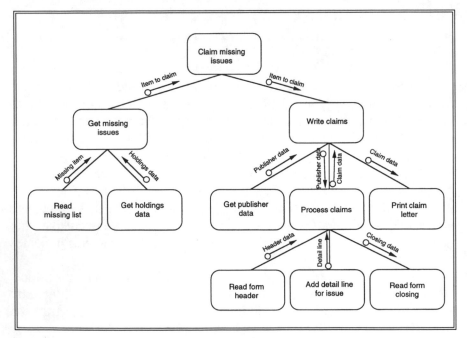

Fig. 8-15.

Entity Relationship Diagrams

Entity relationship diagrams (ERDs) *describe* data. They are clearly related to data flow diagrams but are also clearly separate from them because they do not show flow. They may be used to complement the data dictionary because they are graphic; they may be able to show relationships between data at rest more clearly than the data dictionary (although usually with less detail).

ERDs are made up of boxes called *entities*. These represent classes of data: PATRON, SERIAL RECORD, ADDRESS, SEARCH TERM, and so on. Entities are connected by relationships that may be shown as lines or (according to some conventions) as diamonds with lines on each side. The relationships may be named if they are not obvious; thus, figure 8 16 illustrates "Patrons Borrow Books."

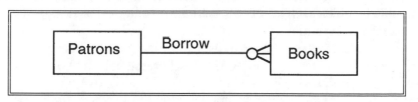

Fig. 8-16.

Since ERDs can be read in two directions, relationships are often more closely detailed. The convention is that for horizontal lines, the relationship is shown left to right above the lines and right to left below them. The left side of a vertical line is read from top to bottom, and the right side from bottom to top (see figure 8-17).

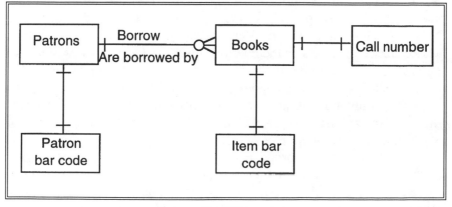

Fig. 8-17.

It is also essential to indicate the quantity of the association: a person can own many books, but a book can have only one owner. In figure 8-17, the fact that a patron can borrow zero, one, or several books is shown by the "crow's foot" to the immediate left of the "Books" entity. While a patron may choose to borrow no books, each patron has one, and only one, bar code. If no valid zero case exists, the crow's foot is shown without the circle. Note that while a patron can borrow many books, a book can only be borrowed by one patron (at a time). This one-to-one relationship is shown by the short crosshatches. The use of two crosshatches shows that each book has only one bar code and that bar code is assigned to only one book.

As shown in the examples above, entities are named as nouns, while relationships or associations are named with verbs. Relationships between associations can be shown with ANDs (both relationships are necessary) or with ORs (one or the other relationship is present). A further refinement of the ERD technique normalizes the data in order to create a structure in which each element is unique. This allows the designer to create efficient data structures.

Analysts have an array of tools in addition to those discussed in this and previous chapters, including HIPO (Hierarchical Input, Process Output) diagrams with visual table of contents (VTOCs); overview diagrams, and detail diagrams; action diagrams; Michael Jackson diagrams; data analysis diagrams; data navigation diagrams; and others. These tools are described in detail and evaluated in Martin's book on structured tools (1988). Yourdon's book discusses some of these tools, as well as state transitional diagrams (1988).

In recent years, other types of models have been developed in response to those who find traditional data modeling insufficient to represent increasingly complex data (Thuraisingham and Venkataraman 1992, 29). Information modeling, for example, combines text and graphics in place of the less complex data modeling represented by such arrays as DFDs. As Thuraisingham and Venkataraman have pointed out, though, lack of consensus exists on the relationship of the various kinds of modeling (1992, 29). A number of the proponents of more complex modeling (e.g., object-oriented design and prototyping) list a specific software program or recommend programs to use as tools to develop a model. Analysts interested in exploring these models will find Marshall (1986) or the collection edited by Loucopoulos (1992) a good beginning.

While all of these approaches have their good points and their proponents, the authors believe that it is most useful to learn one technique well in the beginning. We have selected structured analysis as that technique, because it is the most commonly used in the profession and the best suited to the wide variety of environments in which information professionals work. Other techniques may be acquired, and used, when need arises, and as analysts encounter situations for which they are suited.

Case Study—Fort Memorial Library

The fireworks were over; only the smoke remained, and Nancy was wishing she had a crystal ball. She supposed she had won her first confrontation with Margie, but she didn't feel like a victor.

She had to admit that Dean Tebbits had backed her up. Of course she had paved the way with regular weekly briefings as the analysis phase had progressed, and the fact that she had asked (and followed) his advice freely certainly had paid off. When Margie had dropped her bombshell (or brick), claiming that Nancy had failed to do a thorough job, the dean had been in a position to royally tick Margie off, which he had proceeded to do, in no uncertain terms, by finishing up with "...and if you can't do the job, we'll have to find someone who can!" Margie had left the room ashen-faced, and Nancy had felt sick.

The dean had then taken Nancy to task for not handling Margie better, making her feel even more unhappy, especially when he pointed out that he didn't become a library director to referee boxing matches between bickering hens. He had finished with Nancy by saying, "You'd better come up with a dyno-supreme project!"

Now Nancy had to do just that. She had in front of her a set of data flow diagrams of the old system, a pile of notes on perceived problems, and a large scotch. None of them seemed to be helping very much. She knew what was wrong, but how was she to design something that was right?

Discussion Questions

- What do you think of the dean's approach to personnel management (consider, for example, his comment about "bickering hens")? How should Nancy react?

- How might the confrontation affect Nancy's future at Fort Memorial Library?

- What are some approaches Nancy might use to create a "dyno-supreme project?"

References

Loucopoulos, Pericles, ed. 1992. *Conceptual modeling, databases, and CASE: An integrated view of information systems development.* New York: John Wiley.

Marshall, George R. 1986. *Systems Analysis and Design: Alternative Structured Approaches.* Englewood Cliffs, N.J.: Prentice-Hall.

Martin, James. 1988. *Structured Techniques, the Basis for CASE.* Rev. ed. Englewood Cliffs, N.J.: Prentice-Hall.

Thuraisingham, Bhavani, and Venkat Venkataraman. 1992. "A New View of Information Modeling: A Bridge between Data and Information." *Information Systems Management* 9 (Spring): 29-36.

Yourdon, Edward. 1988. *Managing the System Life Cycle.* 2d ed. Englewood Cliffs, N.J.: Prentice-Hall.

Chapter 9

The Object Orientation "Revolution"

Throughout this work, the authors have stressed structured analysis and design techniques, especially the Yourdon/DeMarco model. We feel that, for the types of analysis that most functioning information professionals will perform, these techniques have definite advantages. The techniques are relatively easy to explain to management and the staff, who can identify with the decomposition model as one they employ in their own activities. The de-emphasis on physical structure encourages innovation on the part of relatively unpracticed analysts, and, as the techniques most commonly used by professional systems analysts, they lend credence to the practitioner's conclusions when presented to others.

Not all situations are ideal for purely structured techniques, however, and some analysts (and professors) have made the techniques rigid to the point where they lose much of their attractiveness. It is always easier to apply an algorithm (or make to an algorithm out of a heuristic such as "a process should have less than seven interface paths"), than to actually think. Recently, especially in analysis and design undertaken as a part of software engineering efforts, a new way of looking at data and its structure has arisen. This change parallels one in programming, away from procedural languages such as COBOL and C, toward object-oriented languages exemplified by C++ and Java. The justification for these methods is similar. As projects become larger (and a simple Java-based Web page may be as complex as many commercial applications of 15 years ago), the difficulty of creating stable systems that are understandable to the analysts and useable by the client becomes greater. While the work being done behind the scenes may be no more complicated than it was in the past, the plethora of panels, radio buttons, scroll bars, and event handlers has made the overall systems much more complex. Much of the emphasis has shifted from *doing something*, to *communicating* what is to be done

133

and what has been done. It is in these areas (the human-machine interface) that object-oriented techniques find their most compelling use. Just as structured analysis and design was originally created to lead to structured program code (although, as we have seen, it has applications far beyond software engineering), so object-oriented analysis and design was developed to lead to good object-oriented programs.

The Object-Oriented Paradigm

As the word "paradigm" suggests, object orientation represents a *different way of looking at the world*. One of the strong points of the structured method is that it fits well with the way most people look at their jobs: a series of processes that feed each other data. The object-oriented paradigm (OOP) looks at the world from a different perspective.

In the OOP, the world is made up of objects. This seems reasonable: suppose someone thinks of his world as being made up of his bed, his coffee pot, his car, and his desk. He gets out of bed, drinks coffee, drives his car to work, works at his desk, drives his car home, and goes to bed. Some of his coworkers drink tea, some take the bus to work, some drive BMWs rather than old Hondas. Some actually take vacations.

But is a vacation an object? In the OOP world it is. Shlaer and Mellor define an object as "an abstraction of a set of real-world things such that all of the real-world things in the set—the instances—have the same characteristics [and] all instances are subject to the same set of rules" (Shlaer and Mellor 1988, 14). They can thus be either physical, such as my desks, or abstractions, such as someone else's vacation. Often, they are representations, such as a picture of a button on a computer screen.

Objects are instances of classes. The Honda and his co-worker's BMW are both objects; they are not identical, but both are automobiles. Simply saying that the co-workers both drive automobiles to work gives some information (e.g., that they don't take the bus or ride motorcycles), and tells something about the characteristics of the kind of transportation they use (e.g., that it has four wheels and an internal combustion engine). This would not be enough to identify one car in the parking lot however. To do that we must specify the particular instance of the class automobile: it is a *Honda* automobile. From that we know to look for a four-wheeled vehicle (we say that the instance of Honda inherits the characteristic of four wheels from the class), with a Honda logo on the trunk. But, of course that is not sufficient either. Hondas are also a class (i.e., there are lots of four wheeled vehicles with "Honda" logos on their trunks). To find this particular vehicle, it is necessary to find the Honda with the Hawaii license number 802-26C.

The value of this approach is obvious. All we have to say is that a Honda (license plate 802-26C) is in the parking lot. We do not have to specify that it has four wheels, or that it is a transportation object. Of course the parking lot is an instance of the parking lot class; Hawaii license plates are an instance of the license plate class.

By using inheritance, we need only specify the unique aspects of an object (its data and behavior), relying on inheritance to supply the remainder. To define an object, we must list the particular categories that it does not inherit from the class to which it belongs (such as make and model for automobiles).

These concepts come easily to those with a library and information background. They are used to working with classes and subclasses and feel at ease with the idea that a subclass inherits the attributes of the superclass. Lest familiarity lead us astray, however, it should be pointed out that the somewhat *laissez faire* way in which, for example, the Library of Congress Subject Headings (LCSH) approach class decomposition would be inappropriate in an OOP setting. LCSH headings are meant to be used by humans, who are much more forgiving of occasional lapses of pure consistent logic than are machines.

We must also specify the way that data may be manipulated within the object. These manipulations are called methods. In OOP, the data and the methods are contained within objects. They neither interact directly with other objects, nor can other objects use their data or methods. As Martin and Odell (1992, 17) state, "an object is thus a thing with its properties represented by data types and its behavior represented by methods." Objects communicate with each other through defined messages sent between them or by explicitly stating that their data and methods can be used by others.

This technique of keeping data with objects and, if necessary, providing techniques for making it available is called *encapsulation* and has been a part of OOP since its inception. The great benefit of encapsulation is that all interactions are closely defined, and data corruption and misuse is minimized. While this sometimes necessitates what appear to be overly complex processes to accomplish simple tasks (e.g., passing data from object to object), the techniques were developed out of a response to what actually happens in large systems without such control: failure, and worse, failure that is extremely difficult to identify and rectify.

Another core concept of OOP is *polymorphism*, the idea that a superclass defines a generic behavior, while specific instances of that behavior are refined when that superclass is referred to by a class. For example, stopping at red traffic lights may be defined at a relatively high level in the hierarchy, but when cars approach such lights, a Honda activates drum brakes, and a BMW activates anti-lock disk brakes.

We may summarize the object-oriented approach by giving the following formula, taken from Coad and Yourdon's *Object Oriented Analysis* (1990, 31):

> Object-Oriented =
> Objects
> > (an encapsulation of Attributes and exclusive Services; an abstraction of something in the problem space, with some number of instances in the problem space)
> + Classification
> + Inheritance
> + Communication with messages

Object-Oriented Analysis and Design

These are obviously useful and interesting techniques, and object-oriented languages such as Java are attaining much popularity. Some would even call them the wave of the present. But how is this related to analysis and design? Object-oriented analysis and design attempts to gain some of the benefits that derive from the object-oriented approach to programming:

- Reusability: Once a class has been defined, it can be re-used in other projects, and lower-level classes and objects may be created simply by referring to the superclass.

- Reliability: Because classes are created once, they can be more carefully tested, and once a superclass is well tested, only the additional behaviors of lower-level classes need be tested.

- Seamless integration with graphical user interfaces (GUIs): GUIs are built on object-oriented models. Using object-oriented analysis and design feeds naturally into such an interface.

- Speedier design: Re-use of preconstructed classes results in ease of construction.

Steps in the Object-Oriented Analysis Method

Object-oriented analysis and design, while hardly a new technique, is not as mature as the structured techniques we have been discussing. A wide variety of models that call themselves object-oriented analysis exists. We have attempted to create a sort of composite description, which draws on several models. As such, it is not as detailed, nor as consistent as the individual methods.

As might be expected, the first step in the process (once the users and uses of the system are identified), according to most experts, is the identification of major classes and objects. This is largely a problem of classification and taxonomy, and the traditional techniques are employed. We can start by working from the top down, looking at a group of objects to see how we can differentiate between them. Division is made on things that make objects different. Essentially, this is the method of Plato and Aristotle, and it is still an effective way to derive classes. A second way to create classes is to work from the bottom up. We may look for a way to group things logically together. Literature may be grouped by time period, by language, by form, by audience, by quality, etc. The groupings are then combined to form supergroups, until a full taxonomy of relationships is created. We may also start with one or more representatives of what we know should be a class and look at what makes them similar. This prototypical approach is especially useful in situations where the classical approaches prove inadequate.

If this discussion is too theoretical, some authors present lists of typical objects. Shlaer and Mellor (1988, 15-19), for example, suggest looking for: tangible things (e.g., airplane, racehorse, power supply, book); roles (e.g., doctor, patient, owner, tenant); incidents (e.g., flight, system crash, accident); interactions (e.g., purchase, marriage); and specifications (e.g., tables that represent a definition—in their example a refrigerator model object might be made up of a specification of model number, cubic feet, power rating, etc.). Coad and Yourdon (1990, 60-70), however, suggest looking for structures (traditional genus/species and whole/part relationships); other systems (with which the system interacts); devices (with which the system interacts); events remembered (what archival data must be retained); roles played (who receives services and who provides it); locations (physical locations or sites the system needs to know about); and organizational units (what parts the hierarchy of the organization structure the system needs to know about or keep track of).

Obviously, these "techniques" are only rough guides that serve to suggest possible ways of looking at a system in order to start defining objects. Much creativity is needed at this point. Booch (1991, 143-45) mentions two other techniques that might be of use. One, suggested by Abbott in the *Communications of the ACM*, is to write an informal English description of the system. The analyst then goes through the description, identifying nouns (potential objects) and verbs (potential operations on them). The second possible technique from Booch, although one he does not think highly of, is to use traditional structured analysis techniques, as previously discussed in this book.

Once the classes and objects are identified and their relationships have been formalized in a (usually) hierarchical structure, the next step is to list the attributes of each object. Attributes are the data elements that specify a particular state of an object (e.g., color). They are those things we must list in order to identify an individual. For the class *car* used in the introduction to this chapter, attributes include make and model. It may also include the attribute *color*. Whether it does or not depends on the system—whether the color of the vehicle has any effect on the system. Generally speaking, useless attributes are avoided.

Having identified the attributes, the designer distributes them in the structure in such a way as to take maximum advantage of inheritance. If all kinds of cars have four wheels, then the number of wheels attribute should go in the car class, not in the Honda class. (This assumes that Honda is used as a subclass of automobiles. If it is shown as a subclass of manufacturers, then it might make sense to include it in order to differentiate Honda automobiles from Honda motorcycles. In object-oriented analysis, as in structured analysis, what is important is to model the important aspects of reality.)

The designer then determines the relationship between objects, often using the techniques of entity relationship diagramming at this point. For example, given two classes—library and book—the relationship "libraries contain (multiple occurrences of) books" might be specified.

Finally, the designer determines the system implementation, specifying the methods for driving the exchange of data between classes. The design is broken into modules and the operation of each part specified. Theoretically, in a programming setting this would result in code being completed. In reality, such a result is not so easily obtained. Several authors emphasize that object-oriented analysis and design is an iterative rather than a linear process. As Booch (1991, 195) puts it: "It is at this point that we often must return to the first step and apply this process again to the inside view of the existing classes and modules. In this way we repeat the design process, but at a lower level of abstraction."

Prototyping

Because object-oriented analysis and design is most often used in the area of software, the design can often be evaluated (and the analysis simultaneously confirmed) by using the technique of prototyping; in prototyping, a working demonstration of the software is created. According to Coad and Yourdon (1991, 10), prototyping is especially useful because:

- it is dynamic,

- it allows the designer to experiment with the human-computer interface,

- it helps discover missing requirements,

- it provides a test for the design, and

- it allows the designer to deliver some functionality early in the project.

These attributes are important in the development of software today. Modern designs are complex, and yet are often judged on the user interface. It only makes sense to develop such systems in an incremental fashion, refining the user interface especially through a series of prototypes that the user has a chance to critique before delivery. This is one more way to induce the client and users to buy into a system prior to its delivery. It is much more difficult for complaints about an interface to be taken seriously if the user has approved of the design throughout the project.

Diagramming Tools

Just as in structured analysis and design, diagrams in object-oriented techniques provide both a way to build a model of the system and a tool to use in explaining and communicating that model. Several schools of diagramming have been developed.

Coad and Yourdon (1990) developed a system based on round-cornered rectangles. The rectangle is divided into three parts by horizontal lines. The space at the top is used for the object's name, the middle space for attributes, and the bottom space for services, which they define as the processing to be performed upon receipt of a message. Objects are then placed in hierarchical relationships, making use of inheritance. Half circles are used to represent the concept of classification (c.g., a MARC record of a bibliographic record, an authority record, or a holdings record).

Martin and Odell (1992, 123-49) also use square-cornered and round-cornered rectangles, but their meaning is completely different from Coad and Yourdon's. In Martin and Odell diagrams, square-cornered rectangles represent data, while round-cornered rectangles represent activities. All of the representations of ERDs are present, as well as special diagramming standards for event types, control conditions, and trigger rules. Separate ways of representing subtypes of objects, operations, and events also exist. Martin and Odell also re-introduce a special type of object and activities, those that are physical rather than symbolic representations in a computer (a MARC record is a symbolic representation; a book is a physical object). Other tools were developed by Booch, Shlaer, and Mellor, as well as by several other individuals and teams.

Thus, as in any area of active exploration, a plethora of competing and complementary tools exists. A good summary of the methodologies available can be found in *Object-Oriented Metamethods* (Henderson-Sellers and Bulthuis 1998), especially in Chapter 5, which attempts to find the essential unity underlying the apparently disparate methodologies and then achieve a synthesis. Often, the choice of a diagramming tool is determined by the CASE tool, which the analyst designers select (or has foisted upon them). The authors feel that to attempt an object-oriented analysis and design project without a CASE tool would be inadvisable. As Arthur Langer states (1997, 112), "Using CASE is the only means of creating and maintaining any central storage of information for enterprise-level systems. [...] Frankly, an IS organization that does not consider CASE cannot provide the long-term support for many of the features and capabilities required by the applications of the future."

Unified Modeling Language

An effort is underway to create a methodology that can be agreed upon by most practitioners in the field. In 1997 the Object Management Group (OMG) released version 1.1 of the Unified Modeling Language (UML), which attempts to synthesize the various competing tools, especially Booch's notation, the Object Modeling Technique (OMT), and Object-Oriented Software Engineering (OOSE). Since it has the approval of the major players in the "OO" field and has been approved by several important organizations (including Microsoft Corporation), it has potential in becoming the most common technique. According to Cantor (1998, 46), "[It] is likely to be the preferred method for specifying object designs for the foreseeable future."

While UML is primarily a modeling tool, it implies an underlying object-oriented approach to the designs it represents. Like the other tools mentioned in this chapter (and indeed throughout the book), it was developed to work specifically on problems of software development but may be used beyond that restricted scope. UML is a rather robust and complex notation, which is only to be expected of a tool that attempts to bring together the work of several active schools of analysis and design. Eeles (1998) summarizes the notations supported by UML as:

- use-case diagrams,
- class diagrams,

- statechart diagrams,

- activity diagrams,

- sequence diagrams,

- collaboration diagrams,

- component diagrams, and

- deployment diagrams.

Perhaps the best source for details of UML are the Web sites maintained by Rational Software <www.rational.com> and OMG <www.omg.com>.

While a full discussion of UML is beyond the scope of this text (the interested reader is referred especially to Harmon and Watson's *Understanding UML: The Developer's Guide* in addition to the sources above), Cantor (1998) provides the following summary of the subtools most useful to relatively inexperienced analysts:

- Use-case diagrams document the systems dynamic requirements.

- Class and package diagrams provide a view of the class design of the system. The diagrams contain a representation of the classes and packages (related sets of classes) and how they are associated.

- Sequence diagrams tie together the use-class diagrams and the class diagrams. They show how the classes collaborate to carry out a use case.

- Component diagrams show how the classes relate to the actual code.

The Utility of the OOP

There is no doubt that object-oriented analysis and design is optimally suited to software engineering projects whose outcome is expected to be computer code in an object-oriented language. The authors, however, believe that its potential to be applied to all systems is limited. As a technique, it is not easily translated by part-time analysts into more human-centered systems, where the main outcome is not expected to be a set of software routines but an integrated package of policies, procedures, and processes. Also, it is not easy to apply successfully when the requisite

CASE tools are not available. It is worth noting that many practicing analysts disagree with this view. For a countering argument, see (Jacobson, Ericsson and Jacobson) *The Object Advantage: Business Process Reengineering with Object Technology.*

It would seem reasonable to use traditional structured techniques to map the big picture of an organization or unit, with specific processes identified for computer implementation. In a circulation department, many activities involve physical objects and humans interacting in a variety of ways. Some of those ways will probably be through computer programs.

Once the overall system is investigated and mapped, those parts that will require coding (or obtaining) software will be identified. If object-oriented languages and GUI interfaces are anticipated (and they almost certainly will be in today's user environment), then those parts can become independent, although obviously related, projects, utilizing object-oriented techniques. This is not to imply that the object-oriented techniques are useless in noncomputer environments. They have a role, but as extensions to structured techniques rather than as replacements.

The techniques of determining classes and specifying their attributes are especially valuable in establishing definitions in the data dictionary. And reasoning out the relationships between objects and how they interact can refine data flows between processes. Perhaps their largest value is as a reaction to the problems that structured analysis has brought on itself through years of use—of becoming the traditional method. We may put too much emphasis on understanding the old system. At some point we must stop analyzing and start designing (since some old systems are so illogical as to defy analysis). Object-oriented techniques act as a counterbalance to this by almost completely de-emphasizing the old system. We may also underemphasize the data dictionary without which (as we stated in Chapter 7), the diagrams are only pretty pictures. In object-oriented analysis and design, the equivalent of the data dictionary is the very essence of the model.

In the end, however, it is not the technique that matters, but the analyst. Individual techniques are merely ways of thinking, not the thoughts themselves. We have emphasized throughout this book that systems analysis is not an algorithmic activity. There are no magic bullets. As Booch (1991, 187) puts it:

The amateur software engineer is always in search of some sort of magic, some earthshaking technological innovation whose application will immediately make the process of software development easy. It is the mark of the professional software engineer to know that no such panacea exists. Amateurs often want cookbook steps to follow; professionals know that rigid approaches to design only lead to largely useless design products that resemble a progression of lies, behind which developers shield themselves because no one is willing to admit that poor design decisions should be changed early, rather than late.

The best technique is the one that produces the best system.

Case Study—Fort Memorial Library

Even though she had "won," Nancy was more than a little depressed over her confrontation with Margie. She really didn't know how to react when Sue, her favorite ex-COBOL programmer, bounced in bubbling excitedly about a required seminar at the computing center from which she had just returned.

"I didn't want to go at first," she enthused, "but now I'm glad I did. They had a speaker from the University of Dover who explained *everything*. There's a great new technique that will solve all our problems. It's a little more complex than what we've been doing, but, after all, how can we explain a complex system with just circles and arrows?"

After a series of questions revealed that Sue meant the University of Dover in Pennsylvania and that the circles and arrows line had been lifted from the speaker (who had probably stolen it from Yourdon), Nancy discovered that Sue was referring to object-oriented programming and UML.

"It's great, I've never seen the computing center so excited. They're making 'OOPs! We've been doing it wrong all these years' jokes and planning to rewrite all the payroll programs in Java! As soon as we put this project to bed, I'm going back there and to get started."

Nancy was interested, but as Sue proceeded to explain what she remembered of the intricacies of UML, she began to have second thoughts. Was this the right time to change methodologies? Was UML the best technique to use for their serials project?

In the end, Nancy decided to use a tried-and-true management technique: she appointed Rachel and Ben to study UML's possibilities and report back. She herself doubted the superiority of UML for their effort, but deep down she doubted her doubts. Was she prejudiced because it hadn't been covered in her master's degree program, or was she merely suspicious of something that arrived that recently with that much hype?

Discussion Questions

- Ignoring the question of UML's utility for this project, what do you think of Nancy's approach to dealing with Sue's enthusiastic support of the technique?

- Sue was not put on the study committee. Was this a good idea or not? Why?

- Assume you have been put on the study committee with Ben and Rachel, and investigate UML on your own. (Many resources are available now, in addition to those listed in this chapter.) What would you report back to Nancy?

- Most library and information science students have contacts in the field. What do your colleagues, instructors, and mentors think about the utility of UML in nonsoftware engineering applications?

References

Abbott, R. J. 1983. "Program Design by Informal English Descriptions." In *Communications of the ACM* 26, 11 (November) 882-94.

Booch, Grady. 1991. *Object Oriented Design*. Redwood City, Calif.: Benjamin/Cummings.

Cantor, Murray. 1998. *Object-Oriented Project Management with UML*. New York: John Wiley.

Coad, Peter, and Edward Yourdon. 1990. *Object-Oriented Analysis*. Englewood Cliffs, N.J.: Yourdon Press.

Coad, Peter, and Edward Yourdon. 1991. *Object-Oriented Design*. Englewood Cliffs, N.J.: Prentice-Hall.

Eeeles, Peter. 1998. *Building Objects*. New York: John Wiley.

Harmon, Paul, and Mark Watson. 1997. *Understanding UML: The Developer's Guide*. San Francisco: Morgan Kaufmann.

Henderson-Sellers, Brian, and A. Bulthuis. 1998. *Object-Oriented Methamethods.* New York: Springer.

Jacobson, Ivar, and Maria Ericcson, and Agneta Jacobson. *The Object Advantage: Business Process Reengineering with Object Technology.* New York: Wiley, 1995.

Langer, Arthur M. 1997. *The Art of Analysis.* New York: Springer.

Martin, James, and James J. Odell. 1992. *Object-Oriented Analysis and Design.* Englewood Cliffs, N.J.: Prentice-Hall.

Shlaer, Sally, and Stephen J. Mellor. 1988. *Object-Oriented Systems Analysis: Modeling the World in Data.* Englewood Cliffs, N.J.: Yourdon Press.

Chapter 10

DESIGNING THE SYSTEM

Introduction

After all necessary data has been gathered and analyzed, the findings are used to create a new system design. This is the creative part of the system analyst's job, the most difficult to explain, and the most fun to perform. The product of this stage is a *system proposal*, a document that describes what the new system is, why it was selected, what it includes, and what resources will be required to implement it. Typically, this document might consist of sections documenting the functional specifications for the new system; a discussion of the alternatives considered; a conceptual description of the new design; a description of input and output and file designs; and a section dealing with resources needed for implementation. The techniques used to create the proposal, like the techniques used in artistic creation, are often highly personal, but some common or standard techniques apply.

This chapter details the techniques for each section of the system proposal.

Creation of Functional Specifications

At this stage, the time spent on analyzing the existing system reaps direct benefits. The data flow diagrams of the existing system should be examined in light of the requirements determined during the data collection stage, with the intent of identifying parts of the existing system that can be salvaged. Obviously, it is pointless to redesign a component that is functioning well. Those parts of the existing system that *cannot* be reused in the new system become, in DeMarco's (1979, 258) terms, "the domain of change." It is important to note that this refers to the existing logical system, not the physical system. This part of the design relies most heavily on the creativity of systems analysts.

At this stage, the domain of change is treated as a new context-level DFD, with the portion of the existing design that can be salvaged serving as a source or sink. This new context level is decomposed to the functional-primitive level to become the specification for the new logical system. As this decomposition takes place, the correctness of the solution should be verified with the client. If the client finds fault, the design is modified and resubmitted until both the designer and the client are satisfied. The new logical design should be completed before physical design takes place. At this point, for example, a circle showing "Print letter," as in figure 10-1, is sufficient; the fact that the client wants a blue LaserTyper X-4 is irrelevant.

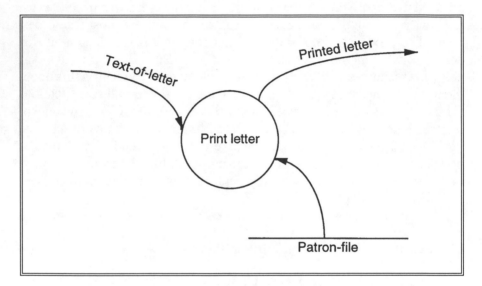

Fig. 10-1.

The order of design is exceptionally important. Analysts must first determine the outputs of the system, then what inputs are needed in order to create those outputs, and only then should they specify processes. A common error is to start with inputs. This leads to questions such as "This data flow comes in. What can we use it for?" It is almost always possible to figure out what to do with data, although the use is likely to be pointless or even counterproductive. This situation is analogous to buying eight-part order forms when you have a use for only three of the copies. You can almost always figure out a use for the other five parts, even if that use is only to sit in a file cabinet. The outputs must fulfill the needs of the users, but redundant or useless outputs should be eliminated. At the same time, the design should allow for modification when feasible so that if a change is needed, it can be accommodated by changes in outputs.

Once the systems analysts have determined outputs, they can identify inputs and document their sources. As with outputs, useless inputs (i.e., those not necessary to create outputs) are eliminated. Only after the analysts have identified all needed inputs and outputs, do they design the processes. Actually, after the outputs and inputs are identified and specified, creation of the process is often trivial; nevertheless, the analysts should consider a variety of process configurations and select the best.

Finally, necessary files should be identified and specified. Care should be taken not to create unnecessary files, and to ensure that all data files are needed for some process or output, except for purely archival data files.

Determination of Alternatives

Analysts have a responsibility at both the logical and physical design stages to ensure not only that a good design is created, but that the design chosen is the best they can create. Seldom is there a single way to do something, and the best way is seldom the first to come to mind. It is especially important during the design stage, therefore, to generate a variety of solutions and to select the best, rather than to generate, test, and implement a single solution. This extra effort is important to create an efficient, effective design, but it is also important when presenting the design to be able to show the client that efforts were made to create the best possible system. Unfortunately, it is all too easy to imagine a solution during the analysis stage and become fixated on that single solution. Often, it is difficult to see alternatives.

One of the most highly respected techniques for generating ideas is brainstorming (Osborne 1963, 166-96). This technique was developed in the 1940s by Alex F. Osborne, and has been the basis of many other idea-generation technologies developed in the last 50 years. Brainstorming has been reinvented under many names, but the essential aspects, explained below, have remained remarkably constant. Essentially brainstorming depends on the power of a group to create and refine solutions for problems. In general terms, the process involves the following steps:

1.   A group of problem solvers is assembled. These people should take their task seriously but not competitively. Although large groups have been used, experience has shown that the most effective size is between 7 and 10 members.

2.   A moderator is chosen or specified. The moderator must be someone who is able to make the individuals in the group feel comfortable and who is able to suggest new approaches, classify solutions, and break complex problems into more solvable, simpler ones.

3. A fact sheet is created and distributed. This memo is particularly important for participants who have not taken part in a brainstorming session before. It sets forth basic rules for brainstorming and gives examples of the sort of ideas needed.

4. The group meets to suggest potential solutions. At this stage, the emphasis is on quantity. If possible, authors of ideas should not be identified. Each idea is written down: overhead projectors or newsprint pads have been used in the past; now computer conferencing systems are frequently employed. Use of computers has the side benefit of helping to preserve anonymity, which can encourage shy participants to express ideas.

5. The basic rules for the session are:

   a. Editing or criticism of ideas is not allowed; suggestions are written down without comment.

   b. Wild ideas are encouraged.

   c. Quantity is more important than quality; the more suggestions, the better.

   d. Combining ideas, or using one as a springboard for another, is encouraged.

6. After the session, a period of incubation occurs, often overnight; additional ideas are then added.

7. The ideas are summarized, duplicates are eliminated, and the suggestions may be categorized or grouped.

8. Either the analysts or the team selects the best ideas for further consideration.

While no theoretical limit to the number of possible solutions exists, utility and time constraints often require that the best three solutions be selected for detailed examination. For example, the team might consider an improvement in the current system (a quick-fix approach), a more extensive alternative approach, and an optimal solution requiring maximum commitment of resources. Each solution is then subjected to a cost-benefit analysis. When the analysts present the system proposal, the analyzed solutions are given in brief form, along with a statement of why each was or was not chosen.

Alternative methods to brainstorming can facilitate creativity in problem-solving. Marshall (1986, 48) lists a number of verbs (e.g., *minify?, magnify?, substitute?*) that can further extend the possibilities suggested in the brainstorming session, and gives examples of applying the verbs. He also describes an approach developed by a researcher (Gryskiewicz 1984) called "brainwriting." In brainwriting, each participant writes down three solutions to a problem and places their paper in the center of the table; each participant then takes someone else's paper and adds three more solutions. The process for organizing verbal brainstorming can then be applied to the written solutions. Brainwriting has the advantage of following brainstorming rules while encouraging the less verbal members of the group.

Marshall (1986, 49) describes the use of an analysis matrix for a structured application to problem-solving. He also refers to analysis tools, such as decision tables and data flow diagrams, as potential problem-solving strategies (50).

Conceptual Design

A statement of the conceptual or logical design should be presented. This may be a combination of the techniques used to analyze the existing system such as narrative, flowcharts, decision tables, and decision trees. The relationship of the inputs, outputs, processes, and files should be included. The detailed DFDs are usually placed in an appendix. As each of the components (inputs, outputs, processes, and files) is refined, its details should be added to the data dictionary, as well as recorded in narrative form. As changes are made, this documentation must be kept up-to-date.

Inputs

Three types of inputs exist: 1) external sources of current information (e.g., book orders from branch libraries); 2) internal sources of current information (e.g., a list of outstanding orders); and 3) systems input (e.g., an automatically generated duplicate item report, or a reminder to back up the system). Each input to and output from the system should be specified. One way of specifying input might be:

1. Name

2. Content and format

3. Frequency of receipt

4. Expected volume

5. Timing (when the input occurs)

6. Medium of transmittal

7. Required validation.

The last component is a critical one. The old catch-phrase *garbage in, garbage out* is still true today. Even the best-written acquisitions system is useless if incorrectly entered ISBNs are used to order books. Validation routines are used to test the relevance and accuracy of the inputs. Inaccuracy usually results from obtaining data from inaccurate sources (the ISBN was wrong in the review source), from typographical errors (the clerk entered it wrong), or from using the wrong data (the LCCN was entered rather than the expected ISBN). Specific routines are outside the scope of this text but might include testing that the data's length is correct (ISBNs should have 10 characters), that it is of the correct sort (ISBNs use only 0-9,–, and X), and that it is correctly entered (the ISBN check digit should be tested).

Outputs

Outputs can also be classified as 1) external (e.g., overdue notice or reserve notice); 2) internal (e.g., inventories or reports for internal consumption); and 3) system. System outputs, such as file size or number of minutes the computer is used, are usually found in a computer system. The specification of outputs might include:

1. Name

2. Content

3. Format

4. Frequency of generation

5. Size

6. Events that trigger the output

Especially in computer systems, analysts should design outputs which humans find pleasant to work with. Many reports created by programmers do not fit into this category. For output data to be useful, it should be:

• designed to supply needed data. If a report is not useful, why produce it?

• edited to strip away extraneous information. Do not make the user search for what he or she needs.

• understandable. Organize the output in a way the *user* finds efficient, not a way that is easiest to produce.

- attractive and neat. Make use of good style, and produce all necessary characters, (e.g., umlauts or macrons).

- checked for accuracy. Validation should take place at output too: no February 30 due dates or invoices for $100,000,000 should be allowed.

Appropriate devices should be specified for both input and output. Input and output devices may include line printers, laser printers, bar code readers, microforms, magnetic tapes, or screen displays. If an inappropriate device (or no device at all) is specified, a good system might be perceived as unsatisfactory. After all, even the best report looks ugly in uppercase-only dot matrix output on green fanfold paper.

Processes

Specifying processes requires first that the action to take place be clearly understood. If inputs and outputs have been properly specified, process specification usually reduces to the question, "How should we take these inputs and most efficiently produce these outputs?"

Use of flowcharts, structured English, or one of the other specification tools will ensure that the design is logical. Ensuring efficiency is more difficult. Often, brainstorming is employed to identify alternative ways of moving from inputs to outputs. Constraints such as budget, availability of hardware, and demographics of the workforce must be taken into account. The practicality of ideas must be validated through discussions with the client and with workers who will actually use the system.

Ultimately, the creation of process specifications is the most creative of the tasks involved in system design, and, as such, it defies detailed description, but the end result of process specification will be a set of diagrams or structured English specific enough to allow a computer program or a procedure manual to be produced.

Files

Specifying files requires the systems analyst to decide the medium for the file. Each of the three types of media offers its own advantages and drawbacks.

Hard copy: This medium is inexpensive and sturdy, involves no machinery, and is the easiest to review (by auditors); however, it is bulky and requires a great deal of storage space. Also, sorting, merging, and changing the information in a hard-copy file is slow and expensive.

Microforms: These files are inexpensive, although they require an investment for filming and machinery for reading. Microforms are sturdy and require little storage space. They are, however, machine-dependent and virtually impossible to sort or merge.

Machine-readable files (tapes, disks, etc.): Machine-readable files involve an even greater reduction in storage space need, they offer great speed and flexibility in sorting, merging, and changing. The disadvantages are the delicate nature of the files and the expensive machine needed to read the files.

The advantages and disadvantages of each form should be considered in relation to the order and frequency of access required of a particular file of information and the volume of information to be stored. A backup of a system, for example, would be an obvious candidate for computer tape, while a backup of the catalog for use when the system is down would more appropriately be put on some microform. Another determining factor will be whether the file has a single purpose (one use only), has multiple purposes (several uses), or is part of a larger database containing other files with a variety of uses.

Specifications for files might include:

1. Sizes (e.g., maximum number of records or maximum length of records)

2. Fields present and whether they are fixed- or variable-length

3. Rate of change of the file

4. Frequency of access to the information in the file

For example, a file might be described as having a minimum of one record and a maximum of 20,000 records, each of which may be between 40 and 99,999 characters. The file might be updated weekly and accessed an average of three times per minute. Files are described in terms of records, each of which is made up of fields and subfields. Often a collection of files is described as a database. These relationships are summarized with examples in figure 10-2.

Levels	Telephone Company	Library
Database	Full set of telephone books, as well as directory assistance	Library as a whole, including staff
Files	White pages, yellow pages, etc.	Bibliographic MARC file, holdings file, etc.
Record	Entry in white pages	MARC record
Items	Name, address, phone number	Main entry (fields)
Elements	Exchange (956-1234)	Author's dates (subfields)

Fig. 10-2.

System Integration

As mentioned in Chapter 1, though a system is considered to be complete in order to simplify analysis and design, all useful systems in the real world are open. That is, data goes into them and flows out of them. During the analysis and design phases the real world is simplified by using sources and sinks that are defined as being outside the system, and in effect, ignored. As the new system is developed, it is essential that it be coordinated with the systems it must connect to. Frequently, this necessitates at least partial analysis of the external systems because they are often poorly documented and not well understood.

For example, if the system must interface with a sink called "District Union Catalog," and a data flow labeled "MARC-record" is going into this sink, it must be determined what the District Union Catalog thinks a MARC record looks like. It would be nice to simply verify that the MARC records meet national standards and then assume that the external system automatically accepts standard MARC records. But it is not infrequently discovered that the designers of the external system were unfamiliar with standards and that (as in the case of MARC records) significant variations exist in "standards" in use.

Thus, before a system is fully designed, its outputs must be checked to ensure that they will be accepted as valid inputs to the system that follows; and the outputs of preceding systems must be checked to ensure that they will be accepted as valid inputs to the system being designed. This often entails creating output and input data "by hand" and then feeding it to the system in question to make sure that it actually works. It is far easier to fix a system during the design stage than during its implementation.

Physical Aspects and Resources

The final part of the proposal is a statement of the physical resources needed to implement the new system. Obviously, this will not be identified in detail at the proposal stage, but a tentative statement of the hardware and equipment, as well as personnel anticipated for the new system, should be provided for the client. A tentative budget should also be designed and presented. Though this information is vital to the client in order to evaluate the proposed solution, analysts should make the client aware the data is *tentative*.

In order to create this final section, designers must bring the system back across the logical/physical split, into the physical realm. Because the physical realm is the part most familiar to the client, diplomacy is often required to prevent the client from placing total emphasis on this aspect while ignoring the logical design. Only after the client has approved the general proposal should detailed physical specifications be made. These, in any case, are often determined by procurement policies, which are beyond the control of the designers.

Case Study—Fort Memorial Library

The serials project group was sitting in a cramped office, becoming frustrated and irritable. The chalkboard was covered with many data flow diagrams (and the partially erased remnants of even more DFDs). The table was littered with coffee cups and cola cans.

Ben was running his fingers through what remained of his hair. "I don't know, with a system as screwed up as this one, it ought to be easy to come up with a better one. Suppose we say that the system anticipates the next expected journal and presents the check-in clerk with that item. Then the clerk can accept it or reject it and go to a detail screen to deal with the problem. Does that sound okay?"

"That's about the stupidest thing I've heard today," answered Maria. "How is the system going to know what issue comes in next? Through telepathy?"

"Yeah," put in Sue, "I'd like to see you write code to anticipate journal arrival."

"Well, if you can come up with a better idea, why don't you do it? We've got a process here that says 'Identify Next Issue.' All you have to do is fill it in."

"It's easy to write a label. It's a lot harder to write a program. Can't we break that bubble down?" Sue asked.

"Into what?"

"I don't know; it wasn't my idea to use DFDs. We should have gone to UML. That's what real programmers use!"

Nancy had had enough. "If you children are finished arguing, maybe we can get some work done. We have to have a proposal ready by next week." *And it's got to be dyno-supreme,* she added to herself. "Now, does anybody have any constructive ideas?" She was met with a stubborn silence. "Well, does anyone?"

Discussion Questions

- Nancy's brainstorming session has started to produce thunder instead of light. What went wrong? How can she fix it?

- What do you think of Sue Schriver's idea of using UML as a tool? Is there a better one?

- A specific item (anticipating serials receipt) is causing difficulties. What would be an effective way to approach that problem?

- To what extent do you think the serials receipt problem is a symbol for a deeper difficulty? If such a problem exists, how should Nancy deal with it?

References

DeMarco, Tom. 1979. *Structured Analysis and System Specification.* Englewood Cliffs, N.J.: Prentice-Hall.

Gryskiewicz, Stanley. 1984. *Brainwriting.* Greensboro, N.C.: Center for Creative Leadership.

Marshall, George R. 1986. *Systems Analysis and Design: Alternative Structured Approaches.* Englewood Cliffs, N.J.: Prentice-Hall.

Osborne, Alex F. 1963. *Applied Imagination.* New York: Scribners.

Chapter 11

PRESENTING THE SYSTEM

Introduction

This is the point in the systems analysis cycle when the analyst is ready to present the recommendations for the new system. The presentation's success will depend on a combination of formal communication vehicles, both oral and written. A presentation with well-organized content, delivered with the aid of tested communication techniques, will go far in aiding comprehension and acceptance of the new system. It is impossible to place too much emphasis on the importance of presenting the design effectively at this critical stage of the process. No matter how well designed the system is, if it cannot be communicated to others, a successful outcome is either compromised or delayed. At this point, the analyst becomes like an advertising agency presenting a new campaign to a client. Agencies put as much energy and communication technique into the presentations as they put into the campaigns themselves. Although the authors do not like to think of the presentation as a sales pitch, it can require the same kinds of techniques.

The importance of effective communication has been addressed previously in Chapters 3 and 5. To be effective is to apply techniques to solicit and convey information and concepts in ways that are mutually understood by each party. To be effective is to listen and to verbalize so that the mental images of each activity or need can be put on paper and expressed in ways that each person can comprehend in the same way (e.g., "Yes, that's what I mean," and "I understand what you are saying"). The presentation is the demonstration of what all the work has led to. The analyst shows how the new design meets the needs. Presumably these needs have been determined in a previous effort. Clearly articulating these needs has been the whole point of the analysis effort so far; now is the time to clearly articulate how the proposed new system meets them. The analyst may uncover new information during the presentation; however, the better the presentation is, the easier it will be to make modifications.

Analysts will be making formal presentations. Up until now, communication has been *informal*, usually talks with individuals or small groups. Informal communication provides the opportunity to make corrections easily, the opportunity to say, "That's not exactly what I meant. Let me clarify." An unproductive interview can be repeated or approached in a different manner. *Formal* presentations, in contrast, are single events. Analysts can hardly say, "We didn't explain that very well. We'd like to try again." Even though the first version of a written report can be revised, with errors corrected and data added, the impression of sloppy work remains. The presentation will be, in a sense, the first impression of the recommendation. And, as the saying goes, there is never a second chance to make the first impression.

This introduction is not intended to intimidate analysts preparing to present the design but to stress the importance of giving as much care and thought to preparing oral and written presentations as to the system design itself. Fortunately, current technology has made effective communication easier and faster. Presentation graphics programs, page layout programs, and color copy machines can all be utilized to inexpensively enhance the presentation. Technology, combined with the basic principles described in this chapter, can ensure a presentation equal to the quality of the design.

Principles of Formal Communication

The underlying principles of formal communication are to consider the presentation's *purpose* and *audience*. This may seem obvious and simple, but many communication projects fail because purpose and audience have never been defined. Simply presenting facts and concepts is not enough. Facts and concepts have different meaning in different contexts and for different people. What is essential to a cataloging clerk may be irrelevant to the interests of the head librarian. Reiterating what people already know may turn a presentation designed to show new concepts into a boring lecture.

Analysts need to consciously identify the purpose and audience before proceeding. For *purpose*, analysts should ask: "What is it that we are trying to get across?" The objectives of the presentation should be put in writing and can serve as a summary outline of the presentation. For example, an oral presentation might be planned to: 1) discuss the nature of the existing problem; 2) share the structure of the design; 3) explain the benefits of this particular design; and 4) list the resources necessary to implement the system.

Analysts must plan the content of the presentation to clearly relate to the objectives. If a topic does not contribute to one of the objectives, it is tangential and will clutter the presentation. Too often, writers and speakers falsely assume that more is better, that the reader or listener will be impressed by a plethora of information, but the *reverse* is true. Busy managers resent wading through verbiage to find the essence of the presentation. In addition, an oral presentation that is not on track will either put people to sleep or be merely entertaining. Also, uncomfortable speakers may tend to talk more to hide their nervousness; sticking to an outline of essential information can keep the presentation on target.

Knowing the purpose of a presentation is not enough. The analyst must also know who the intended audience is in order to tailor the presentation to them. Is the audience managers who want a broad overview of the project? Operators who need specific details? Will the listeners or readers understand technical terms or acronyms? Analysts need to identify the specific audience and its needs, and keep the target audience firmly in mind while preparing the presentation.

The Oral Presentation

Oral presentations effectively share information about the design and can establish a positive climate for acceptance of a subsequent written report. A typical oral presentation at this point in the systems analysis process might be a 20-minute presentation to between 10 and 30 people in a classroom-type setting. (The inexperienced speaker might welcome a brief oral presentation; more experienced speakers will recognize that the time limitation will require very careful and selective planning.) To design an effective oral presentation, do the following:

1. Gather data. The speaker must have a broad understanding of the entire design, not just the topic to be presented. If a team of analysts has worked on the design, the member(s) selected to present the proposal must be prepared to answer questions on areas that other team members may have taken responsibility for.

2. List relevant topics to be covered. All relevant topics must be addressed, but unnecessary details should be omitted.

3. Organize topics. Presenters should decide on a logical sequence of topics and the amount of time to be devoted to each topic.

4. Develop topics. Speakers should present each topic concisely but in sufficient detail to inform listeners. Concrete examples help to clarify the topic and to link the design to the current environment.

5. Develop topic summaries. Briefly summarize the topic to ensure that the listener understands the main point of the topic.

6.   Provide transition between topics. Speakers need to show the relationship between the previous topic and the current one to establish mental outlines for the listener. Examples include "The next step in the conversion process would be ..." or "Another factor that led to our recommendation is ..." Speakers may also choose to distribute or display a copy of the agenda of the presentation as a written outline, referring to it when moving to another topic.

7.   Use graphics. Graphics can supplement and enhance the total presentation, but avoid gratuitous graphic gimmicks. The audience is accustomed to seeing sophisticated graphic images, but presenters, though eager to use desktop graphic tools, may be less sophisticated about the techniques they use to create them. Poorly conceived graphics can insult and bore people. Media aids (e.g., charts, transparencies, video tapes) must not merely parrot what the presenter is saying, but rather convey information more effectively. It is annoying to endure a presentation of bullet statements read from an overhead transparency. But the same information supplemented with an illustration, a flowchart, or a photograph leaves a stronger impression.

It is not a bad idea to consult a graphics specialist for assistance on format, typography, and layout. Sometimes elements that make for good graphic presentations are subtle and not easy to identify. A simple, unified but flexible presentation format can be designed by the specialist and then expanded with details by the analyst. Video production is especially challenging. No video at all is better than a tape of someone's talking head with a bad script and sloppy editing.

If analysts do execute their own graphics, they should keep images and text simple and large in scale and make good use of color and composition. Text should be legible and large, with key words highlighted. Presenters should avoid using transparencies that have text too small to be seen by viewers, especially transparencies of text also provided as handouts. Above all, the message of the graphics should be obvious. Graphics should explain, not need to be explained.

An extra word of caution: if equipment is needed for any visual materials, it should be set up in advance, tested, and focused. Replacement parts, such as overhead projector bulbs, should be on hand. If a computer is to be used, the presenter must ensure ahead of time that the projection device will function properly with the actual hardware, software, and lighting.

Public Speaking

Most people approach their first experience in public speaking, even before a small group, with nervousness. If there is a team of analysts, the most confident and accomplished speaker may be selected to present the major portion of the talk, with other members in supporting roles. A combination of speakers can be effective, adding the variety of a different face and voice for the audience and drawing on the strengths of each team member. For example, one team chose to have the member most familiar with the current system provide the problem statement, the most confident speaker presented the proposed system, and the member who enjoyed challenging questions took over for the question-and-answer portion. The time allotment for this presentation was 45 minutes. If less time was allotted, only one or two speakers would have been slated. Using too many speakers in a short time results in a choppy and confusing presentation. Neophyte speakers will do well to adopt the following strategies, recommended and used by more experienced public speakers and performers:

1. Know the material well. Remember that, in general, a speaker knows more about the topic than an audience, and that the audience will benefit from the information being given.

2. Practice aloud, either alone or with another person, especially other team members. However, *do not* practice in front of a mirror. Practicing in front of a mirror seldom helps; it only tends to make the self-conscious more uncomfortable and does not aid in achieving a natural delivery. If feed back is desired (and it can be quite useful for speakers with some self-confidence), friends or members of the analysis team make a much more useful audience. Check the timing of each section, but add some extra time as a buffer.

3. Anticipate problems, such as topics that will elicit questions. Prepare the answers in advance; decide in advance how to handle tough questions if the answers are readily available, but do not try to cover up ignorance. It is better to say, "That's a very good question. I'll need to do some research to give you the exact details, but I'll get the information to you right away," than to say, "I'm not sure, but I think…" In fact, questions provide valuable feedback for the whole project.

4. Be relaxed. If nervous, *pretend* that you are a confident, poised speaker and play that role. A few minutes of solitude and deep breathing from the diaphragm before you go "on stage" can have a calming effect.

5. Accept your nervousness. Remember that even experienced stage performers suffer stage fright before performances. Try to use your nervousness as a stimulus.

6. Use your own words and actions that come naturally. Avoid stilted speech or unnatural vocabulary. Use notes to keep on track; practice your presentation so that you are familiar with the flow, but don't try to memorize it. Unless you are an accomplished actor, reciting a memorized text will almost certainly sound stilted and unnatural and will make it even more difficult to react comfortably to questions, interruptions, or unusual events such as blown projector bulbs or out-of-order transparencies. Imagine that you are sharing information with a friend rather than a group of strangers.

7. Introduce yourself at the beginning. Write the introduction into the presentation if necessary.

8. Spend more time practicing the beginning and the end of the talk. People pay more attention to introductions and summaries; these are your first and last chances to grab the audience.

9. Develop enthusiasm for the topic, and do not be afraid to show it. It is easier to sell others a product that is personally valued.

10. Dress well but in clothes that do not require fussing. A stiff jacket that does not move easily, a scarf that slips, or a jacket with pockets that are a tempting place to hide shaking hands will be a distraction.

Written Reports

Reports are written explanations of aspects of a project. Preliminary reports tell the client where a project might go; progress and status reports tell the client the project is or is not on track; and final reports tell the client what happened in the end. The specific report, at this point in the systems analysis, is for explaining and justifying the recommended design of the project; it may take the form of a proposal.

Content

Like the oral presentation, a report will be most useful if it is prepared with the purpose and audience clearly in mind. Because it is a more or less permanent document, take care to make it:

- *concise*: logically organized, easily referenced

- *readable*: written in standard English, without unnecessary jargon, and in a straightforward style

- *accurate*: in every detail

The writer of the report must try to answer the following key questions:

1. What is the report about? What is to be communicated?

2. What effects will the report have? Will the report give an impression of a carefully designed project?

3. What is the tone? Is the report too casual or too stilted?

4. What previous reports will it follow? What prior knowledge can the writer assume?

5. What time period is covered? Are time limitations clearly defined?

6. What are sources of the data? Does the report detail the tools used to gather the data?

7. How reliable is the data? Does the report offer proof of data validity?

8. Who will write the report? Is one member of the team best qualified, or will the report be effective if several people collaborate?

9. How long will preparation of the report take? Is enough time allowed to prepare a good report but not so much that it delays the total project?

10. Who will receive a copy? Are enough copies being prepared to cover dissemination to relevant persons? Is anticipated distribution so wide that problems are created?

11. Does the report meet user requirements? Does the report provide sufficient information without being too lengthy?

Failure to address these questions will result in a report that does not effectively represent the design.

Style and Format

A report can be quite solid in its content and still, if written poorly and presented in an ill-defined format, look flimsy. Today's desktop publishing tools are invaluable in producing attractive and professional documents. The report text should be divided into three major portions plus appendixes:

- The executive summary. The summary, one to three pages in length, should state the problem, the proposed solution, the cost, and the time required to implement. It is somewhat like an abstract. If the client reads nothing else (and a busy executive may indeed read no further), this section should explain the crucial elements for the top decision maker.

- The main body.This portion includes the introduction, which contains the background and environment of the problem, and the text, with details of the proposal; data; and alternative solutions not selected.

- The conclusion.The summation should include the best solution, a cost breakdown, the time required to implement, and the reasons for choosing this particular solution. It is not necessary to include a bibliography, and usually not desirable to use footnotes, although direct quotes and paraphrases in the text must be cited.

- Appendices. This portion can include information that is not critical for the client but that was used in the analysis (e.g., DFDs, a data dictionary, flowcharts, a glossary).

Production

Use a word processor to provide ease of editing. Run the spell-checker, but be sure to proofread the report as well. Grammar-checking programs may be helpful for enhancing writing ability. If the grammar checker notes sentence after sentence in the passive voice, consider doing some rewriting. It is always good to have someone who is not too close to the project read the document for meaning and style.

When writing the report, bear in mind that the purpose is not to provide a mass of prose to wade through, but to present information in an easily comprehended manner. Run-on paragraphs can often be converted to straightforward bullet statements that are easier to grasp and comment on in discussions.

Effective use of typography can enhance the appearance and the clarity of reports.

- Most document production systems allow a writer to make use of typographical devices (e.g., boldface for major headings, italics for emphasis or contrast).

- More sophisticated systems simulate typesetting, allowing old typewriter conventions to be replaced by the richer convention they were designed to approximate; thus, underlining for emphasis can be replaced by italics.

- For the body of reports, tried-and-true serif typefaces like Times should be used.

- Use of boldface or larger type sizes for headings is appropriate.

- Consider using a contrasting sans serif face for headings and titles (e.g., Helvetica headings with a Times body), but be careful when mixing fonts. It is very easy to create clutter and confusion. The page should appear to be even and balanced.

- If there is a doubt that something looks right, it probably does not. Keep it simple.

- If a typographic element is not needed for understanding (a colon after a subhead, for example), leave it out.

- Numbering systems for an elaborate report are useful, especially if linked to a detailed table of contents.

Printing and Binding

To make the most of the effort expended in writing, editing, and designing a report, print it on the highest quality printer available. Because even small organizations now have laser printers, this is the ideal choice. Bond papers slightly heavier than the usual stock used in laser printers and photocopiers are available and contribute greatly to the appearance of the document. Showthrough (visibility of type through a page) is minimized and the feel of the paper is more substantial. If you need multiple copies of the report, try the laser bond in your copier; otherwise, use the "quality copy" as your presentation original.

To give the report a final touch of style, design an attractive cover. Laserprint or photocopy cover-weight stock (many laser printers and photocopiers accommodate heavy stock as a manual feed) with a design incorporating the project title, names of the client and analyst, a date, and a logo or perhaps a significant illustration. If a fully printed cover is not an option, at least present the document with a standard binding cover, perhaps with a window to the title page.

Always have the report bound, not stapled. Depending on the size of the report, choose a post or spiral binding. Copy centers offer many types of binding systems. Post-type bindings are professional looking but do not lie flat. If the report is a working document for a committee discussion, a spiral or comb binding that allows it to lie flat may be more appropriate. If the document is part of a series, or if revisions are anticipated, a three ring binder with sleeves on the cover and spine for cover pages may be more effective (though more expensive).

Documentation

Documentation provides the how and why for the operators who will actually work within the new system. It is intended to be informational, not promotional, and is as concise as possible. Documentation should include an explanatory narrative of the process, structured English instructions, and decision tables or trees as needed. Because the documentation will be the principal means by which operators will learn the system, it is especially important that it be accessible, complete, and correct.

It is important to realize that documentation serves the dual purpose of *instruction* and *reference*. In its instructional function, the documentation must clearly explain each phase of the system. This explanation must be logical, leading from the start of the system to its outputs. In computer documentation, for example, each major function (perhaps input, editing, and saving a document) might occupy a separate chapter. These chapters may take the form of a tutorial, with exercises to show each aspect of the system operation. Once the system is learned, however, the documentation serves as a reference on how to perform each operation. For this use, the tutorial format is not particularly helpful; an item-by-item listing (or command-by-command for computers) is much more functional. An index that leads the user to the correct description of the procedure is critical.

The documentation must also contain a section that discusses possible system failures (the ubiquitous error messages). Methods of avoiding or solving problems must be provided for each potential failure. Obviously, no designer would intentionally provide a system with fatal errors.

Despite the notable efforts of technical writers and editors, computer software documentation is notorious for instructions that appear to have been written by the programmer—with false assumptions of user expertise, no organization of the information into logical chapters or sections, esoteric terminology and jargon, and a primitive index, if any. Analysts should make every effort to avoid these negative examples. A good strategy is to have a totally uninformed reader try to follow the instructions, just as it is useful to have a naive reader or listener critique all written or oral presentations in advance.

Propaganda

Presenting a design may require the production of materials or verbal communication intended to convince others of the value of the design and to promote the acceptance of the new system. These materials may take the form of flyers highlighting the progress of the project, bulletin board postings, articles prepared for an in-house newsletter, announcements at staff meetings, or other creative ways to keep everyone informed of the value of the new system design. Propaganda, or promotional communication (as practiced in advertising and public relations and rooted in rhetoric, or the art of persuasive communication), requires an understanding of the target person or group, and an awareness of the benefits of the system to the audience. The same communication fundamentals that apply to formal reports and presentations apply to promotional materials.

Obviously, analysts will present the system in a favorable light in order to "sell" it. It is important to emphasize, however, the need for honesty. If 51 percent of the operators liked a screen design, it is correct to say, "This screen was preferred by most operators," but stating that "all" or "an overwhelming majority" preferred the screen design is dishonest. If only 49 percent or fewer preferred the screen design, it is misleading to say that it was preferred by most. Such tactics are unethical and eventually damage the credibility of the analysts and acceptance of the system. *Never* lie.

One danger with propaganda (and it is largely to emphasize this danger that the authors prefer to use *propaganda* rather than *promotion*) is that the people who produce it may come to believe it. Analysts should always retain a core of cynicism about their efforts—they should remain unsure and questioning throughout the project. To believe one's own propaganda is to court complacency. While the majority of users may have preferred the screen design chosen, the analyst should always have the other 49 percent firmly in mind.

Summary

The quality of communication between the analysts and those within the existing system has a great effect, negative or positive, throughout the process but especially at the point of presenting the design. Careful planning, use of effective and proven communication strategies, and confident presentation contribute greatly to the overall success of the project.

Case Study—Fort Memorial Library

"That was a lot of fun!" said Bai.

"And a lot of work," put in Maria.

"But look at what we've got." Bai tapped the thick pack of paper she held in her hands. As the edges became flush, she stroked the cover lovingly. "It's as beautiful a proposal as was ever produced."

"It works, and it's elegant," agreed Sue.

Nancy brought them down to earth. "Now all we have to do is convince the rest of the world." She smiled as their faces fell. "It's not as bad as all that. We think the proposal is great. The proposal *is* great. Now all we have to do is make that as obvious to Dean Tebbits, Margie, the fiscal officer, the heads of Readers' and Technical Services..." Nancy counted off on her fingers the people who would be at Monday's meeting. Suddenly the butterflies returned to her stomach.

"Okay," she said firmly, "we're getting a late start—only three days to prepare the presentation. Let's divvy up the jobs."

"I'll make transparencies of all the DFDs," said Bai.

"And I'll get copies of the proposal for everyone," put in Ben.

"Okay, I'll coach Nancy on the computer stuff, so she'll look like she knows what she's talking about," said Sue, with a grin. "Not that anybody else that'll be there knows anything. What do you think, Nancy? A half-hour's worth for them? We'll whomp up a script and put it on your Power-Book to read."

"Wait a minute," said Maria. "This was a democratically created document. I think we all should take turns presenting it. We can each do the part we know best!"

"Well, if you think I'm going to talk in front of that bunch of bigwigs, you can think again," replied Sue.

Nancy looked at each of them. "Let's figure out what we want to do, and then we'll figure out how to do it, okay? For example, I don't think we need transparencies of all the DFDs, even if we think they're lovely. Now, what's the most effective way to win these people over to our design?"

Discussion Questions

- In the last chapter the group was at each other's throats. Now they seem cohesive again. Based on your experience in working with groups, is this normal group behavior? What might Nancy do to encourage this attitude to continue?

- Maria wants to talk. She wants everyone to talk. Discuss the effect of acquiescing to her suggestion. What might be the effect of turning her down? How can Nancy handle *this* one?

- Do you think the DFDs would make an effective graphic tool for the presentation? If not, what would be better? How would you organize the graphics for a presentation like this?

- How would you answer Nancy's final question?

Chapter 12

Introduction

The first chapter emphasized that *systems* in systems analysis did not refer to hardware or software, but to an existing environment of processes, practices, and procedures. The systems analyst will often find, however, that the design of a new system may require the selection of hardware and software to resolve inadequacies in the existing system. Especially when the existing system is complex, use of modern technology may be critical. The use of the term *system* in this chapter, therefore, will relate to the selection of hardware and software if these are a part of the new design. Several basic considerations govern the choice of the best hardware and software for the new design.

Existing Versus Custom Designed Systems

Selecting a system that is fully developed offers major advantages. First, the buyer can evaluate the actual features of the system. Features promised by a vendor—"vaporware"—may or may not be developed within the desired time frame and to the exact specifications of the buyer. In other words, selecting an existing system is safer. Second, existing systems are usually less expensive because vendors can spread development costs among many buyers. If a system costs $1,000,000 (a low figure to develop an integrated library system), it can be sold to 1,000 libraries for $1,000 each (ignoring costs of sale and profit, if any). If a system is being designed for one site, the buyer must cover all the personnel cost and any other costs involved.

The disadvantage of selecting an existing system is that the product tends to be generic, meeting the average needs of a number of similar situations. Specialized needs of a particular design may not be fully addressed by the existing system.

173

Package Systems Versus Component Systems

It may be desirable to purchase a system that will replace an entire existing system. For example, a library may purchase an integrated package that includes an online public access catalog, a cataloging module, an acquisitions module, and a serials module. However, if systems analysis shows that the problem is confined to a single process, it may be possible to select a component that will replace only that process (e.g., to buy a new "bubble" for the DFD). This option allows the client to spread the purchase costs and the necessary training for each component over a longer period of time.

Pursuit of Perfection

Whether an existing or custom designed system is selected, it will be virtually impossible to buy or create a system that is ideal for every person and operation. Instead, the evaluators will need to determine mandatory requirements, oppose them to desireable ones, and select a system that meets all of the former and provides as many as possible of the latter.

System Selection

Four options are open to the purchaser of a system. First, the buyer may choose to produce custom software and then purchase hardware to operate it. In this case, "system selection" means simply "hardware selection." A second option is to select software that is compatible with existing hardware. In this case, compatibility with existing hardware would be one of the system specifications. Another option is to buy the hardware and software separately and then merge them. This may offer the advantage of negotiating a lower price for the two separate purchases. However, if problems are encountered when the software is loaded, it may be more difficult to establish which vendor is responsible for resolving the problems. A fourth choice is to select a turnkey system, buying the software and hardware from the same vendor. The vendor then assumes responsibility for successful implementation of the system. However, the vendor is not faced with active competition on the hardware and software and can often command a higher price for the convenience of the combined system.

Within the four possible options, analysts need to be familiar with the choices available in the marketplace. Visiting trade shows provides an opportunity to view the latest products. Analysts should be aware, though, that only the positive features will be presented. Also, not all products may be represented at local shows. Computer stores generally display hardware and software suitable for small businesses. In addition, discount stores may offer the close-out models rather than the most recent hardware and software. Again, analysts must filter the information presented through a broader perspective of the field. Sales representatives vary in their technical knowledge of the computer hardware and may, in some cases, recommend a system based on their hope for a higher commission rather than the needs of the customer. For a general overview of the products available, however, trade shows and computer stores are interesting and sometimes helpful; knowledgeable sales representatives can share useful information. Trade journals provide a more reliable and broader perspective of available products. Analysts should create a general knowledge of the field through wide skimming of relevant articles and a more detailed understanding for specific projects through a search of current literature that includes reviews.

Determining Costs and Benefits

Analysts should keep in mind the adage, "There is no such thing as a free lunch" when determining the costs and benefits of alternative systems. All benefits have costs associated with them, and much of our life is spent deciding between benefits based on their costs. For example, a couple may decide to wait for a bus in the rain in order to have enough money for a movie ticket, or they may decide to invest in a taxi ride and forego the movie. The money paid to the bus driver, taxi driver, or box-office attendant is easily compared. These quantifiable costs include anything that can be counted (e.g., dollars, inches, minutes). A problem arises in the fact that to establish a basis of comparison, costs must be expressed in the same units (usually money). Of course, no natural conversion factor exists between dollars and minutes. Being paid ten dollars to listen to thirty minutes of recorded music is much more attractive than being paid ten dollars to spend thirty minutes undergoing a root canal procedure! In the example of the couple, more costs are involved than merely the money paid: if the couple takes the taxi they are also paying the price of missing the movie. But attending the movie has the cost of an uncomfortable drenching. It is difficult to reduce these costs to numbers, and they are therefore called nonquantifiable factors.

In the library setting, there is the question of which is a better implementation: a system that requires four hours of cataloger's time to produce a catalog record, or one where the record is purchased from OCLC at a cost of four dollars. In effect, the question is whether four hours or four dollars is worth more—an unanswerable question. If the cataloger's time is converted to dollars at a pay scale of twenty dollars per hour, the comparison becomes a choice between eighty dollars for one book for the cataloger, or four dollars for a record from OCLC. The answer is obvious.

A library might conduct several *kinds* of cost analysis:

1. Maximizing benefits for a given cost. The library may be on a fixed budget and trying to select the "best" system possible within that budget.

2. Minimizing costs for a given level of benefits. The library may have fixed specifications and select the least expensive system that meets the specifications.

3. Maximizing the ratio of benefits over costs. The library may select a system that costs twice as much as another but gives three times the performance.

4. Considering the costs of money. In an inflationary environment, the library may choose to pay a larger amount in the future rather than a lower amount immediately. If money can be borrowed at an interest rate lower than the interest rate paid on savings, a profit can be made (see "Cost of Money" below).

The first three kinds of cost analysis can be accomplished by using relatively simple, if tedious, mathematics. Following is a formula for determining unit costs:

$$(a+b+c+d+e+f...+n) / x = y$$

where *a* through *n* are specific quantifiable yearly costs (e.g., personnel costs, fringe benefits, supplies, contractual costs) and *x* is the total output of the system (e.g., number of books cataloged in a year). Matthews, in an early work (1980, 100-1) lists twenty five possible cost components; there are certainly others. The costs (*a...n*) over the benefits (*x*) is the cost to benefit ratio, or *y*. Logically, the system with the lowest unit cost should be selected. Unfortunately, this fails to take into account three factors: the costs of selection, the cost of money, and nonquantifiable costs.

Costs of Selection

Hidden costs are often associated with deciding whether to change systems and which system to buy. These can include the cost of a consultant, travel to vendor sites, or legal advice. For example, in one school with which the authors are familiar, ten teachers met for five afternoon meetings to decide which of two word processing programs would be selected for the school. The teachers were expected to examine both packages, rate them, and produce a report on their findings. These reports were typed by the school secretary, reproduced, and given to each member of the faculty.

At a conservative estimate the selection process alone cost over $5,000, without the purchase of the software. The cost of the decision-making process would have paid for copies of both of the programs for the teachers.

Costs of Money

Even more hidden costs are associated with money itself, especially when the costs are not a one-year investment. More often, decisions involve multiyear investments such as deciding whether to purchase a product or service over several years, factoring in the cost of annual maintenance, or comparing the advantages of lease or purchase of equipment.

Few discussions of cost of money occur in a library setting. Of these, the best is Michael Koenig's *Budgeting Techniques for Libraries and Information Centers*. As Koenig (1980, 19-20) points out, even in noninflationary times, dollars spent or not spent lose value over time. For example, in the early days of microcomputers, some consumers decided not to purchase a computer in hopes that the prices would come down. If they postponed buying a computer that cost $1,000 and would be used for at least five years, they sacrificed $1,000/5, or $200, in computer usage during the wait period. If the price of the computer remained constant, the cost would still be $1,000 but the discounted value would be only $800. Other factors could also discount the value of the future $1,000, such as the consumer's failure to keep the money set aside for purchase.

The value of money depreciates even more during inflationary times. In the 1970s, double-digit inflation was the norm. If buyers could have purchased a software program priced at $1,000 in 1970 and postponed payment until 1980, the program would have cost the equivalent of $350 (based on the worth of a dollar in 1970). Despite the fact that $1,000 changed hands, that $1,000 would have bought 1,000 hot dogs in 1970 but only 350 in 1980 because the money was worth less in 1980. In other words, given the choice of spending $350 in 1970 or $1,000 in 1980, the astute buyer would have chosen the $1,000. This is the concept of net present value (NPV). In 1990, the net present value of the $1,000 to be spent in 1980 was only $350.

Koenig (1980, 20) suggests using a 3 1/2 percent to 4 percent inflation-free discount figure (as shown in the microcomputer example) and adding that to the current rate of inflation (as shown in the software example) to arrive at a reasonable discount rate to use in decision-making. Using the NPV gives more reliable costs for projects that are paid for over several years or that continue to accrue costs over several years. Most spreadsheet programs include a function for computing NPV. These require a quantification in dollars of costs and benefits; the length of time over which the money will be spent; and the time value of the money (what the money could have earned if invested in something besides the project). This last quantification is a complex concept, but the current rate of one-year certificates of deposit is often used.

In all of these techniques, the following rules of thumb apply:

1.   Include all reasonable quantifiable costs.

2.   Reduce costs and benefits to dollars and cents.

3.   Be conservative in estimating benefits and liberal in estimating costs.

Koenig (1980, 15-16) also touches on the concept of "sunk" costs—the amount of money already invested in the present system, relevant only when determining the costs and benefits of upgrading the current system or when a decision-maker has a political investment in the current system. For example, a school librarian considering purchase of an upgraded circulation program might discover that her computer is inadequate. She can prepare for the objections of her principal to replacing the computer by listing the added features of the newer program and the cost (or feasibility) of upgrading the existing computer.

In a business setting, the costs of money become even more complex with factors such as the cost of borrowing money, the loss of opportunity for other uses of assets, and the amount of return expected by the organization for any investment. The Koenig reference is a useful source of information on these and other business-related issues (1980).

Nonquantifiable Costs and Benefits

Nonquantifiable costs include such elements as quality of service, currency of materials, accuracy, aesthetics, or job satisfaction. These are important considerations, but they either defy measurement or cannot be easily converted to dollars. The factors are important, but should not be used as the major consideration in a decision.

One technique for factoring in nonquantifiable costs and benefits is to list them and then assign priorities to them. If ten nonquantifiable factors are identified, these should be assigned numbers from ten for the most important to one for the least important. Each alternative should then be ranked on a scale of one to ten, based on how good it is in that category. The rankings are multiplied by the priorities, and the categories are then totaled. The nonquantifiable elements can then be compared, with the systems with high scores being better than those with low scores. For larger numbers of nonquantifiable factors, weights (perhaps from a high of five to a low of one) can be assigned to each, based on a judgment of how important each is to the library. Like prioritization, these weights are usually determined through some consensus-building technique. Weights and priorities are evaluated in the same way. Figure 12-1 shows that, between system A and system B (based on the criteria shown), system B is the better choice.

Criterion	Priority	System A Score	System A Weighted	System B Score	System B Weighted
Easy to use	10	8	80	6	60
Attractive screens	9	4	36	8	72
Documentation easy to use	8	6	48	3	24
Fits in our current workflow	7	6	42	8	56
Upgrade path is acceptable	6	4	24	4	24
Commands are "intuitive"	5	1	5	8	40
Quality of vendor's ALA parties	4	10	40	2	8
Hardware matches decor	3	6	18	4	12
Vendor is socially responsible employer	2	4	8	6	12
Friendly sales staff	1	10	10	5	5
TOTAL SCORE			263		313

Fig. 12-1.

Designing Specifications

It is critical to differentiate between what is needed and what is desirable in a new system. Features that are needed become the mandatory requirements in the list of specifications; desirable features are secondary specifications. Since no system will be able to meet all the specifications, it is important to determine at the outset what requirements are absolutely essential to the successful implementation of the design, and which ones are features that would be welcome but whose absence would not hamper operations. Designers of specifications must also be aware that assumptions of common sense are dangerous. What seems like common sense to the ones drawing up the specifications may not be common sense to the vendor.

The specifications must live up to their name: they must be so specific that there will be no misunderstanding between the parties involved. One library, for example, simply specified IBM-compatible computers for a project. The low bid was for a system that ran IBM programs but used nonstandard components that were expensive and difficult to obtain: the motherboards were two inches smaller than the ones on typical clones; thus, standard replacements purchased from normal suppliers could not be used. The next time bids were prepared, the component sizes were listed.

Using existing specifications can speed up the process and remind designers of features that they might otherwise overlook. For example, the specifications drawn up for the Tacoma Public Library (Hegarty n.d.), although now out of date, are recognized as a useful model for others. Another useful source of information is *Proposals and Contracts for Library Automation: Guidelines for Preparing RFP's* (Cortez 1987). *Library Technology Reports* published a sample Request for Prposal (RFP) (Model 1990, 657-749). Finally, some major consultant firms sometimes make their boilerplate specifications available for purchase. Care must be taken when using these "canned" RFPs to employ them as models and not merely copy them. The level of detail should be consistent with the needs of the library, and unnecessary specifications should be deleted. At least one vendor of low cost (*circa* $3,000) systems simply ignores thick RFPs, knowing that the cost of preparing a response will be greater than the profit on a sale.

Vendors are often willing and eager to supply a set of specifications. Again, these specifications can provide a description of a system that may make the prospective buyer aware of additional desirable features; however, they will usually be designed to favor what the vendor feels is important and may not lend themselves to a fair evaluation of other systems. It is a good idea to identify a list of systems that might meet the requirements of the libraries and then send each a Request for Information (RFI). An RFI, as its name implies, is a request that the vendor supply information on its system. RFIs usually include details of the library environment (size of collection, number of circulations, and so on), as well as any other information, such as anticipated schedules, which the library feels the vendor might find useful. Vendors generally respond with information on any of their system configurations that might be useful, and occasionally they respond that none of their systems would be suitable.

The best set of specifications combines information from all of the above suggestions, thus tapping more than one source of potential specifications. Good specifications are realistic in expectations and include no false assumptions. The specifications should be grouped, as needed, to develop categories of functional components, sequences of services, or other logical divisions, and when possible, some indication of the relative importance of each specification should be given.

Requests for Proposals

Once the specifications have been written, a Request for Proposal should be developed and disseminated to vendors. A typical RFP will consist of several sections:

1. A section describing the library and its environment, a tentative timetable, contact people, and so on.

2. A section containing the specifications for the system that is to be purchased.

3. A section detailing standards which must be adhered to and definitions for terms used.

4. An administrative section explaining how bids are to be submitted, what the deadlines are, whom to contact for clarification, and so on.

Two very different types of RFPs exist. In one case, the library is asking for the vendor to provide the system it thinks will best suit the needs of the library and to specify how much such a system will cost. The library then selects the proposal that it feels has the best cost-to-benefit ratio. This kind of RFP is common in private and commercial organizations. The other kind of RFP is more properly called a Request for Bids (RFB) or Request for Quotes (RFQ). In this system, which is common in governmental agencies, the library specifies what it wants the system to accomplish and then must choose the lowest bid which meets the specifications.

Obviously, specifications for RFBs must be much more specific. If a library issues an RF*P*, which demands authority control, and one vendor takes that to mean use of MARC Authorities format, another takes it to mean ability to make global changes to the database, and a third interprets it to mean the ability to produce an alphabetized list of all headings, the library can compare costs and features and select whichever it feels meets its needs. In an RF*B*, if "authority control" has not been precisely defined, the library may find itself forced to either accept the cheapest system or begin the RFB process again.

Writing RFPs is a specialized task. Most organizations have a legal or procurement office which must check each RFP before it is released. These people often have extensive experience in large purchases, even if they lack knowledge of libraries, and if approached as allies, they can be very helpful in the purchasing process. The RFP is one area where consultants are often used to advantage: a librarian may do two or three RFPs for large systems during a career; a consultant may do that many each year, or even each month. Even if a consultant is engaged, however, the responsibility for creating specifications rests with the library. Some librarians try to save time and money by copying another library's RFP, and some consultants use a stock RFP with little or no modification beyond changing the library name. Use of "boilerplate" specifications simply leads to vendors using "boilerplate" responses. One vendor with which the authors are familiar has a file of responses keyed to specific paragraphs used by a well-known consultant, which they simply copy to their response. If the consultant produces a stock RFP, and the vendor gives stock responses, the unique circumstances at the library are never addressed.

Proposals must get to the potential vendors if responses are to be received. Lists and evaluations of vendors in various areas of librarianship are often given in *Library Technology Reports*, *Library Journal*, and *Library HiTech*, among other periodicals. RFPs should be sent directly to vendors which can be identified as likely candidates. In addition, it is proper to advertise the existence of RFPs in library periodicals to allow additional vendors an opportunity to respond. Finally, it is common to advertise the RFP in local newspapers. In some cases this may be a legal requirement, but in most cases it serves to avoid the charge of "not buying locally," which can hurt a library in fund-raising efforts.

Once the deadline for submittal of proposals is reached, the proposals should be evaluated using a four-step process:

1. Any proposals that do not meet the mandatory requirements should be eliminated.

2. Each of the remaining proposals should be judged to determine to what degree the vendor meets the specifications.

3. A financial review of the company should be conducted, based on vendor statements and information gathered from other sources, such as the annual "Library Automation Marketplace" review in *Library Journal*.

4. Subjective opinions should be added. One vendor's search screens may be more aesthetically pleasing than another's. These concerns should not be underrated because they will affect user satisfaction, but they should not be the only criteria considered.

Again, cost and cost-effectiveness are not the same. Selecting a vendor only because they quoted the lowest price may not result in the selection of the system that will best serve the buyer's needs. The selected system must meet the mandatory requirements, but of those that are flexible systems, some systems may meet more than others. At the same time, some of the flexible requirements may be more important to the library than others. One way to compare the costs more effectively is to determine a *weighted* cost by assigning a value or weight to each nonmandatory feature, based on its importance to the library. The scores for features present in the proposal are then totaled and divided into the total cost of the system. The most cost-effective system is the one with the best cost/feature ratio. The difference between this approach and that illustrated in figure 12-1 is that the factors are binary (see figure 12-2). For example, a system either can load holdings from the 049 field or it cannot. If desired, scores can be given as to *how well* each requirement is met as shown in figure 12-1, and weighted scores can be compared. This approach is preferable when local procurement regulations allow, because it provides a finer gradation of compliance.

		System A		System B	
Specification	Weight	Complies	Score	Complies	Score
System loads holdings from 049	1	X	1		
System loads holdings from 082	5	X	5		
System loads holdings from 911	3		0		
System downloads from OCLC	5	X	5		
System downloads from BiblioFile	3		0		
System downloads from LC CDs	1	X	1		

Fig. 12-2.

The decision to purchase a particular system is rarely made by one person. Since no one person has the expertise for all factors that go into the selection process, a committee is usually appointed. The committee often includes individuals who will be affected by the system or who have special areas of responsibility or expertise. There may be representation from each library department, from professionals and staff members, from end-users, from the university or municipal data processing center, from the board of directors of a public library, and perhaps from the agency that will provide the funds if there is one. The committee must include all the important constituencies but must not become too large. It is probable that the committee will be without authority, but it will make a recommendation to the library director. The director's decision should be reviewed by the institutional legal staff and perhaps by the data processing department before being forwarded to the group actually responsible for the purchase (e.g., board of directors regents). This group probably knows little about the system and its requirements but should understand that an effective selection process has taken place.

In spite of size constraints of the selection committee, strategies are available for involving a larger group of end-users. For example, determining the priority order of the evaluative criteria offers an opportunity for expanding participation in the process. When a large school district was developing a short list of approved automation software programs, sessions were held in several geographic locations to provide information about software features and to allow the librarians to state which were essential, desirable, or unnecessary features. They also determined the priority order of the features. The information provided valuable feedback to the selection committee, increased the knowledge of software for the librarians, and made the end-users a part of the selection process.

Contracts

Once the system has been approved for purchase, a formal contract should be prepared with the assistance of a lawyer who specializes in contract law. Sometimes a board of directors has a lawyer serving on it, but that individual may be primarily concerned with criminal or real estate law. It is critical that a lawyer with experience in contracts review the document that formalizes the commitment of client and vendor. Libraries have the contracts checked by lawyers to ensure that they codify what has been agreed to.

It should be noted that the contract is simply a clear statement of the understanding of both sides. Its purpose is to ensure that both parties agree on what is taking place. It is not a proper arena for trying to gain advantage or to hide expectations, but it should clearly state what is being agreed to. Therefore, terms such as "record," "MARC format," "authority control," and so on, which are open to various interpretations, should be clearly defined. It should also clearly state which party is responsible for such factors as site preparation, hardware installation, shipping costs, and so on.

During this stage of the procurement process it is common for negotiation to take place. For example, the vendor may wish to receive all payment before shipping the product, while the library obviously would prefer to defer all payment until the system is installed and tested. While such negotiation can become intense, little will be gained by refusing to compromise on any points. Such behavior only sets the stage for an unpleasant relationship that may last for years.

Exercise in Evaluation and Selection

You have been given responsibility for choosing a new automation software package for a large furniture store to manage accounting, sales, delivery, and inventory. What are the steps you will follow in the process?

Who will be involved and how? How will you balance budget constraints and product quality? See Appendix B for some possible answers.

Case Study—Fort Memorial Library

Nancy and her group were holding a coffee break discussion about their new system. They had created a set of generalized requirements that had been approved by both Dean Tebbits and by the Serials Department. These had been codified in a systems proposal. The proposal had been presented to general acclaim; even Margie seemed to like it. With Sue's coaching, Nancy had come across as a seasoned veteran. She *felt* like a seasoned veteran.

"Thank goodness that's over," opined Nancy. "Now we can get some work done rather than spending all our time in third-world diplomacy."

Maria started to say something, but Sue cut her off. "Right. A couple of lines of COBOL and they'll have a new system that'll knock their eyes out. Last year I worked on the student registration program we were implementing, and this is just about the same. We can steal whole routines from it; just substitute journal titles for student names and issues received for courses taken. It's a cinch; it'll only take a couple of weeks."

Bai looked up from her cup of hot water. "But when we were looking at circulation systems in my unit two years ago I spoke with many librarians across the country. They felt that there were many good circulation systems already on the market. There was a feeling that writing your own wasn't a good idea. Wouldn't that also be true for serials systems?"

"That's what they told us in library school back in the sixties," agreed Ben.

"But this isn't the sixties," said Sue. (Nancy could see Ben mouthing, "More's the pity.") "Why pay thousands of dollars for a system we can develop right here. No system we can buy will meet all of Margie's requirements; I can tell you that without even checking. Writing a serials routine can't be too hard. It'll be a lot of fun. Let's do it!"

Nancy was sorry she had opened her mouth. Two weeks ago Sue had been adamant that she could not write such a program. Besides, as Nancy remembered it, the new class registration system had been a fiasco. Did she really want to base a system on that?

"Okay," Nancy said decisively. The group stopped talking and looked at her. They had learned over the past months that when she used that tone she usually had something meaningful to say. "Let's use what we've learned to decide which path to take. Sue, you work up a cost/benefit analysis on the local/purchased question; check the literature for current prices. Bai, I want you to find out what is available in the marketplace that might come close to matching our needs. Maria, I want you to find libraries that have developed their own systems and get them to tell you whether they're glad they did it that way or not. I'll talk with the head of the computer center here and find out what kind of support we can expect if we decide to do it locally. Let's get the information, make a decision, and get on with getting a system in here."

Discussion Questions

- What are some of the trade-offs you see in in-home vs. purchased systems for this library? If the decision is made to purchase a commercial system, what problems might be expected from Sue? From Margie (because the system probably wouldn't match her desires exactly)?

- What do you think of Sue's enthusiasm? How could Nancy channel it into more productive paths? Do you think Nancy handled the situation well, or not?

- How should Nancy proceed in order to get the best possible system while avoiding intra-group conflicts.

References

Cortez, Edwin. 1987. *Proposals and Contracts for Library Automation: Guidelines for Preparing RFP's.* Studio City, Calif.: Pacific Information.

Hegarty, Kevin. n.d. *More Joy of Contracts.* Tacoma, Wash.: Tacoma Public Library.

Koenig, Michael E. D. 1980. *Budgeting Techniques for Libraries and Information Centers.* New York: Special Libraries Association.

Matthews, Joseph. 1980. *Choosing an Automated Library System.* Chicago: American Library Association.

Model Request for Proposal. 1990. *Library Technology Reports* (September-October): 657-749.

Chapter 13

MANAGING A PROJECT

Introduction

Project management has been defined as the process of achieving project objectives in spite of contravening factors, or more simply stated, the process of accomplishing something. A project (often called a *pro gram* in government operations) is a special kind of task: it is an activity that is not within normal functions of a system, and it has a beginning and an end. Whether it is a group of students planning a class picnic or the government developing a nuclear weapon, it is an additional endeavor that is not part of the daily work of the people involved, and will not become an unlimited ongoing activity. A project may or may not involve the use of computers.

Although project management is not a part of systems analysis, it determines the ultimate success of the design created *through* systems analysis. The new systems design will fail if the management of the implementation project is ineffective. In practice, project management may be assigned to the systems analyst who can ensure that the design is implemented according to plan. Project management is performed under what Rosenau (1992, 15-22) has called the "triple constraints": performance specifications, time, and budget. When these constraints can be reconciled with the approved design, a project can be successfully completed (see figure 13-1). The authors have attempted to adapt Rosenau's general concepts to the library arena.

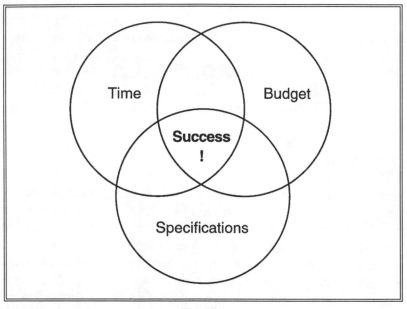

Time

Budget

Success
!

Specifications

Fig. 13-1.

Performance Specifications

The first constraint that must be addressed in project management is the performance specification of the system. Many projects never meet the performance specifications that were created during the design stage. Many reasons exist for problems related to system performance. Quite frequently, the design itself is faulty. Obviously, a faulty design will result in a difficult implementation. In addition, a design may be well conceived, but so poorly described that it is hard for the project manager to determine what the designer had intended. For example, if system design simply specifies use of "the classification number in the MARC record," this may refer to the 050, 082, 852, or another MARC field, and time must be spent in removing the ambiguity that should have been resolved during the analysis and design phases.

Relying on vendors or suppliers to provide the service or product exactly as promised also produces problems. For example, one school library purchased a microcomputer-based circulation program from a vendor who had previously developed a successful mainframe product. The specifications were virtually identical to those for the mainframe version, but it was to be implemented on an AT-class machine. The vendor assumed that by the time he had ported the program to the DOS environment, a sufficiently fast and powerful machine would become available, and that machine would be substituted for the 80286 machine. After six months, the vendor reached the conclusion that continued development would not be profitable since no suitable machine was on the horizon. The vendor's "solution" was to encourage the school to purchase their minicomputer-based product. Eventually, large, fast microcomputers appeared, but not soon enough to rescue that school's automation project.

Time

It is true that projects rarely are completed on time. A major barrier that affects the timely installation of the new systems design is insistence on exactly meeting or exceeding the design specifications. If decision-makers are seeking the "perfect" system rather than an effective one, additional demands may be placed on the new system even before its installation is complete. Acceding to these demands will result in delays in completion of the project. The earlier emphasis on getting official signatures on the acceptance of the design can help overcome this tendency—at least the project manager can point out that agreement on what the system should do has already been reached. While it is never possible to completely "freeze the specs," ensuring that responsible parties sign off on the design as it is created will minimize the problems of non-ownership. At best, the design will become the client's design, motivating resistance to unnecessary changes. At worst, the project manager will be able to point out that the project is meeting the specifications the client agreed upon.

The lack of necessary staff working within the organization can result in frustrating delays. Absences among personnel, poor communication between the project manager and the people whose assistance is needed, employees' disinterest in the project, or active opposition to the change, can sabotage the project schedule. Project managers can make use of many of the techniques for gaining and keeping commitment discussed in Chapter 3.

To finish on time, necessary materials must be available on schedule. Delays in delivery of promised goods or services or failure to find qualified applicants for a project position will seriously hamper meeting project deadlines. One library planned to install an automated catalog during the fall semester of the school year and evaluate user satisfaction in the spring. The federal funds targeted to purchase the software were held up from September to December. Then, the commercial delivery service responsible for shipping the program suffered a warehouse fire and, in the aftermath, shipped the package to Virginia instead of Hawaii. Installation of the program was completed the week books were due back in the library at the end of the spring semester, six months after the project should have been completed.

Budget

All of the time problems detailed above will probably result in budget problems. Delays in meeting the project timeline result in cost overruns for the total project.

The process of bidding for products and services, while designed to cut costs through open competition, can have the opposite effect. A vendor may be aware that competitors have a higher-priced product and raise the bid price to their range. The asking price then becomes higher than the list price. One school district prepared bid specifications for a purchase of twelve microcomputers. Because of the terms of the contract (i.e., penalties for delays in delivery, extended warranty requirements, etc.) the only vendor who fully met the specifications increased the price of the microcomputers 30 percent over the price charged to a walk-in buyer. Faced with their budget constraints, the school district had to select another microcomputer with fewer desirable features.

Unrealistic estimates of the cost of the project will create problems in the budget. Such estimates are often made by people who truly *believe* in the project, often without conscious desire on their part to lie. They hope that, though the project would not be allowed if the true costs were admitted, once the project is started it will be allowed to continue, and, in the end, its merits will be so great that the cost overrun will be forgiven. Obviously, unless costs are accurately determined, and plans made for unforeseen additional costs, the project will not remain within budget. As one of the author's former students, now working for a major library system vendor put it, "In this business everybody lies. They lie about what they need and what they want; they lie about how much they can spend and about how much things cost. They lie about when they need something and when they can deliver it. They even lie about whether they are satisfied." Rosenau goes so far as to claim people and vendors engage in a "liars contest" (1992, 19).

Simple errors in computing the cost of the project can create major problems. For example, in one project, a library using simple, single-entry cost accounting accidentally listed the FICA (social security) payment as an income item rather than an expense. Once the error had occurred, it was copied the next quarter, resulting in a grossly inflated credit balance. The inevitable crash of the budget occurred, accompanied by bouncing checks. *This really happened.*

Indeed, many libraries show an almost total lack of cost control with poor or no cost management. For example, some libraries that do not receive state or federal grants actually put all their income into a single checking account and spend the money until it is gone—without an expenditure plan or accounting system. When the time comes to spend money on the project, it is discovered that the funds have already gone for something else.

Changes in funding priorities and patterns within the duration of the project can create major problems, especially when the funding agency is not the same as the organization performing the project. Government agencies (e.g., universities, public schools, and government departments) are particularly vulnerable to situations where the objectives of the funding agency, such as the state legislature, may differ from the organization's.

Overruns

In addition to the constraints that a project manager must take into consideration, factors beyond the manager's control exist that may add to the total cost of the project. These include strikes; new legal requirements after the design is completed (e.g., government regulations, such as a new fire code that required plenum cable rather than the PVC-insulated type several libraries had budgeted for, causing them to be hit by a 30 percent increase in wiring costs); unusual inflation; and so on. Some financial margin should be included in the project plan, but if extraneous factors threaten to add considerable costs, this information should be shared with the client, and a plan for additional funding or a reduction in expectations should be determined.

Some projects seem nearly doomed to failure, while others seem to sail through to success despite problems. It has been the authors' observation that projects which everyone wants to be a success are usually perceived as successful. This leads to the conclusion that, when possible, success-prone projects should be sought, and those that are prone to failure should be avoided. The Venn diagram in figure 13-2 shows factors affecting commitment to success.

When given a choice, a wise manager will seek to be associated with projects that fall in the intersection of the three sets. Projects that fall in the intersection of just two sets can often be successful if public relations (propaganda) efforts are expended on the group that is not committed, but projects falling outside any intersection should be avoided if possible.

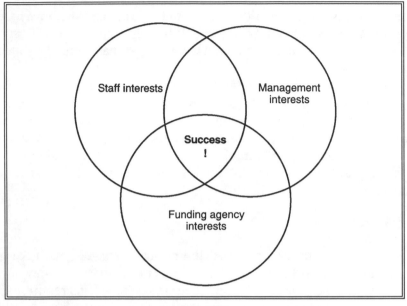

Fig. 13-2.

Steps in Project Management

Careful planning for the project enables the project manager to minimize the effects of the triple constraint. The steps in project management are: (1) define the work; (2) plan the implementation; (3) perform the implementation; and (4) complete clean-up tasks.

Statement of Work

The definition of the project is called a "statement of work." Often a statement of work is prepared by the library before a project manager is assigned or hired, but, if not, the project manager should prepare a definition and have it approved by the library's management. The statement of work should include a description of the work to be accomplished, a briefly outlined statement of a plan for implementation, and a statement addressing the triple constraints. Care should be taken with this document because it forms the basis for deciding whether the project (and hence the project manager) is successful or not.

The Implementation Plan

The implementation plan is a model of the project. Its basic purpose is to help avoid unexpected occurrences that prevent success. It does this by allowing project managers to make their mistakes on paper rather than on the project itself. The plan, therefore, is anything but a mere formality. It is the essence of the project, distilled and arrayed in print. Plans *do* work; they do keep projects on schedule, on budget, and within the specifications, or as close as possible.

In order to be effective, however, plans must be taken seriously. The worst kind of plan is one that is made simply to fulfill a requirement. For example, a library director may say, "We need to have a plan to get the grant. Sally, make up a plan for us, and we'll insert it as Appendix B." Not only is this library in the same position as not having a plan at all, as far as control is concerned, it is actually in a worse position because project managers may take the plan seriously and make decisions based on it. An ill-conceived plan is worse than none at all.

An effective plan should include:

1. A summary of the project, including the statement of work

2. Network diagrams (covered later in this chapter)—each event and activity covered by the network diagram should be listed; if the plan is modified as the project proceeds, each change, and the reason for it, should be recorded

3. A list of milestones (observable events that allow the project manager to identify what stage of the project has been reached)

4. A list of exactly what tasks are to be accomplished and who will be responsible for each task

5. A budget

6. An acceptance plan that details the tests that will be applied to determine success (e.g., criteria of evaluation)

Project managers will find that they have to strike a balance in the amount of time spent on the plan. On the one hand, so much time can be devoted to planning that the actual implementation is delayed by the planning process. On the other hand, enthusiasm for "getting on" with implementation can result in hasty planning, with the consequence of costly mistakes in the implementation. A balance needs to be struck between "analysis paralysis" and "if you're too busy to do it right the first time, how will you find time to do it over?"

The Implementation Process

Implementation is best accomplished by a knowledgeable team of workers who have worked on the design, are familiar with it, and have the needed skills. Unfortunately, this is seldom the case, and project managers must make the best of the staff they have to work with. In addition, project managers seldom are in the chain of command; they usually have to accomplish their mission by *convincing* people outside the implementation team to help rather than by telling them to. Eventually, implementation boils down to making sure the plan is followed and dealing with situations where the plan can not be or is not being followed.

Project Control

Control in this sense means keeping track of how well the plan is being implemented. Maintaining the control of the project requires that project managers know what is supposed to be happening in a project and what is actually taking place. The breakdown of the work involved, network diagrams, and cost estimates provide the information that project managers need to work effectively. Management skills are needed to allow managers to choose subordinates wisely and to give them sufficient authority to carry out their part of the project.

Ongoing project management requires that project managers keep informed of progress through reports from their subordinates. These reports should be the minimum number needed. They are sometimes limited to oral reports, or they may be formal written documents. In either case, any interaction should be nonthreatening. If project managers kill the bearers of bad news, soon no one will be willing to report problems. Probably the most pleasant way to manage a project is to allow subordinates to follow the plan on their own to the greatest extent possible, with the manager receiving periodic reports, as well as special reports when an exception must be made to the plan. Unfortunately, this is sometimes not sufficient to maintain good progress. In cases where subordinates cannot be trusted to follow the plan, critical elements of the plan are being implemented, or the plan has proven to be nonfunctional, the manager must establish tighter control, require approval upon completion of one task or phase before beginning the next, conduct a periodic review, or get directly involved in a component that is the responsibility of a subordinate.

In general, though, the mentality of "all authority is mine because all responsibility is mine" should be the exception. Managers who give the impression that they lack trust in their subordinates lose the best workers and the originality and insight those subordinates might have provided.

Problem Solving Within a Project

When problems arise in the course of managing a project, and they will, a six-step approach should be used:

1. Discover and state the *real* problem.

2. Investigate the problem and its environment.

3. Consider alternative solutions.

4. Select the best solution.

5. Communicate the solution to the personnel who have been affected by the problem and who will be implementing the solution. Document changes in writing.

6. Evaluate the solution.

In other words, standard system analysis techniques should be used to solve the problem.

Completion of the Project

Projects should eventually be completed. There should be some point at which it can be said, "The project is finished." This seems obvious, but often no such official acknowledgment exists, and projects just seem to fade away. Such a situation prevents a clear assumption of the duties of the implementation staff by the regular library employees. If something goes wrong under such circumstances, no one knows who is in charge. It means that project staff cannot get back to their real jobs, and that whether or not final payments for systems may be released is ambiguous.

Once a project has been completed, an astute project manager should carry out a number of tasks as part of the termination process:

1. Formally state that the project is complete and that acceptance tests may begin.

2. Receive formal acceptance from the client library following successful acceptance tests (see Chapter 14).

3. Provide a final report on the project and deliver any documentation.

4. Release staff members to their previous tasks and release or find new jobs for personnel hired for the project.

5.   Determine how continued assistance and support to the system is to be provided.

6.   Conduct post-completion audits for self-protection.

Tools for Project Control

Planning for and controlling a project effectively will depend on the degree to which the project manager knows what is supposed to happen and what is actually happening. A number of tools have been used to accomplish these aims (e.g., Gantt charts, the program evaluation and review technique [PERT], and critical path methodology [CPM]).

Gantt charts display planned tasks through use of horizontal bars. They indicate the degree to which the task has been completed in a number of ways, most often by darkening the bar to an extent equal to the percentage of the task that is completed. Figure 13-3 shows a Gantt chart with bars not yet darkened.

Gantt charts are an effective communication tool because they display the desired actions and current progress and are often used as illustrations in reports. They do not, however, provide an effective means of control since they fail to show the interdependence of the tasks, do not indicate that some tasks are more difficult than others, and can be ambiguous. For example, if 50 percent of a bar is darkened, this could indicate that a) 50 percent of the task is completed, or b) 50 percent of the time allotted to that task has passed. Because of these disadvantages, Gantt charts have been superseded for planning and control purposes by network diagrams, although they are still useful communication tools.

Like Gantt charts, network diagrams are useful in a gross sense to communicate the stages of a project; however, unlike Gantt charts, network diagrams are rigorous enough to supply guidance for the project manager, especially when resources must be allocated. Two common types of network diagrams are CPM and PERT. While they differ in their specifics, they are enough alike to discuss together. They are combined into a single discussion below. For simplicity's sake, they are called CPM charts.

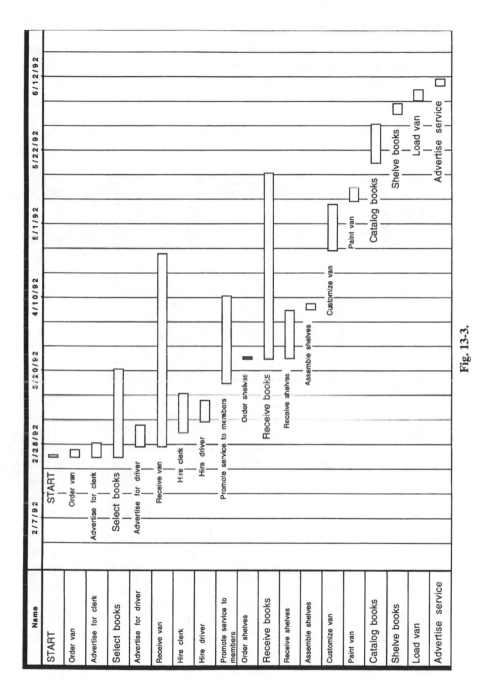

Fig. 13-3.

The most useful feature of a CPM chart is the determination of the critical path in a project (hence the name of the tool). The critical path is defined as the operations that must be accomplished on time in order for the entire project to finish on time. The oversimplified CPM chart in figure 13-4 demonstrates this.

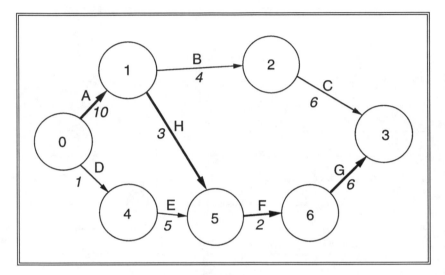

Fig. 13-4.

Events are shown as circles and are designated by numbers. *Activities* are shown by arrows and are given names (represented here by letters). The numbers associated with the arrows are the estimated times those particular activities will require to complete. This diagram shows that, assuming all the estimates are accurate, it will take at least twenty-one days to finish the project: Activity A takes ten days; Activity H, three days; Activity F, two days; and Activity G, six days. Any delay in any of the activities on this path will result in a greater overall time spent on the project than was estimated. This is, then, the *critical* path; it is shown with bold arrows.

Obviously, the other activities must also be completed, but if Activity B takes five days rather than four, the project can still be finished on time. If Activity D takes five days rather than the estimated one, the project can still be completed on time. This time buffer is called *slack*. The ABC path has one day slack (the times for A, B, and C add up to twenty days, while the critical path is twenty-one days), and the DEF path has seven days slack.

There are two reasons why the determination of the critical path is so valuable. First, it allows the manager to shift resources when necessary. Shifting of resources is necessary if any activity on the critical path falls behind schedule. In the example above, if Activity H takes four days rather than three, the project is in danger of being completed behind schedule; the fact that H is on the critical path makes this evident. If the project manager diverts effort from C (making it take seven days instead of six and using the one day slack) and adds that effort to F or G (thereby subtracting one day), the project may still be completed on time. Knowledge of the critical path and available slack helps the manager to make rational decisions on where to concentrate efforts.

The second valuable aspect of CPM is the determination of the date by which the project must be started in order to be completed on time. For example, a library may receive a grant for a project with a deadline for completion and for expending money. If the project manager knows that the critical path is forty-seven work days long, and the deadline for completion is June 30, the manager knows that the project must begin by April 27, resources must be reallocated to shorten the critical path, or the project must be redesigned to eliminate some activities on the critical path. It is almost as valuable for a manager to know what is *not* on the critical path. Speeding up the completion of activities off the critical path will not benefit the total project schedule.

Drawing CPM Charts

Reference was made earlier to events shown as circles (nodes) and activities shown as arrows. A single node should represent the starting point, and another single node should represent the ending point. Traditionally, the beginning node is labeled Ø and the last node is given the highest number, but other nodes may be assigned arbitrary unique numbers.

As a first step in drawing CPM diagrams, each activity in the project should be identified and listed. This should not be a major additional task if the project plan and statement of work has been carefully completed. If a CPM diagram proves impossible to construct, it is a sign that the plan is inadequate. Once the steps are listed, the relationships between them should be identified. For example, if one step is to bar code books in a collection, and another is to select barcodes, and a third is to buy bar codes, obviously the relationship is that: (1) bar codes must be selected; (2) then bar codes must be purchased; and (3) finally, bar codes must be applied to the books. Some relationships are as easy to identify as this one, while others are more subtle and may not be discovered until the diagram is being completed.

The network itself may then be drawn. Like data flow diagrams, CPM charts are not usually correct on the first try. Scratch paper and a pencil are the essential tools for the first draft, and a willingness to start over as needed. Redrawing is almost inevitable, since crossovers should be minimized for maximum clarity. There are several drawing tools available to ease the task of creating network diagrams. Most of them fail to conform exactly to the appearance of hand-drawn diagrams created in accordance with either CPM or PERT rules (see, for example, the diagram shown as figure 13-10). Few systems analysts are purists. The authors recommend using the tool that works best for your system.

The basic network configurations are shown in figure 13-5. This diagram shows a linear relationship: selecting, purchasing, and applying bar codes. In other words, the direction of the arrows indicates the time dependency of the activity. Node 1 marks the event of ordering bar codes; node 2, receiving bar codes; and node 3, completing of bar code application. Ordering bar codes has to precede receiving them; receiving bar codes has to precede applying them. These are logical events to use as milestones.

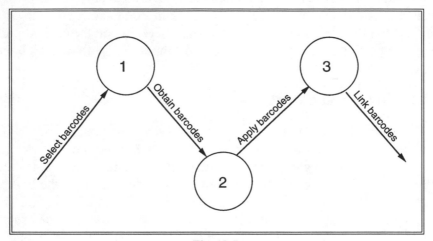

Fig. 13-5.

Figure 13-6 shows a merge node; that is, both activities "Obtain software," and "Obtain hardware" must be completed before the resulting activity, "Install software" may be accomplished. One of the basic aspects of CPM charts is that the output of a node cannot occur until the *all* inputs have happened (i.e., the earliest time an activity can occur is equal to the longest path leading to it).

Figure 13-7 shows a burst node. This is a situation where two activities can occur once a preceding activity is completed. Once a system has been selected, both advertising and training can be initiated.

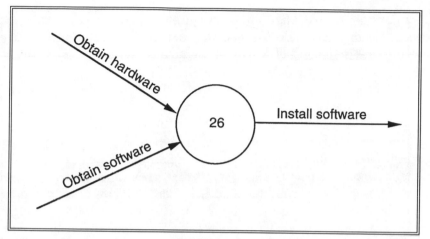

Fig. 13-6.

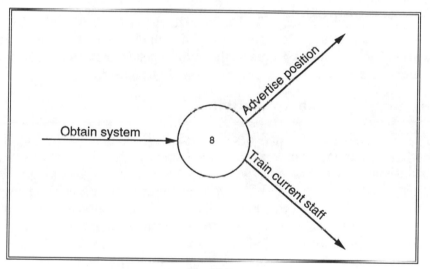

Fig. 13-7.

Occasionally, it may be necessary to show dependency where no real work connection exists between nodes. In such cases, "dummy" activities, shown as dashed arrows, are used. In figure 13-8, an administrative decision has been made that the work on documenting Phase 2 will not begin until documenting Phase 1 is completed, even though no real connection between the two exists.

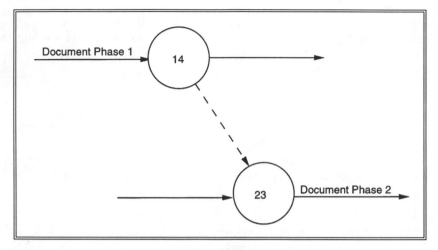

Fig. 13-8.

Once the preliminary CPM diagram has been drawn, it is wise for the project manager to review the steps with both the clients and the project staff. When everyone concurs on the basic dependencies, estimates of the time necessary to complete each task should be added.

Estimating Time for Activities

Some advocates of network diagrams insist on making the length of each arrow proportionate to the time estimate. An arrow showing an eight-hour activity would be twice as long as one for a four-hour activity. This gives the satisfying result of showing the critical path as being physically longer than any other but can result in some oddly structured diagrams. More typically, the nodes are adjusted for maximum aesthetics and clarity, with the times indicated as numbers next to the activity.

It is generally agreed that accurately estimating time is the foundation for a successful project. If time estimates are inaccurate, the critical path is not dependable. Correct estimation of time is essential but often poses a challenge. If the activity is one that has been carried out before and has no extenuating circumstances, estimating the required time is simple. If common practice is not available for the estimate, though, the project manager must use a formula to determine the probable amount of time required. Based on a special case of the standard deviation formula, this technique suggests obtaining three expert opinions for every task: the most probable (T_{mp}), the most optimistic reasonable (T_o), and the most pessimistic reasonable (T_p). T_o and T_p were originally defined as the 1-percent fastest and slowest times (i.e., out of 100 times, the fastest time and slowest time; and out of 200 times, the two fastest and slowest times).

The estimated time, T_e, was computed using the formula $T_e = (T_o + 4*T_{mp} + T_p)/6$. The standard deviation for this estimate is obtained by using the formula $sd = (T_o - T_p)/6$. The value of this is that, assuming accurate estimates, the project manager can be reasonably confident that the estimate is accurate to within +/- 1 sd about 66 percent of the time, within +/- 2 sd 95 percent of the time, and within +/- 3 sd 99 percent of the time.

Of course, the accuracy of the entire estimating process is dependent on the "expert" mentioned above. Experts may be those who perform the task (the experts on how long it takes to catalog a book *should* be the catalogers), authors of published accounts of similar projects, or charts published by some industries. Many people (including some "experts") have difficulty understanding the difference between an estimate and a guess. Therefore, whenever possible, an effort should be made to verify the estimate. In one retrospective conversion project, the staff "estimated" it took them thirty seconds to locate an item in the database and confirm it as matching the item being searched for; actual measurement showed that this estimate was off by a factor of four.

It is important to realize that this estimating technique rests on shaky theoretical grounds, is only as good as the initial estimates, and is very time consuming. Still, it has proven useful in situations where time constraints are very tight and where a substantial disincentive exists for exceeding the allotted project time (e.g., where late penalties are involved). Since time estimates are so important, some writers have argued that estimates should not be made from left to right as the network diagram is constructed, arguing that if it *appears* that the project cannot finish on time, there will be a tendency to underestimate the tasks that fall toward the end of the critical path. These authors advocate a random approach to choosing the order of tasks to be estimated. One factor that is often overlooked is the necessity for reducing all times to the same form: for example, calendar days (twenty-four hours), payroll days (eight hours), or work days (six hours, at best).

You may want to try the following exercise in network diagramming. An answer and discussion is found in Appendix B.

Assume you have been asked to implement an automated catalog in a small library. After speaking with vendors, reading books, peering at worthless Web pages, and so on, you have come to the conclusion that the following must be done. (Assume you have plenty of people on the staff so that some steps can be done simultaneously.) The steps necessary are given below.

For this project: (1) draw a CPM/PERT chart; (2) show the critical path; (3) comment on what you should change in the above process if the critical path exceeds the available time; and (4) discuss what the advantages and disadvantages of these changes might be.

Steps:
    Select software (6 weeks)
    Once this is done you can:
        Order software (2 weeks)
        Receive software (2 weeks)
        Mail-order computer hardware (6 weeks)
        Prepare computers (2 days)
        Buy network software (2 days)
        Install network hardware (4 days)

Once the software and hardware have arrrived you can:
    Load the software (1 day)

Having done that and installed the network hardware (above), you can:
    Test the system (1 day)
    Load the MARC records (4 hours)

At that point you are finished!

Other Benefits of Network Diagrams

In addition to the critical path itself and the latest possible start time, network methodologies can provide many additional details for each activity. Typical data include the earliest and latest time that an activity can be started, the earliest and latest time it can be finished, and the slack time for the activity. The calculations for these times can be complex. Fortunately, many computer programs exist, such as the Microsoft Project for Windows and MacProject for Macintosh, as well as minicomputer and mainframe programs that can be used for computing and drawing CPM charts. Since mistakes in project management can cause great difficulties, the wise project manager uses one of these programs.

Project management tools *do* work. In one case with which the authors are familiar, a library was given a grant to establish an intrasystem delivery service. Three parts made up the grant: purchasing of a van to transport books, hiring a driver to drive the van and a clerk to supervise and publicize the service, and allocating about $40,000 for the purchase of books.

The project was planned for the July to June fiscal year. Typically, the money was released in March and had to be spent by July 1. The project had to be completed in ninety days or canceled completely. In that time, the project manager had to:

1. Order and receive the van

2. Advertise and fill the driver's position

3. Customize and paint the van

4. Select, order, and receive the books

5. Buy and assemble shelves to store the books

6. Catalog and shelve the books

7. Load the van

8. Advertise and fill the clerk's position

9. Promote the service to the library staff

10. Advertise the service to the public

It became clear that three basic paths were in the network; after dependencies were established, times were estimated, and the following diagram was created (figure 13-9).

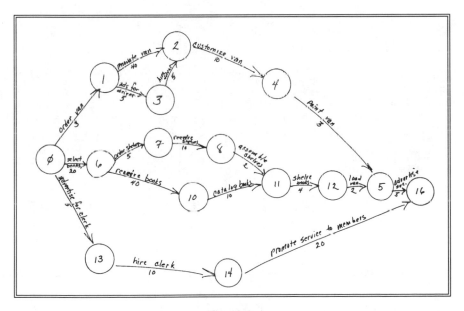

Fig. 13-9.

The diagram was done by sketching. An equivalent diagram from a computer printer would have been neater but no more useful (see figure 13-10). The critical path is shown as the bold line on the chart.

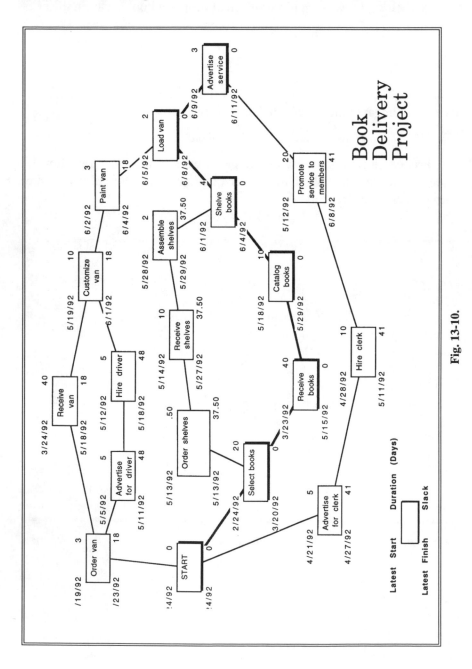

**Book
Delivery
Project**

Fig. 13-10.

The diagram confirmed that the project could be completed—barely—in the time available (i.e., the last start date had not been passed). The value of the CPM approach was proven when a postal strike interrupted delivery from the book jobber to the library. Since receiving books was on the critical path, efforts needed to be diverted to that task. The van was then in the process of being customized, but that step was not on the critical path. The library retrieved the van from the garage, drove it to the jobber's warehouse, and got the books to the library in time to stay on schedule. The van had to be rescheduled at the garage, but the delay presented no difficulty because adequate slack was available in that path. Later, when the clerk had an emergency and had to take several weeks' vacation, there was no anxiety in the project crisis because the CPM chart showed sufficient slack in that path to allow for the leave time.

The value of network diagrams is obvious.

Exercise in Project Management

Green Team Landscapers is owned by two very talented designers. Susan is innovative in designing landscape plans that turn problem-ridden sites into works of art. Her horticulture knowledge guarantees that the plants will flourish in the local climate.

Her partner, Phil, is an equally gifted artist in soil and stone. He easily solves problems of drainage, erosion, and uneven terrain as he turns Susan's designs into reality. His construction experience is used to install outdoor outlets for landscape lighting and pond pumps.

In spite of their considerable talents, however, the company has a roster of disgruntled customers. Susan sometimes has to cancel appointments because of poor scheduling; Phil is often weeks behind schedule because of rain delays or unavailability of rental equipment; and Mary, the officer manager, fends off customers upset because they have been given no start date or because Phil doesn't return phone calls. Determining the cost of plants is very accurate, but jobs often go beyond the cost estimate because of unforeseen labor costs. In his efforts to provide maximum quality, Phil sometimes decides independently to add features that increase the final cost. Because no written contracts exist, customers are left with little defense against cost overruns.

Mary keeps a wall chart of pending jobs and is instructed to keep Phil apprised of the schedule. Phil, however, enjoys his role of crew boss and resents Susan and Mary for their efforts to direct his activities.

1. What are the first tasks systems analysts need to undertake in resolving the company's problems?

2. Where would each of the project management tools be appropriate?

3. How can the costs be estimated more accurately?

4. How should the issue of written contracts be addressed?

See Appendix B for suggested answers to the above questions.

Case Study—Fort Memorial Library

The members of Nancy's group were busy going about their individual investigative paths. Meanwhile, she had to find out if the computer center would help the group develop a software package. Off she went to the university's computer center's analyst to pick his brain, but she found instead that he wanted to pick hers.

"You're the only one over there that makes sense," was how Ed Kleindeinst, the senior analyst, had put it. It was both incorrect and impolite, but Nancy wasn't given time to object. "We've got a full-scale analysis going on here, and they've got you duplicating a quarter of my people's work," he said.

"Look, here's what we plan to do. We've got six or seven good commercial integrated systems. Here are the details of what the library is doing now, and here's what these systems will do. As far as I can see, with a little modification of work routines, we can just drop one of these babies in, and the library wouldn't even notice. Except for serials," he said. "We're stymied in serials. First of all, we can't get a straight answer out of the witch who runs it. Second, while all the vendors insist their systems work, their customers all have horror stories about serials check-in and claiming. Take a look at this and see what you think." He tossed down a two-inch-thick document.

"If this holds up we've got money to buy until the end of the year," he said.

Automatically, Nancy looked down at her watch, but she knew it was already November.

The analyst continued, "Tebbits has come around, but I don't know if we can get the stuff up and running by the deadline to expend the funds. Look, you've got your job to do, but forget all about writing your own program. Even if we had the expertise, we wouldn't have the time to help you." The beeper on his belt went off. "Look, take this with you and see if you think it's feasible to put in a system by January. And feel out serials. Are they as crazy as they seem? I gotta go!" he shouted over his shoulder on his way out the door. "Try to get a report to me by Friday."

Nancy was left sitting in his office feeling more than a little over-whelmed. She came for help and was asked to plan an installation. At least she got an answer to the question of whether the computer center would help them.

Discussion Questions

- The computer center won't help. In what ways does this make life more difficult for Nancy? Does it make her life easier? Does she have a problem (review Chapter 4)?

- She has been asked to determine if the computer center's schedule can be met. Is this possible? How would she go about it?

- The revelation that the computer center's project is well advanced will have a major effect on her group. How should she break the news to them? How should they proceed?

References

Rosenau, Milton D. 1992. *Successful Project Management*. 2d ed. New York: Van Nostrand Reinhold.

Chapter 14

PROVING THE SYSTEM

Introduction

Not all systems analysis projects involve computer systems, but those that do present special concerns addressed in this, and the following, chapter. As seen in previous chapters, there are many determinants that lead to selection of a particular system for implementation: examining sales literature of the vendors, talking with sales representatives, speaking with people who have installed the system, asking the vendor to respond with a proposal to our requirements, and so on.

All of these determinants share a common characteristic: we are trusting others. Experience shows that even with the best intentions, people may not perceive reality the same way. As one librarian who had emerged from an automation attempt with enhanced wisdom and experience put it:

> I trusted [the president of the company] because it was obvious that he was honest and sincere. It appeared that he believed every word he told us. By the end of the third year I came to realize that he *was* honest, and *did* believe every word. It was just unfortunate that reality present in the rest of the universe wasn't the same as in his part. I said it didn't work; he said it did. I reported bugs; he explained they were features.

At the same time, system vendors complain that librarians refuse to acknowledge that a system is operational if there is a scratch on one terminal. This is a matter of critical importance to library system vendors because few of them are overcapitalized. A lengthy delay in a library's payment could cause serious cash flow problems for a vendor.

211

So how can we ensure that a system functions according to *our* sense of reality rather than someone else's? How can system vendors be sure that eventually the client will acknowledge that delivery is complete? The answer is in *testing*: clear statements, agreed upon by both parties, as to what will be done to agree that "the system has been delivered." The term we use for this proof that the system is operational is "acceptance testing." It is desirable to ensure that the system is "correct" in the sense used by the British Standards Institute's definition of *correctness*: "a system is correct if it does what it is supposed to do and does not do what it is not supposed to do."

Two caveats must be given about testing. One is the negative assumption of testing. Basically, we assume that if the system cannot be shown to *not* work, then it is error-free. This is obviously not true: flaws can and do remain hidden in complex systems for years. The second caveat is a corollary to the first: few systems are tested for every possible combination of variables. Just because a flaw has not been found does not mean a flaw is not there.

Pre-Release Tests

Of course it is assumed that the vendor believes the software works. Unless a library has agreed to be a beta test site for a system, the software should be free from known bugs. This is important because of the massive amounts of time necessary to test the basic functions of a system. It is generally assumed that the vendor has done this (i.e., it is assumed that the vendor is sure it works). Analysts and clients test to make sure it works *for them*.

Ordinarily, the pre-release testing function within the development organization is done by a quality control or quality assurance group. While the quality assurance group may work closely with the developers, it is more common for the developers to test the system (or modules and submodules) when the developers think they are finished. It is the responsibility of quality control to ask two questions: "Does it do what the specifications said it should do?" and "Does it work?" Recently, there has been much discussion of how to improve testing. Much of this has been the result of applying systems to dangerous or critical environments where humans traditionally were in control: nuclear power plants, aircraft, and so on.

Ad Hoc Testing

The traditional method of pre-release testing may be termed "ad hoc testing." The quality assurance group puts the system through its paces. Trying every action that occurs to them, they try to make the system crash. If they fail, the assumption is that the software works. Unfortunately, failures of systems show that this technique is insufficient to ensure reliability:

obscure combinations of values continue to cause airplanes to drop out of the sky, trains to jump their rails, and elevators to fall to the basement without warning. At the same time, it is important not to underrate this technique. When applied by knowledgeable and conscientious people, it will deliver systems that most people will agree are satisfactory. To go beyond the merely satisfactory requires more rigorous tests.

Functional Testing

Functional testing is a more rigorous application of ad hoc testing. In this technique test cases are generated based on what the system is to accomplish. For example, if Boolean logic is to be used to search for titles, then a title search using Boolean logic is executed to ensure that the "correct" titles, (and only those), are retrieved. Theoretically, if all possible cases are tested, it can be proved that the system works. Unfortunately, testing all cases is impossible due to what is termed the *combinatorial explosion*: the number of tests is equal to the possibilities of each choice multiplied together.

Therefore, modifications are usually introduced. Rather than testing all combinations of all variables, selected cases are used: the largest and smallest values allowable (boundary values); values larger and smaller than the permissible values; zeros; blanks; alphabetic, numeric, and special characters. Use of these techniques will pick up errors which ad hoc testing would probably ignore. Such tests, if applied in the 1950s and 1960s, would have prevented the Y2K panic in the waning years of the twentieth century. Many systems produced in those times are still being used (especially operating systems). Some of these systems cannot handle dates after 1999: when the system was developed, 2000 was more than a human generation away; it never occurred to anyone to test such outlandish dates in an industry where three years is an eternity.

Despite its improvement over ad hoc testing, functional testing does not have the admiration of system theoreticians nor the acceptance of regulatory systems for critical applications. This is because, while functional testing may *create* error-free systems, it cannot be *proven* to do so.

Structure Testing

Structure testing is an improvement over functional testing because it shows that each part of the software actually works. In structure testing, the execution of a program is tested down every line of code. By following execution of the software, it can be shown that 1) no path leads to unacceptable results and 2) all code is actually used. The reason for the first of these is intuitively obvious, but the second is equally important: inaccessible code could represent functions that should be implemented but aren't, or it could be a Trojan horse—a piece of software designed by a nefarious programmer that does nothing until it is activated and then wreaks havoc on the application.

Other Techniques

As the opportunities for malfunctioning computer systems to cause disasters increases, so does the insistence that systems be proved error-free. The most obvious way that this can be done is by combining functional and structural tests. There are also methods that involve formal mathematical proofs for the system's performance. These techniques are only beginning to become practical as computing power increases. In any case, the fact that the system performs perfectly on a vendor's development machine, using the vendor's test database, in the vendor's home environment says little about whether it will work in a given library. When acceptance tests are performed upon implementation, it is not an attempt to validate the vendor's software; it is an attempt to make sure the system works where it will, in fact, be used.

Implementation Tests

Over the past ten years or so, agreement has been reached on the types of tests that are appropriate to test library implementations. Several kinds of tests should be performed on software that the vendor has delivered. They include tests for *reliability* (does the system crash every time the coffee pot is plugged in?), for *functionality* (does the cataloging module export real MARC records?), and for *capacity* (will the system work with seven million records as well as it does with the vendor's 20,000-record test set?). It cannot be overemphasized that these tests must be performed by the individual libraries after implementation. The results of similar libraries' experiences cannot be substituted, nor can the vendors give the library this information. The point is for *the library* to test *its own* system. At the same time, testing should be an ongoing function. The library should not wait until the system is completely installed to begin. Instead, each portion should be tested as it is brought up. In this way, the final acceptance test would be to ensure that everything works well together.

Reliability

If there is any kind of test that cannot be hurried, it is the reliability test. Simply put, this test checks to see whether the computer system will continue to operate acceptably over a period of time. Clearly, two factors must be negotiated here: how long a period of time, and what constitutes acceptable operation. The first of these is generally given in terms of days—typically 60 to 90 days. The second is given in terms of "percentage of downtime"—typically somewhere between 5 and 0.1 percent (depending on whether the situation is being viewed from the vendor's or the library's perspective).

It is important to realize that no system has 100 percent uptime forever. Some systems, however (such as those that use multiprocessor technology and mirrored storage devices), come close. Sometimes a system fails within the time period for the reliability test. Generally, this does not result in the return of the system and a request for the library's money to be refunded. Instead, vendors are commonly given several chances to meet the reliability requirements. The number of chances and the stringency of the requirements are subjects for negotiation but typically are in the range of four to six months.

Superficially, the outcome of the reliability test is easy to interpret; in reality there are difficulties. Reliability tests might be compared with roadtests on an car. If the engine stops while the car is being test driven, the car has clearly failed the reliability test. But what if a tire goes flat? What if the rearview mirror falls off? What if the cigarette lighter fails? What if the lighter fails and the driver is a nonsmoker?

The same sorts of "degrees of downtime" exist in computer reliability tests. Clearly, if the computer melts down, this is a more serious failure than if an OPAC keyboard suddenly starts producing multiple characters. The most common way around this dilemma is to have an agreement between the vendor and the library on the relative importance, or weight, of each class of failure. A failure of the central processing unit (CPU) might get a weight of ten, while a bad keyboard on an OPAC terminal might get a weight of one-tenth. Multiplying the weighting by the time the component was down and summing all the occurrences provides a measure of the "distributed" downtime. If the total is less than a previously agreed upon number, the system has passed its reliability test.

The effects of failing this test are so severe that duplicate logs are generally kept by library and vendor staffs. These are compared frequently to ensure that neither party is confused about the actual status of the test. A formal structure should be in place for reconciling differences of opinion on items where disagreement occurs.

Functionality

Does the system do what it is supposed to do? That is the question answered by the functionality test. The basic documents needed to determine functionality are the system specifications and the vendor's proposal. In many ways, functionality tests repeat the work of the vendor's quality assurance group. Of course, a single library operating over a relatively short period of time cannot do as thorough a test as (it is hoped) the vendor did. Still, it is important that the library staff systematically exercise each function to the best of its ability.

Because the functionality test is predicated on the library staff understanding the system, it is usually performed after any vendor-supplied training has taken place. At the same time, the test should be conducted primarily based on the provided written documentation rather than on class notes. After all, library staff does change, and the vendor will not be around to conduct training forever.

Capacity

These tests fall into two categories: the ability of the system to function under maximum usage, and the ability of the system to store and handle the maximum number of records and terminals.

The first of these is not too difficult to achieve, at least in theory. When functions and peripherals are accessed at once, the system should still function acceptably. While it is possible for a heavy load to actually cause the system to crash, a more typical system accommodation is to lengthen the response time for each transaction. A circulation that takes a half second when it is processed on the only terminal being used may take minutes when the system is heavily loaded. Note that this test is a real-life test. That is, the terminals should actually be used to process realistic transactions. Projections of response time based on mathematical models are no substitute.

Thus, response time must be specified for normal (average load) situations, as well as maximum load situations. Both aspects are important, and there is generally a trade off between them. As in all tests of this type, agreement must be reached on the basic definitions before the test is begun. Response time, for example, can be measured from the time the transaction is initiated by the user until the first system message appears on the screen, or from the initiation until completion of the request. "Being processed" messages can be used to reduce user frustration; though these are useful, they do not constitute a meaningful response to a request from a response-time perspective.

The second type of capacity test, which tests whether the system will handle the full number of records and peripherals, is especially difficult. Often a library has not finished retrospective conversion when the system is delivered. Often the system is purchased to allow for expansion into additional areas and libraries. Can it be known that the system will continue to function well? In simple terms, no. This information can only be extrapolated from the current situation. Though hard and fast rules cannot be given, it is wise to assume that response time does not vary linearly with load; that is, when the number of terminals and/or records is doubled, response time is more likely to increase by more than a factor of two.

Though the problem is insoluble in an exact sense, two techniques may possibly help. In one situation, response times are generated for increasing numbers of terminals and records. This data is then plotted, and the curve extended to include the maximum configuration, which is used as an estimate. Another possibility, which may occasionally be feasible, is to find another library (with the same system) whose size approximates the maximum configuration of the library in question. A ratio of response time at acceptance of the system to the current response time at the other library can then be applied to the measured acceptance test response time in order to predict future results.

Some vendors may also have functional systems that libraries can use to simulate capacity tests. Care should be taken to identify where these systems differ from the user's potential installation. The more differences exist (e.g., type of CPU, number of terminals, or record type mix), the less easy it is to extrapolate from a given system. This is especially true if, for example, transactions are speeded up by computer to simulate larger systems.

Incorporation of Tests

Testing is not something that can be considered in a vacuum; the foundation must have been laid during the earliest steps of analysis and then formalized during the system development or selection phase. It is essential that the tests be specified in the contract, along with the consequences if the tests are passed or failed. The mix of transactions (Boolean vs. non-Boolean searches, catalog maintenance vs. catalog search, circulation check-out vs. check-in) should be specified, as well as number of terminals and length of the test. Equally essential are clear definitions of the items being tested. The definition of *downtime, response,* or *search* may decide whether a system passes or fails. Both parties should agree *before* the test begins.

Typically, a library agrees to pay a proportion of the contracted system price upon successful completion of the acceptance tests. If the system fails to pass the tests, then the money is withheld until the system does pass. If worse comes to worst, the library should be released from the contract if the vendor fails the acceptance test. This is not as useful an option as it might first appear, because the library generally has invested large amounts of money in reaching this point and would be forced to try to collect damages in court to cover them.

Clearly, the more money the library withholds, the more pressure can be brought to bear on an unsatisfactory process. However, failure of several libraries to pay a vendor may precipitate a cash flow problem for the vendor, which might prevent necessary work being done to fix the problem. The amount of money to be paid upon acceptance (or, from a vendor's standpoint, the amount withheld until the system passes) is a matter for negotiation and must be specified in the contract.

Case Study—Fort Memorial Library

Nancy had come back from the computer center feeling very depressed and, she believed, with good reason. An hour-long talk with her team had restored her humor. They had a good system proposal. The computer center's efforts might or might not reach fruition, but meanwhile, there was work to be done.

She spent the next few nights working on a rough project outline for Kleindienst, figuring that keeping on the good side of the computer center was never a waste of effort. However, most of her effort was devoted to shepherding the team's decision process.

Even Sue had acknowledged that without the help of the computer center they could not develop software in-house, so the work had boiled down to selecting the best system. In the end, they had found a system that ran on a microcomputer and had what they considered to be an acceptable serials module, even though it did not exactly match their specifications. It meant buying an integrated package and only using one small part of it, but it was the best solution they could come up with. Dean Tebbits had authorized installation, and the vendor had agreed that they would defer payment until the system was in place and tested.

Margie, however, was not happy. The system was undergoing testing in her department, and it failed to meet her expectations.

"It went down again," she wailed to Nancy.

Nancy explained quietly that since Margie had accidentally pulled the computer's cord from the electrical outlet, she could not blame the system. And the fact that it did not produce a sorted list of serials checked in that week wasn't a failure either, since the system didn't claim to do so. "But it was one of our *requirements*," Margie replied.

Then Margie had pointed out that the computer was in the way, and people kept bumping into it. When Nancy pointed out that it was exactly where Margie had insisted on it being (so she could "keep an eye on it"), Margie had accused her of "plotting" and had burst into tears.

Nancy hated it when people cried at her, but she was near crying herself.

Discussion Questions

- What is going on here? Is it a problem of inflated expectations, failure to understand the limitations of purchased software, or something deeper?

- Nancy is confronted by a weeping client. What should she do? What should she *not* do?

- Nancy herself is under stress. The results of her team's efforts are being negated by the client. How should she react to this? How would you be likely to react under such circumstances?

- What do you think of the way the acceptance tests are being conducted? What improvements would you suggest?

- Nancy has been imposed upon by the computer center's analyst. Did she do the right thing by giving him the report he asked for? What are the possible consequences of refusal and of acquiescence?

Chapter 15

STRATEGIES FOR IMPLEMENTATION

Introduction

While the topics in the preceding chapters cover much of the material that falls within a strict definition of "systems analysis and design," functioning systems analysts in library and information environments must deal with operational issues as well. The following topics are typical of the issues with which systems analysts must cope.

Site Preparation

As mentioned in Chapter 12, the seller of a computer or computer system frequently requires that a special environment be created for the new hardware. While this work might be entrusted to contractors or to facilities specialists within an organization, the analyst/designer must be aware of the issues involved so that an implementation is not jeopardized by improper site preparation. It is especially important that the analyst ensure compliance with local construction and electrical codes.

Generally speaking, the more costly and elaborate an implementation is, the more detailed must be the site preparation. Mainframe computers may require elaborate special rooms. Minicomputers generally require much less preparation. Microcomputer-based systems need very little in the way of special environments. Nonetheless, the better the environment for the system, the more dependable it will be and the longer it will last. The following discussion generally addresses a major installation, but the concepts, at least, are important all the way down to microcomputers.

Physical Layout

The room itself should be large enough that all major system components are accessible, with space for maintenance both in front of and behind the major units. Ample room must be provided for peripheral equipment (e.g. printers, and so on), as well as for expansion. Often a suspended ceiling and raised floor is created to allow convenient and concealed wiring, as well as to promote air flow. Doors should be large enough to wheel in the largest piece of equipment anticipated. Steps should be avoided, with ramps greatly preferred. These points apply not only to the room itself but to the entire delivery path from the loading dock to the room: having a wide door on the computer room does not help if the computer will not fit through the front door. Since water is not good for operating electrical equipment, care should be taken to place the room away from overhead pipes.

Power

Power is also of prime importance: it must be *correct, clean,* and *constant.* *Correct* power means that the voltage be as specified for the equipment being installed. This will generally be 110 volts in the United States, although larger equipment may require 220-volt service. In addition, power must be supplied in sufficient amounts: the amperage rating of the circuit must be sufficient to power the equipment, with an additional safety factor to prevent frequent blowing of circuit breakers. Large installations may require three-phase service, but such installations would almost certainly be overseen by a specialist. Nonetheless, the analyst should be aware that such requirements exist and ensure that the proper installation is provided.

Clean power means that the voltage at the outlets should not have sudden variations (spikes), which can be imposed on the current by lightning, heavy switches opening elsewhere, or even by such common sources as automatic coffee pots. Clean power can be promoted by using surge suppressors in line with the outlets. For small units these may take the form of special extension cords or outlet blocks; larger installations would have surge suppression built in as part of a special power handler.

Constant power is power that maintains the correct voltage within narrow limits. Voltage that is too high (surges) or too low (brownouts) can cause components to burn out and data errors to occur. Power can also fail completely, causing loss of data and, sometimes, physical damage. Protection is generally provided by an uninterruptible power supply (UPS)—a unit that uses batteries to supply power at a constant voltage.

Of course, regardless of the size of the installation, the outlets should be well grounded, and the power outlets should be sufficient in number and conveniently placed. An accessible emergency power shutoff switch should also be available.

Communications

All computer areas should have a dedicated telephone line. Even better would be two lines: one for data communications so that the system may be maintained remotely via modem, and one for human communication. Even systems with Internet connections will find multiple telephone lines useful under some circumstances. The lines coming in from terminals and those used for dial-up access to the system should be neatly cabled and should terminate in a patch panel to allow flexibility. Obviously, each line should be labeled at both ends, and a map of cables should be maintained.

Lighting

Since computer maintenance often involves close inspection of small parts, lighting should be adequate and without glare. Battery powered emergency lighting should also be installed.

Climate Control

While modern computers can operate over wide temperature ranges, air conditioning is still advisable and is essential in large installations. Since computers often function better in temperatures too low for human comfort, a separate thermostat, or even a separate system, is preferred for the equipment. The system should have an automatic shutdown feature to respond to any potentially damaging rise in temperature in the event that the air conditioning fails.

The optimum temperature for computers is generally 65 to 75 degrees. At this temperature, however, the humidity often drops below the 40 to 60 percent range suitable for computers. Provision, then, should be made for adjusting the humidity to maintain the computer's optimum climate. The lower humidity common to air-conditioned rooms may also require the use of anti-static mats, or even grounding straps for personnel, to prevent static electricity damage to circuitry.

Noise Control

While the actual operation of computers is silent, associated equipment (e.g., fans, printers, or disk drives) can be quite noisy. Acoustical tile can help alleviate this. However, ear protection is sometimes necessary for operators exposed to computer room noise for long periods.

Security

Security is essential to prevent accidental or intentional damage to both data and equipment. Its purpose is not to catch villains, but to prevent damage often it succeeds by merely being obvious.

Hardware Security (Accidents)

Many accidents can befall computers. It is important to secure hardware against the variety of accidents that can occur. This type of security involves identifying and monitoring vulnerable areas and providing a response to threatening conditions. In addition to the security of power discussed earlier, protection against fire and water must also be considered. All computer facilities should have fire and smoke detectors, and all but the smallest should have water detectors. These detectors, as well as those for power loss, should be wired to an audible alarm and connected to appropriate agencies. In addition, automatic telephone dialers may be installed to call predetermined numbers and report problems automatically. Fire extinguishers appropriate for use on computer equipment must be readily available. In large installations, a whole-room extinguishing gas is often used (although a movement to eliminate these devices is under way because of the potential damage to the earth's ozone layer if the gas is released).

Hardware Security (Sabotage)

Sabotage does occur in library settings, perpetrated by disgruntled employees, angry patrons, and career saboteurs. The single most effective way to prevent sabotage is by restricting access: the computer should not be in public view or in a public area if at all possible. Only authorized personnel should have access to the computer, and these people should wear badges or tags that identify them and show their authority. Paradoxically, an empty room invites vandalism. The best security is reached when several trustworthy people are always in the room. Obviously, the room should be locked, and keys or combinations should be strictly controlled and changed frequently. Dropped ceilings should not allow easy access from other parts of the building.

Surveillance forms a second line of defense to access control. Most effective is human monitoring, but few libraries can afford sufficient guards; hence, electronic monitoring is often used. Often, surveillance cameras are placed to observe the computer room, but of course, someone must watch the monitor. Surveillance can also be done in the absence of humans either through active devices, such as sonic or microwave motion detectors, or passive means, such as magnetic switches, infrared detectors, pressure sensitive devices, or sound detectors. In any case, surveillance should be visible to convince the potential saboteur not to attempt any damage.

Data Security (Accidents)

The library's database is essential to its operation. If the computer is destroyed, it can be replaced in a matter of days. If the data is destroyed, it can take years to rebuild.

The most effective security against accidental data loss (beyond simply being careful) is the backup. Libraries should back up their systems at least weekly, with the day's changes being backed up each day (incremental backups). As a minimum, three backups should be maintained at all times—the current one, the previous week's, and the week before that. In addition, many libraries do a complete backup of all data and programs and place these in long-term storage. The important thing to remember about backups is that all the work done since the last backup will have to be redone or replaced if the system fails. For this reason, backups must be tested. In at least one case known to the authors, a library which had been doing backups faithfully found out, when their system crashed, that the backups included everything but the bibliographic data files. Backups should not be stored in the computer room, and at least one should be kept off-site.

Data Security (Sabotage)

The best data security is to have good physical security. If the potential saboteur cannot gain access to the data, it becomes much more difficult to harm it. Also important are frequent, well-protected backups. Finally, truly paranoid system administrators never allow anyone to work alone in the computer room.

Unfortunately, physical access to the system may not be required to harm it. One of the most effective tools for saboteurs is the telephone line or Internet connection (it was recommended above that at least two be installed). While no system that is connected to a network can ever be truly secure (military systems containing highly classified material are isolated from the public telephone and Internet systems), the danger can be minimized by securing cables all the way to the pole. Points to protect include the point where all the lines from outside the building are connected to the ones inside. This may be called the "wiring closet," "punchdown block," or "demarc" depending on local usage.

In addition, frequently changed passwords should be required to access all nonpublic functions, and any built-in shortcuts (back doors) to the operating system (e.g., the Escape or Break key) should be disabled on terminals accessible to the public. Often, system suppliers are eager to help secure their system, and will provide many helpful suggestions. Some operating systems have centralized organizations to publicize new-found security problems along with their fixes.

Disaster Planning

Any system that relies on a computer should include a plan to cope with the loss of that computer. Because of their complexity of design and dependence on external sources (e.g., electricity), it is very likely that any given computer will be inoperable at some point in its lifetime. Though every effort should be made to avoid computer downtime, realistic managers will also have a contingency plan ready to go into effect as needed. The disaster plan should be in writing, and should detail the responsibilities of each individual, the resources to be used, and the steps to be followed. It should be written to take into account several levels of disaster. Finally, it should be reviewed at regular intervals, as well as when major changes are made to the system (new software, change of computer vendor, and so on). Some of the responses that might be included in a disaster plan include:

1. Revert to a manual system (for example, use a microfiche version of the catalog if the system is down). The microfiche catalog would have to have been created previously, if used as part of the disaster plan.

2. Create a special temporary system (write down the borrower's ID number and the bar code number of the book if the circulation system is down). It is important that this system be designed *before* the disaster when sufficient time can be spent to design a workable system.

3. Maintain a second computer as a backup. For example, in many smaller implementations, if the server for the library's local area network (LAN) goes down, a computer being used as an OCLC terminal might be pressed into service to act temporarily as the network server. In addition, many systems attempt to minimize

the kinds of units they use and then maintain a full set of spare parts for them. The identification of necessary spares and their procurement is part of the disaster plan.

4. Move the operations to another location. If a fire guts the library's computer room, for example, the entire library computer operation might move to another location, using borrowed or leased data processing equipment. Most larger cities have commercial computer centers (hot sites) whose sole function is to support temporary operations. This option implies that copies of the necessary data, programs, forms, and so on be maintained off-site, that proper operation be tested beforehand, and that communications links to the library be available.

5. Stop operations. This is a viable option in the case of overwhelming natural disaster, war, or other cataclysmic event. The plan should detail the orderly shutdown of the system so that it can be resumed with minimum difficulty once conditions return to normal.

Bringing Up a New System

Making a new computer system operational is a satisfying, if difficult, task. Several methods have been used to provide a smooth transition from the old system to the new.

One technique is *paralleling*: keeping the old system in place until the new one is operational. This has obvious attractions, because if the new system fails, the old one is still in place to take over. A less obvious advantage is that if the new system is better, that fact is driven home with each transaction. Paralleling does, however, have some pitfalls: it is very expensive, the work is doubled (sometimes for patrons as well as staff), and staff may fail to learn the new system while the old one is operational. If proper analysis, design, and testing have been done, paralleling should not be necessary except in the most critical environments (e.g., medical facilities and air traffic control centers).

A second technique is *phasing-in*. The most obvious example is a library system with branches, where a system may be brought up one branch at a time. This technique is much more efficient than the paralleling technique, because work is not being duplicated. In a technical services area, modules are often phased in, for example, with acquisitions first, then cataloging, and finally serials.

The third technique is *total immersion*. On a certain day the old system stops operation and the new system begins functioning; no transition is made. This technique has the advantage of being clear and unambiguous.

It is potentially the least expensive technique, but it implies a great amount of confidence in the new system.

The choice of which technique to use is partly determined by the person in charge of implementation, and partly by circumstances. For example, a lack of funds might preclude paralleling; a single site, single function system would prevent phasing the new system in.

First-Time Automation Efforts

In many ways, first-time implementations are easiest. The excitement of computerization, the ability to customize the installation (e.g., the computer room), and the fact that all the hardware and software is new all work to the system's advantage. Unless difficulties have arisen during contract negotiation, relations with the vendor(s) should be excellent. Of course, all necessary training, documentation, forms, and public relations must be complete *before* the new system comes up. Procedures should also be in place to detect problems and to deal with them quickly.

Subsequent System Implementations

When a library is migrating from one system to another, many of the advantages enjoyed by first implementations are no longer present. The staff is used to the old system. The computer room was designed for a different set of machines (and is often still full of those machines). The vendor whose system is being replaced may harbor resentment.

Under such circumstances, planning is doubly important. A complete plan for the orderly transition from one system to the other should be established. Network diagrams detailing removal of old equipment and installation of new are vital. At one library, newly installed hardware had to be removed to allow older equipment behind it to be taken out. A vigorous public relations campaign may be necessary to explain the need for and the advantages of the new system, because some disruption is inevitable. Finally, all reasonable effort should be expended to maintain good relations with the old vendor, because personnel often move from one company to another, and the library may find itself dealing with the same person in a brand new vendor's shop.

Retrospective Conversion

Libraries have a problem that most industries do not: they have thousands of paper records for items in their collections. Unlike most organizations, libraries cannot simply wait until the old records are useless and then discard them. Instead they must retrospectively convert the old paper records to machine-readable form. This retrospective conversion is necessary for all of the major files in use in the library: bibliographic data, authority records, and holdings records.

Bibliographic Records

Retrospective conversion can be done in-house by downloading records with the use of tools such as OCLC, BiblioFile, or LaserQuest; or it can be done out-of-house through vendors such as OCLC, RetroLink, or Marcive. In-house efforts may be less expensive in dollars spent from a budget item for conversion, but they seldom are less expensive than commercial efforts when staff time is taken into account. Generally speaking, vendors who specialize in retrospective conversion also maintain better quality control. In any case, libraries should not resort to manual entry for any but the smallest collection (e.g., fewer than a thousand items).

Whether the effort is done locally or through a vendor, the goal is to obtain MARC records that perfectly match the item in the library's collection. Usually, this is done by using the library's shelflist cards. If "magic numbers" (ISBN, LCCN, or ISSN) are retained on the shelflist cards, the task is made much easier. Unfortunately, many libraries either failed to retain this information or modified printed cards (which included ISBN or LCCN) in order to use them with other editions, with the result that the number on the card does not match the number in the book on the shelf. Therefore, a match with ISBN or LCCN does not necessarily represent a match with the book; comparison of the bibliographic data is necessary.

The first step in the retrospective conversion process is to conduct a thorough weeding and inventory of the collection, because it is pointless to pay from fifty cents to several dollars for records for books the library does not hold, or which should be discarded. This is the most efficient time to accurately bar code the collection, using duplicate bar codes: one on the book and one on the shelflist card to indicate that the book was present. (Another common practice is to bar code the books as the last step in the process after records have been obtained; this requires extra care to match the item bar code with the shelflist card number.)

After the inventory has been completed, the conversion proper is ready to begin. If a conversion vendor is being used, the shelflist (or a copy of it) is sent to the vendor. From that point, the steps are similar. Using a database of LC MARC records (or a database of LC records plus member-contributed records for some databases), a first run-through of the shelflist is accomplished using inexpensive clerical staff. This step identifies perfect matches (usually a book is considered to match a record if the author, title, publisher, date, and edition all match). Local data, such as call number and bar code number, are then attached, and the record is saved. For items not found in this step, a second attempt is made, using more highly trained staff. Near-hits and very similar records may be modified to conform to the library's holdings at this step. Once again, the local data is added. Those records still not found must be added as original cataloging. Some libraries make a final determination whether to retain the item at this step; others simply key in those items, along with the local information. This residuum seldom exceeds three percent of the entire collection.

As a final step, if bar coding was not done during inventory, bar codes may be generated in shelflist order, and the number automatically inserted into the record. The barcodes are then affixed to the books in the library, and the records indexed into the catalog database.

Authority Records

An authority file is simply a specialized data dictionary used in cataloging. Authority control is usually maintained over names, subjects, series, and uniform titles. It is especially important in automated systems, because computers lack the human ability to match "close" hits. Some systems use standard MARC authority records and allow uploading of authority records from the full LC file, which is available on tape or CD-ROM. Other systems require human matching and editing of the authority-controlled terms, which may be included in the bibliographic record. Upgrading of authority records should always be considered, because automation permits (and some systems allow) full advantage of the broader, narrower, and related terms in the syndetic structure, as well as more elaborate cross references.

Holdings Records

Holding records, or item records, generally contain local data such as bar codes and call numbers. There is a MARC format for holdings, but it is relatively recent, and many system vendors use a proprietary format or include the information in the bibliographic record. Thus, conversion of holdings information is especially problematic when migrating from one vendor to another because standards are often not adhered to. If movement of item records from one system to another is anticipated, careful planning, discussions with both vendors, and tests with sample records must be done before full-scale conversion is attempted.

Migration Conversion

Of course, many libraries have long since completed retrospective conversion and may feel their problems are essentially over. Unfortunately, this is not the case. When the decision is made to move from one vendor's product to another, many of the same problems crop up. Exporting records is frequently not a priority for programmers, and the export function is often not specified or tested by librarians eager to get their new system up and running. The consequences of this shortsighted attitude are realized when system migration becomes necessary. Before purchasing a system, buyers should always export sample records and attempt to import them into a system known to accept real MARC records. If a system does not properly export records, it should be rejected, just as a system that would not import such records would be.

Unfortunately, even this does not ensure a smooth migration. Some of the most complex data (e.g., patron and vendor files) *have* no standards. Part of any system migration planning should be the identification of such files and records and the creation of a plan to move each to the new system. If planning is begun early enough, re-keying can usually be avoided.

System Maintenance

System maintenance is necessary to correct incorrect data, to fix bugs in software, and to install upgrades and new versions of software. To make maintenance easier, a list of what hardware and software has been installed, along with its version or release number, should be maintained. For each product, a statement of responsibility for maintenance should be attached. A schedule of maintenance and a maintenance log of actions taken should be maintained for each piece of hardware. Mission-essential hardware should be under maintenance contract, although many libraries save significant amounts of money by not entering into maintenance contracts on nonessential or redundant equipment such as terminals, personal computers, or modems.

Locally produced software must be maintained locally. For such software, a copy of the source code (the program itself) is essential. This code should be well documented, both with comments within the code and with external manuals. If at all possible, the person who produced the code should be responsible for maintaining it. Ideally, source code should also be available for commercial systems, but vendors are understandably reluctant to release this data. Vendors have, however, stopped supporting software or gone out of business, leaving libraries without a means of maintaining their programs. One compromise that has proven workable in many cases is for the source code to be held in escrow and made available to libraries should circumstances warrant it. The amount of local modification to system code, and the responsibility of both parties for software maintenance should be clearly and formally spelled out.

One problem that has cropped up time after time is in deciding whether a problem is in hardware or software. For example, a system may simply stop operation (hang) at apparently random times. This may be caused by hardware or by software. If the vendor has not supplied both, the hardware vendor may blame the software, and the software vendor may insist that the hardware is not functioning properly, and the problem remains unsolved. If the system was purchased as a turnkey operation, the contract should clearly state that the vendor is responsible for maintaining its operation, including both software and hardware. The conflict then no longer arises, because one party is responsible.

Unfortunately, this is not possible when the hardware and software are purchased from different vendors. In such cases it may be necessary to remove all software from the system, except for the operating system and necessary files. If the problem continues, it clearly was not software-related; however, if the problem stops, then the software can be tentatively blamed. Unfortunately, this involves shutting down the system and is not foolproof evidence. A source of help can sometimes be found in user groups that maintain databases of common failures and solutions to them.

One point that must be made is that vendor-supplied maintenance is not free. Even if it is not paid for directly by the library, it still must be covered by the purchase price. At one point, the provision of "free" maintenance for an indefinite time was the norm in the library software market. More recently, as the market matures, software maintenance contracts have become more common. In either case, the library staff should become familiar with the system and with their responsibilities for maintaining it, and should check for minor or obvious problems (unplugged cables, dead power outlets, and so on) before calling their vendor's maintenance number.

Vendor Relations

If problems arise in the terms of the contract not being met, the buyer should make an effort to solve the problem amicably, realizing that the vendor has a stake in the success of the project. Though the buyer has made an investment of financial resources, time, and personnel, the vendor has made an equal investment in the reputation of the company and its products and services. Bargaining honorably to resolve any problems brings better results than using a contract as a threat.

The buyer must also realize that any problems that arise are probably not an effort on the part of the vendor to take advantage of the buyer. For example, a failure to deliver a component of the hardware on time is probably due to slow delivery by the vendor's supplier, rather than a deliberate attempt to avoid fulfilling the terms of the contract. An objective, collaborative, problem-solving attitude is more effective for resolution than an adversarial one.

If all else fails, disputes should be referred to the institution's legal department. (It is at this point that the value of a clear contract becomes evident.) The legal department then assumes responsibility for settling the problem. Usually, an attempt is made to settle without recourse to the courts, because civil suits can be so expensive and time consuming that no real benefit is ever gained. In any case, the library staff must not take personal offense at the fact that the vendor disagrees with them; it is better that the lawyers, with their professional expertise, handle the problem. It is the responsibility of the library staff to continue running the library— often a difficult job if relations with the vendor have deteriorated. Even as a lawsuit is being settled, the library staff must deal with the vendor on a day-to-day basis.

Conclusion

It is the authors' hope that this textbook has prepared the potential systems analyst/designer with some of the tools she or he will need. It cannot provide everything that analysts must know, especially in an evolving field where, by definition, systems analysis and design is constantly changing along with the system under consideration. Wise systems analysts never become fixed on any single technique or technology, realizing that these change over time (sometimes over quite short periods of time). On the contrary, analysts are well advised to continually learn and to constantly prepare themselves for change followed by more change.

At the same time, analysis and design is a practical field, dealing with what *is*, not what ought to be or will be. Analysts who cannot recognize and accept reality are doomed to failure. Often they may not like the reality of the system, and sometimes they can change it, but frequently they must adapt the system to unpleasant facts. Analysts may have to make recommendations that are painful for them or for others. Realizing that perfection is for a higher power, analysts must be confident that logical application of rational rules will yield the best solution from a set of possible outcomes, even if that solution is sorry enough in itself.

This constant matching of desires against reality is a painful process, yet it results eventually in wisdom. Perhaps the process becomes one of natural selection because, generally, long-time systems analysts, harassed and stressed as they may be, tend to be satisfied and happy individuals. The lessons learned in systems analysis are ones that easily translate to problem solving and informed decision making in a much broader, life-application context. Few professions are able to offer more than this.

Case Study—Fort Memorial Library

Nancy felt as if she has been delivered by the *deus* to end all *deus*, and straight from the *machina* of the university's systems shop. She had been in the middle of yet another tearful meeting with Margie when she had received a call from Dean Tebbits asking her to come to his office immediately to confer with the computer center's representatives. Now she was waiting outside his office under the sympathetic eye of his secretary.

"He says to go right in, dear," the secretary prompted.

As she entered, she saw that Ed Kleindienst was there, along with several people she had not previously met.

"I'd like you to meet Ida Wheelock and Phil Dortor. They work with Ed Kleindienst," the dean said. "You've already met Ed, I think."

Nancy nodded.

"I've been telling them about your efforts here," the dean went on. Nancy noticed that her team's report was open on the desk. "Unfortunately, your efforts will never be implemented. The systems office has recommended, and the trustees have approved, that we purchase a Marconix integrated library system," he said. "I'm afraid that will mean we won't need your system. We'll pull it out and ship it back."

Nancy was stunned. All that work for nothing. Of course she had known it was a possibility, but it still hurt.

"However," he said, "I've shared your work with Ed and his people, and they agree that you've done an outstanding job. Ed tells me you have a logical mind, and you're willing to help out, even if it means extra work for you. Anyway, I've got a new position of systems librarian to fill, and I've decided to offer it to you." He hefted Nancy's documents and reports. "This is first-rate work, and it deserves a reward. What do you say?"

Discussion Questions

- What *does* Nancy say?
- What about her team?
- What about Margie?

Appendix A

NQA OVERTHRUSTER PROJECT

Phase II Subcontract No. 123-456-789-00
Delivery Order No. 1234
Purchase Order No. 56778

I. Phase II Progress

Task 1. Build Six Improved Overthrusters

• Design work is finished. The components are on order. Significant development refinement of the Phase II instrument has gone into the swing arm and suspension design for the optical head. Design verification testing is in progress and has resulted in a few modifications, including the addition of motor control. Additional changes were made to replace key nylon bearings with steel.

• Electronic design has been finished. Boards are in layout and parts have been ordered; many are coming in already. Original prototype circuitry was on vector (perf) boards, and these units will have production circuitry, shielded cabling, and standard protocol interfaces.

• Design verification tests (DVTs) for the system have been conducted and were successful. The design for the complete overthruster controller is now in layout. First production copies are expected by the first week in April.

• DVTs in the area of the instrument head are concentrating on the focus system, zoom, and illumination subsystems. All DVTs should be completed before the end of March so that results can be incorporated as soon as possible.

- Fabrication parts are on order. **Important parts are behind schedule** and lead time is expected to be six weeks. Sufficient slack exists in that path to enable the project to be completed on time.

Task 2. Continue Support

Data for the next IPR has been collected.

Task 3. Plan Beta Site Tests

- This task was started in December following discussions on the method of approach.

Task 4. Conduct a Statistical Evaluation

- This task is being evaluated prior to obtaining results from the Phase IB upgrades.

Task 5. Submit Monthly Progress Reports

- This task is complete through February 1998.

Task 6. Conduct Program Management Reviews

- This task is complete through January 1998.

- The IPR is planned during the week of April 1,1998 to review

II. Problems

- As the analysis continues, the need to add additional dimensional control is emerging. This will be further analyzed and reported on in March.

III. Plans for March and April

- Continue processing available data to further investigate the preliminary results.

- Make adjustments as necessary to continue improving performance, as described above, and support testing of the instrument in its new configuration.

- Continue beta site road testing.

Appendix B

RESPONSES TO BRIEF CASE STUDIES

Chapter 4

Autoshop Case Study

Problems:

1. Insufficient parking.

2. Retail customers incur no delivery costs and minimal bookkeeping, but pay substantially more than professionals. The most profitable customers receive the worst treatment.

3. Customers with delinquent accounts are allowed to continue purchasing.

Recommendations:

4. Provide validated parking at nearby lots.

5. Give discounts to retail customers who do not require deliveries. Example: "That's $10.00 if we deliver; $8.00 if you pick it up."

6. Use a billing system which allows sales staff and accounting staff to view the same documents. (In the actual project, completed in the 1970s, a paper "one-write" order and billing system was specified. Today, the solution would probably involve a networked billing, sales, and inventory package.)

Chapter 5

Practice in Selecting Data Collection Methods

1. Examination of the facility's instructions for employees, followed by observation of the facility's operations in allowing access, showed that company procedures were not being followed. Training sessions for employees and closer adherence to the procedures reduced thefts.

2. A survey of the trainers to determine the reasons for training sessions still pending revealed that 67 percent of the sessions were delayed due to lack of response by the sites to scheduling requests. By sending short questionnaires to the training sites, the director discovered that the contact persons listed on the original purchase orders were no longer at the site or were financial officers not directly involved in training. Direct contact with educators using the software resulted in training sessions being scheduled.

3. Perusal of attendance statistics showed that absenteeism was much higher in summer than in winter. A series of interviews with staff and managers of the department was scheduled. Nothing unusual was uncovered during the interviews, but during their progress the analyst was disgusted by the smell coming from the hospital's waste collection point next door. Discussions with management showed complaints had been made to the hospital but that they were unwilling to do anything about the smell. Employees had been counseled to "live with it." Improved air conditioning resulted in absenteeism returning to normal.

4. Interviews with catalogers showed that a large gift of (almost worthless) books and other materials from a wealthy donor had disrupted workflow. The library had a "first-in, first-out" policy which normally worked well, but which was overwhelmed by the donation. The interviews uncovered the fact that normal acquisition procedures, which would have resulted in most of the gift being weeded before cataloging, were not followed under the direct orders of the head librarian. An interview with the librarian determined that he hoped for a large bequest from the donor, a bequest which would be put in jeopardy if the donor's gift did not become part of the collection. The analyst suggested quick (minimal) cataloging by clerical staff, because most of the materials would be discarded upon the donor's death.

5. Analysis of "bad search" logs showed that students were not so much browsing as floundering. Observation and informal interviews showed that many of the students at the workstations did not know how to conduct a search and were not locating needed materials. Additional instruction increased intervention by librarians when students appeared to be having problems, and setting a reasonable time limit for each student resolved the problem.

Chapter 6

Practice in Drawing Flowcharts

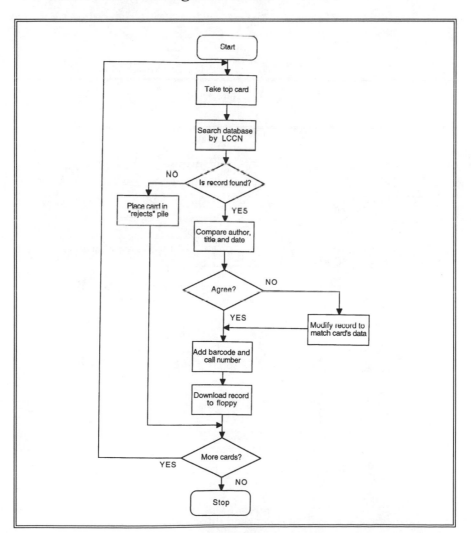

Fig. B-01.

Chapter 7

Practice in Drawing DFDs

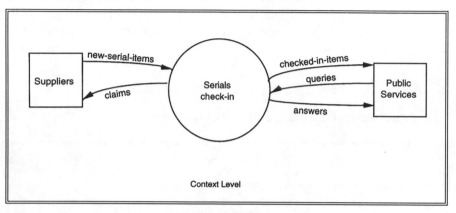

Fig. B-02.

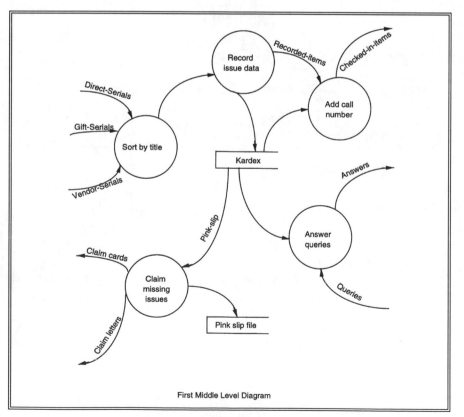

Fig. B-03.

Questions and clarifications (you may think of additional ones!):

1. What is the pink slip used for?

2. Is any purpose served by different card colors?

3. Is there some reason why claim letters are sent to donors?

Chapter 8

Structured English for Circulation Example

FOR EACH borrower
   Obtain books and ID
   Scan patron bar code
   IF borrower is blocked
        Refer patron to Circulation Librarian
   ELSE
   FOR EACH book
     Scan bar code
   Return books and ID

Practice in Constructing Decision Tables

A decision table for Unseen University is shown below:

	1	2	3	4	5	6	7	8	9	10	11	12
Track	A	A	A	A	A	A	W	W	W	W	W	W
Applicant	M	M	W	W	C	C	M	M	W	W	C	C
Associate Degree?	Y	N	Y	N	Y	N	Y	N	Y	N	Y	N
Right	X	0	X	0	X	0	1	2	2	3	X	0
Left	X	5	X	5	X	0	2	3	1	2	X	0
Brainstem	X	2	X	2	X	5	2	2	2	2	X	7

Track: A=Alchemy, W=Wizardry
Applicant: M=Men, W=Women, C=Creatures
Outcomes are given in terms of the number of courses of each type that must be taken.
X represents "impossible" rules.
Bold columns are valid rules. Non-bold columns are impossible rules shown for completeness.

Decision Trees

A decision tree for the same problem, after trimming impossible branches, might look like this:

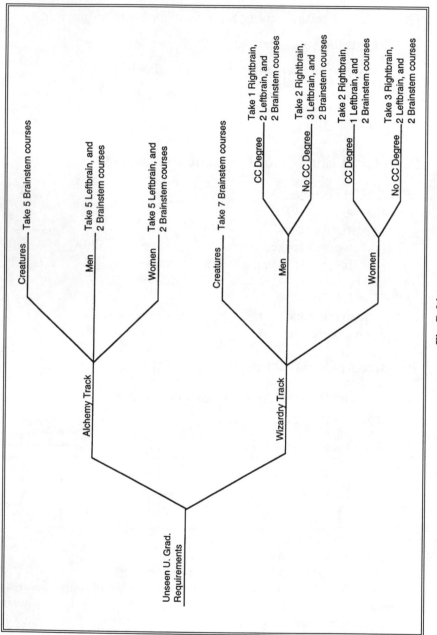

Fig. B-04.

Chapter 12

Exercise in Evaluation and Selection

Steps to follow:

1. Determine needs of the store accounting department. Identify essential, desirable, and additional features. Set priorities.

2. Determine budget.

3. Research available programs in professional journals.

4. Prepare a request for proposal or programs with positive reviews within the store's budget.

5. Evaluate programs using the objective criteria determined in the first step.

6. Narrow the selection list to fewer than five.

7. Demonstrate the programs for store personnel.

8. Reach consensus on final selection.

People to involve:

1. Bookkeeper and any assistants

2. Store owner

3. Representatives of sales staff

Chapter 13

Exercise in Network Diagramming

Note that all times have been reduced to work days (one week = 5 days, 4 hours = .5 days). It is obvious that the process of obtaining and installing the computer hardware defines the critical path, especially the six weeks (40 days) necessary to mail-order the hardware. For this reason, if it is necessary to shorten the process this would be the area to attack, perhaps by buying hardware locally. Doing this, however, might have the disadvantage of costing more and perhaps reducing the features available.

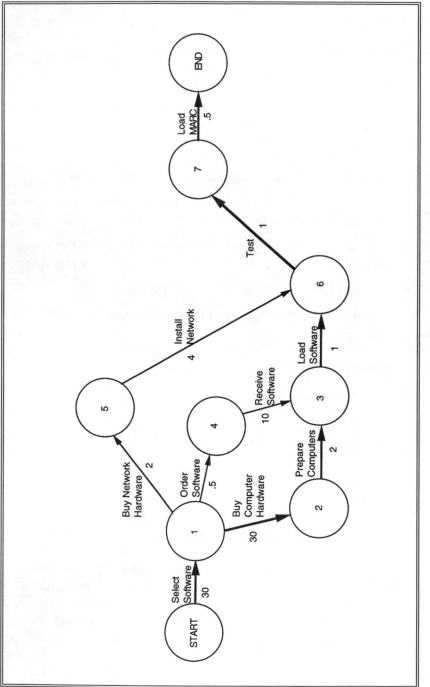

Fig. B-05.

Exercise in Project Management

1. It will be important to ensure that Phil sees himself as a major decision-maker in solving the company's problems. Unless the systems analysts succeed in involving him in setting up the project management, the effort is bound to fail. If the systems analysts convince Phil that he is in control and is the key person to turn the company around, he will support the effort.

2. A Gantt chart would be a useful tool for displaying the current and pending projects. A PERT analysis will provide data for the tasks involved in the individual projects. The CPM will be more effective in scheduling operations so that they can be completed within the scheduled time frame.

3. Since labor costs have often been higher than projected, the systems analysts will need to work with Phil to determine the average amount of time required for each of the tasks involved in landscaping a site. If records have been kept for previous projects, they will provide useful data for the determination. Using a calendar of rainfall averages in the area for each month will provide information about the number of rain days that should be factored into projects. With worst-case estimates, the company may find itself finishing projects early, allowing them to fit in small projects ahead of schedule or beginning the next large project earlier than anticipated.

4. With sound data for estimating, the company is better equipped to prepare written contracts before work begins. Contingency clauses can protect the company from unexpected costs (e.g., removal of large boulders discovered while terracing). Similarly, the clauses protect the customer from Phil's on-site additions, requiring written agreement from the customer for the added features, with clearly stated additional costs.

Appendix C

JAVA PROGRAM
TO DETERMINE SAMPLE SIZE

The program below should be transcribed carefully (assume all capitalization, punctuation, and spacing is important) using an ASCII text editor, or a word processing program. If a word processor is used, the document must be saved as ASCII (or DOS) text. The file name must be Samsize.java.

```java
import java.io.*;
class Samsize {
    public static void main (String[] args) throws IOException {
        int popin;
        double pop;
        String confin;
        double conf;
        double xsq;
        double samsize;
        int sam;
        String more  = "Y";

        BufferedReader kb = new BufferedReader
            (new InputStreamReader (System.in));
                        //* figure as many samples as desired
        while (more.startsWith("Y")) {
            System.out.print("Enter population size: ");
                popin = Integer.parseInt (kb.readLine());
        System.out.print("Confidence interval (.01 or .05): ");
            confin = kb.readLine();
        System.out.println();
                        //* allow for variations in entering
                        //* decimals from keyboard
        if (confin.equals(".01") || confin.equals("1") || confin.equals("01")){
            conf = .01;
            }else{
```

```
            conf = .05;
            }
    pop = popin;          //*  convert population from integer to decimal
      if (conf == .05){   //*  now determine chi-square value
        xsq = 3.841;      //*  for 1 degree of freedom at desired
        }else{            //*  confidence interval
        xsq = 6.635;
        }
                        //*  perform the actual math (based on
                        //*  Krejcie & Morgan), then convert to a
                        //*  whole number for sample size
    samsize = (xsq*pop*.5*(1-.5))/((conf*conf*(pop-1))+((xsq*.5)*(1-.5)));
    samsize = Math.floor(samsize+.5);
    sam = (int) samsize;

    System.out.println      //*  give answer
       ("Sample size for "+conf+ " confidence interval is "+sam+".");

    System.out.println();   //*  loop if more sample sizes are desired
    System.out.print ("Determine more sample sizes (y/n)? ");
      more = kb.readLine();
      more = more.toUpperCase();
    System.out.println();

    }  //*  close loop for more sample sizes
  }  //*  close method main
}  //*  close class Samsize
```

Once the program is entered, it should be compiled using a standard java compiler. Compilers are available free from http://java.sun.com as part of the Java Development Kit (JDK). The result will be a file called samsize.class. This program may be run using the standard java interpreter, also part of the JDK, from the command line by typing **java Samsize**, or (if system supported) by dragging and dropping.

Index